TIBCO Spotfire – A Comprehensive Primer

Create innovative enterprise-class informatics solutions using TIBCO Spotfire

Michael Phillips

[PACKT] enterprise
PUBLISHING   professional expertise distilled

BIRMINGHAM - MUMBAI

TIBCO Spotfire – A Comprehensive Primer

First published: February 2015

Production reference: 1130215

Published by Packt Publishing Ltd.
Livery Place
35 Livery Street
Birmingham B3 2PB, UK.

ISBN 978-1-78217-640-4

www.packtpub.com

Credits

Author
Michael Phillips

Reviewers
Andrew Berridge

Colin Gray

Sameer Sheth

Tommy O'Dell

Commissioning Editor
Amarabha Banerjee

Acquisition Editor
Subho Gupta

Content Development Editor
Anand Singh

Technical Editor
Ryan Kochery

Copy Editors
Pranjali Chury

Puja Lalwani

Nithya P.

Adithi Shetty

Project Coordinator
Akash Poojary

Proofreaders
Maria Gould

Kevin McGowan

Jonathan Todd

Indexer
Tejal Soni

Production Coordinator
Shantanu N. Zagade

Cover Work
Shantanu N. Zagade

Foreword

Before I begin, I need to make a quick disclaimer: although I am a Spotfire consultant working for TIBCO, this foreword and the rest of the book have been written completely independently of TIBCO, and any views or opinions expressed herein are my own and those of the author and do not represent TIBCO's official policy or statements in any way.

I met Michael Phillips, the author of this book, during my first Spotfire consulting engagement. Very quickly, we established an excellent working relationship and were always bouncing ideas off each other as to how we could exploit Spotfire to its fullest!

Spotfire is unique in the business intelligence market in the way that it supports (and encourages) ad hoc data exploration and in the degree to which it is extensible and customizable. Michael and I used these capabilities (and many other Spotfire features) to deliver a first-class reporting, analytics, and data exploration system during that consulting engagement. I believe the system we delivered was truly innovative in its approach. It provided an unprecedented combination of data analysis and free-form data exploration in a highly regulated environment. It guided the users in their analysis, enabling them to monitor and report on clinical events and findings, and yet allowed free-form exploration of the underlying data, enabling the users to understand why the data was showing what it was. Critically, we also allowed users to take action on the data from within Spotfire itself and monitor the results of those actions over time.

In my experience as a Spotfire consultant, customers are passionate about the technology. They quickly embrace the product and form centers of excellence and Spotfire communities within their organization. The ease with which the platform can be customized and extended, combined with the extensive range of built-in tools and features, means that Spotfire analysts are always finding new ways to embrace the technology and use it to deliver amazing value for their business. It never ceases to amaze me every time I see how a new Spotfire analysis solves a critical problem for a business. Michael's enthusiasm and desire to write a book about Spotfire is another example of how customers and users become passionate fans of the platform.

This book is a comprehensive primer to Spotfire. It is a fresh approach to working with Spotfire because it (uniquely, in my opinion) combines reference material with practical how-to hints and tips and real-world experience and advice. Michael's authoring style is vibrant and involving. It really feels like he is taking the reader on a journey—right from the very start of working with Spotfire to the analytics, best practices, and practical examples of how to construct powerful and flexible visualization and reporting solutions.

Michael also covers some advanced topics that often don't get to see the light of day. For example, he provides a comprehensive introduction to development using IronPython, the scripting engine within Spotfire. In my experience, this is the single most under-utilized part of Spotfire. It is very powerful, and yet, many people choose not to exploit it. Using IronPython, you can configure visualizations, create custom reports, write data to a database, and call out to external systems, to mention just a few applications.

He also touches on statistical programming, predictive analytics, and event analytics, providing a few practical examples in each case. Again, Michael's unique approach means that these topics—often considered advanced and not well-understood—are made accessible and understandable to the reader. After reading this book, you will be a confident Spotfire user and report author, and you will be more familiar with the terminology of data analytics and understand where to go next to get further information.

Finally, all that remains for me to say is, enjoy the book! I hope you find it useful.

Andrew Berridge
Senior Industry Analytics Consultant, TIBCO Spotfire

About the Author

Michael Phillips has worked with TIBCO Spotfire on a daily basis for the past 3 years, designing and building solutions for complex clinical informatics challenges. He has a strong mix of scientific, business, and technical experience. Having gained a PhD in biochemistry, Michael worked as a general science and medicine editor for 10 years, and also as an IT manager for 15 years, specializing over time in business intelligence (almost 10 years now). He currently works as a clinical informatics product manager in a dedicated innovation team at ICON plc, a large global clinical research organization with a very strong product offering in clinical informatics. His work spans a comprehensive range of activities from business, commercial, and scientific analysis and strategy right through to the technical work of building solutions in Spotfire.

He has a passion for business intelligence, particularly data visualization and self-service data exploration. Although his IT experience is wide-ranging and he is very comfortable with technology, he retains a strong business focus and believes that self-service informatics is a difficult but absolutely essential challenge in today's culture of "big data" and information on demand.

Many thanks to my friends and family for their support and encouragement.

About the Reviewers

Andrew Berridge is a senior Spotfire consultant. He currently works within a team of dedicated industry analytics specialists within TIBCO. He has more than three years' experience working with Spotfire full time, but he first touched a much earlier version of the product back in 2000! After graduating with a first-class honors degree in computer science from the University of Kent, he worked as a software developer for a large pharmaceutical company for 13 years before moving to TIBCO. During his time at the pharmaceutical company, he transitioned to a consulting role by way of many projects and technologies. His final endeavor at the pharmaceutical company was a data warehousing project, where he developed a solution automatically to transform hundreds of widely different specified datasets from clinical trials into a single, homogenized data warehouse for visualization in Spotfire. Andrew is well versed in a wide range of programming languages, including C#, Java, IronPython, JavaScript, and many others. Since joining TIBCO Software in 2011, he has used the arsenal of tools and skills at his disposal to create innovative and powerful business intelligence solutions for the most demanding of customers and users.

> Andrew is very grateful to Michael Phillips for his invitation to work on this book. Working together with him in person and on this excellent and informative book has been a very productive partnership and always a pleasure.

Colin Gray has had 15 years of experience in data analysis and informatics, and has worked in industries such as pharmaceuticals, environmental, and IT. Throughout this time he has led data analysis projects and development methods to make better use of data and communicate it better with others. To this end, he has heavily employed web-based technologies and statistical packages. In more recent years, Colin has focused on developing informatics and data analysis projects through the use of the TIBCO Spotfire technology within the environmental sector.

Sameer Sheth has been practicing as a senior business intelligence and data warehousing consultant since 2004 with a proven track record of maturing business intelligence and data management practices while conforming to evolving business models, shifting priorities, demands, and timelines.

His primary focus has been on architectural design, development, and implementation of enterprise performance management, business intelligence, and data warehousing solutions across various domains, such as oil and gas, the education sector, retail, the financial spectrum, health care, and airline industries.

Sameer has been a technical reviewer for a few books published by Packt Publishing, such as *IBM Cognos TM1 Developer's Certification Guide*, *IBM Cognos 10 Business Intelligence*, and *IBM Cognos Business Intelligence 10.1 Dashboarding Cookbook*. These books were developed for a user to successfully understand, implement, and obtain best return on investment on their business intelligence solution.

Tommy O'Dell is a Canadian electrical engineer turned statistician living in sunny Perth, Western Australia. He works as a senior analyst in value-chain planning and analysis for a large mining company. You can find him occasionally blogging about his love of data at `http://datalove.org/`.

I'd like to thank Mandy, my wonderful and beautiful Aussie bride, for her support and understanding while I work by day and pursue my nerdy passions by night.

www.PacktPub.com

Support files, eBooks, discount offers, and more

For support files and downloads related to your book, please visit www.PacktPub.com.

Did you know that Packt offers eBook versions of every book published, with PDF and ePub files available? You can upgrade to the eBook version at www.PacktPub.com and as a print book customer, you are entitled to a discount on the eBook copy. Get in touch with us at service@packtpub.com for more details.

At www.PacktPub.com, you can also read a collection of free technical articles, sign up for a range of free newsletters and receive exclusive discounts and offers on Packt books and eBooks.

https://www2.packtpub.com/books/subscription/packtlib

Do you need instant solutions to your IT questions? PacktLib is Packt's online digital book library. Here, you can search, access, and read Packt's entire library of books.

Why subscribe?

- Fully searchable across every book published by Packt
- Copy and paste, print, and bookmark content
- On demand and accessible via a web browser

Free access for Packt account holders

If you have an account with Packt at www.PacktPub.com, you can use this to access PacktLib today and view 9 entirely free books. Simply use your login credentials for immediate access.

Instant updates on new Packt books

Get notified! Find out when new books are published by following @PacktEnterprise on Twitter or the *Packt Enterprise* Facebook page.

Table of Contents

Preface

Big data is not new, nor are data visualization and analysis. Around 5,000 years ago, the Babylonians were using a symbolic number system and mathematical tables not only to record and analyze mundane market information, but also to record and process astronomical data to reach conclusions about the nature of the cosmos.

Technology has advanced considerably since the clay tablets of Babylonian times, and more data is available then ever before, but data volume and complexity and the techniques available to handle data are relative concepts. It has always been challenging to derive insight and meaning from data, and it always will be.

TIBCO Spotfire is one of a handful of general-purpose analytics platforms that bring data integration, transformation, analytics, and visualization together in a single, enterprise-class development environment. The rich feature set and enterprise architecture allow you to create simple, centralized dashboards from spreadsheets or develop sophisticated self-service business intelligence frameworks that integrate multiple "big data" sources or model specialized and varied data through advanced analytics algorithms to develop and test new informatics hypotheses.

I have been working with Spotfire since 2011 to do all of the above in the field of clinical research, where good data analysis and insight lead to healthier and longer lives. I wrote this book to share my experience with you and give you a solid grounding in the use of this amazing analytics product. I deliberately avoided using any examples from my clinical background and instead chose to use more general, and I hope interesting, examples to illustrate Spotfire's many capabilities.

Whether you want to do mundane business analysis or push the boundaries of data science, this book is the beginning of your journey into Spotfire's panoramic analytics landscape. Fasten your seatbelt if you wish but keep this chart at hand at all times!

You can download all the data and IronPython scripts used in the examples from
`http://www.insidespotfire.com`.

Who this book is for

If you are a business user or data professional who wants to learn how to use TIBCO
Spotfire to develop business intelligence (BI) and analytics solutions, this book is
for you. The book assumes no prior knowledge of Spotfire or even basic data and
visualization concepts. If you are a data novice, it will hold your hand through
those early tentative steps and give you the confidence and skills to become an
independent analytics practitioner with this powerful tool. If you are already a
skilled data analyst and wish to learn how to apply those skills through Spotfire, this
book will teach you the required Spotfire techniques but also challenge you to think
more deeply about how you can deliver insight in as agile a way as possible to your
BI community.

Conventions

In this book, you will find a number of text styles that distinguish between different
kinds of information. Here are some examples of these styles and an explanation of
their meaning.

Code words in text, database table names, folder names, filenames, file extensions,
pathnames, dummy URLs, user input, and Twitter handles are shown as follows: "
The `Spotfire.Dxp.Application` namespace has a class called `Visual` "

A block of code is set as follows:

```
# Get marked rows as a row selection
for marking in Document.Data.Markings:
  if marking.Name == "Marking":
    rowSelection = marking.GetSelection(dataTable)
```

When we wish to draw your attention to a particular part of a code block,
the relevant lines or items are set in bold:

```
# ChangeDataTable
# Declare libraries
# Define the metadata table objects
# Set up cursors for columns in MetadataKpis and MetadataBusinessRules
```

Any command-line input or output is written as follows:

```
# cp /usr/src/asterisk-addons/configs/cdr_mysql.conf.sample
    /etc/asterisk/cdr_mysql.conf
```

New terms and **important words** are shown in bold. Words that you see on the screen, for example, in menus or dialog boxes, appear in the text like this: " Select **Unique values** as the **Color mode**, which assigns one color to each region."

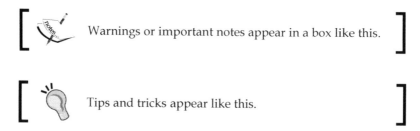

Warnings or important notes appear in a box like this.

Tips and tricks appear like this.

Reader feedback

Feedback from our readers is always welcome. Let us know what you think about this book—what you liked or might have disliked. Reader feedback is important for us to develop titles that you really get the most out of.

To send us general feedback, simply send an e-mail to feedback@packtpub.com, and mention the book title in the subject of your message.

If there is a topic that you have expertise in and you are interested in either writing or contributing to a book, see our author guide on www.packtpub.com/authors.

Customer support

Now that you are the proud owner of a Packt book, we have a number of things to help you to get the most from your purchase.

Downloading the example code

You can download the example code files for all Packt books you have purchased from your account at http://www.packtpub.com. If you purchased this book elsewhere, you can visit http://www.packtpub.com/support and register to have the files e-mailed directly to you. You can also download code from http://www.insidespotfire.com.

Downloading the color images of this book

We also provide you with a PDF file that has color images of the screenshots/ diagrams used in this book. The color images will help you better understand the changes in the output. You can download this file from: `http://www.packtpub. com/sites/default/files/downloads/1234OT_ColorImages.pdf`.

Errata

Although we have taken every care to ensure the accuracy of our content, mistakes do happen. If you find a mistake in one of our books—maybe a mistake in the text or the code—we would be grateful if you could report this to us. By doing so, you can save other readers from frustration and help us improve subsequent versions of this book. If you find any errata, please report them by visiting `http://www.packtpub. com/submit-errata`, selecting your book, clicking on the **Errata Submission Form** link, and entering the details of your errata. Once your errata are verified, your submission will be accepted and the errata will be uploaded to our website or added to any list of existing errata under the Errata section of that title.

To view the previously submitted errata, go to `https://www.packtpub.com/books/ content/support` and enter the name of the book in the search field. The required information will appear under the **Errata** section.

Piracy

Piracy of copyrighted material on the Internet is an ongoing problem across all media. At Packt, we take the protection of our copyright and licenses very seriously. If you come across any illegal copies of our works in any form on the Internet, please provide us with the location address or website name immediately so that we can pursue a remedy.

Please contact us at `copyright@packtpub.com` with a link to the suspected pirated material.

We appreciate your help in protecting our authors and our ability to bring you valuable content.

Questions

If you have a problem with any aspect of this book, you can contact us at `questions@packtpub.com`, and we will do our best to address the problem.

1
Show Me the Data

When you start Spotfire for the first time, your first task is to load some data. This data can come from a file, a database, or even the clipboard. This chapter will show you how to get started quickly with a Microsoft Excel spreadsheet and move on to work with other data sources.

Data is at the heart of all analysis, and it's important that you know, not only how to load data into Spotfire, but also how data works. If you handle a lot of data in spreadsheet form, you will no doubt understand its content and meaning very well. You might even have developed advanced and insightful representations of your data. However, there is so much more you can do with Spotfire to improve the handling of this subject matter.

Importing data into Spotfire is just the beginning. To progress into its rich analytic world, you will have to become familiar with the **relational database model**. You will have to learn some formal data concepts. We will therefore spend some time taking a look at some basic database principles to set you on your way to advance quickly beyond the limited world of the spreadsheet.

At the end of the chapter, you will have built a solid foundation to work through the more visually exciting tutorials in this book, and indeed, for your future use of Spotfire as an everyday analysis tool. What's more, you'll be very pleasantly surprised at how easy it is to get started.

Before we begin, please read the preface if you haven't already done so. It contains some important prerequisites for the examples we will cover in this and later chapters. This chapter does not go into any detail about the Spotfire platform, focusing instead on the manipulation and analysis of data. You should find this a more rewarding and productive starting point. We will cover the TIBCO Spotfire platform in detail in *Chapter 4, The Big Wide World of Spotfire*.

In this chapter, we will cover the following topics:

- Adding data to Spotfire from files
- Key data concept—basic row/column structure of a data table
- Key data concept—date types
- Using the inbuilt filters in Spotfire
- Key data concept—data relationships
- Linking data in Spotfire
- Connecting directly to a database
- Key data concept—data queries

Adding data to Spotfire from files

There are usually several ways to achieve the same result in Spotfire and, as you learn to use the tool, you will develop your own preferences. When you launch Spotfire, you will see all the main options to load data.

From the opening menu, you can use the **Open File** icon or the **Add Data Tables** icon. If you look at the main menu bar, you'll notice the **File** option. If you select this option, you should see the **Open** and **Add Data Tables...** options. Similarly, if you look at the icon bar just below the main menu bar, you'll notice symbols to open a file and add data tables. Hover your mouse over the icons and you will get a description of their functions.

Whether you want to use the menu options or the icons is a personal preference. The difference between opening a file and adding a data table is important, however.

Opening a file means opening a datafile or a saved Spotfire analysis file and closing any open Spotfire file in the process. Spotfire will prompt you to save your file before you open the new file.

Adding a data table means adding data content to an open Spotfire analysis file, keeping all its existing content. If you simply launched Spotfire, opening a file and adding a data table amount to the same thing but, if you want to add additional data tables, you must use the add data table option.

Importing a Microsoft Excel spreadsheet into Spotfire

Let's open a Microsoft Excel spreadsheet in Spotfire.

The data used is `BaseballPlayerData.xls`, which you can download from `http://www.insidespotfire.com` or copy from the TIBCO Spotfire professional client installation directory (`~TIBCO\Spotfire\#.#\Example Data\Baseball`) on your PC. The TIBCO file is in text form, so you will need to convert it to Microsoft Excel first.

1. Start by clicking on the folder icon (on the far left in the previous screenshot).

2. You will be presented with a standard Open file dialog, allowing you to navigate to the spreadsheet file.

3. Spotfire will open a dialog window asking you to confirm or change key aspects of the Microsoft Excel file.

4. The first thing to notice is the **Worksheet** selection dropdown at the very top of the dialog window. Spotfire can only import one worksheet at a time. There is only one sheet in our file, so we can ignore this option.

5. The next thing to notice is the preview of your data and its structure. Spotfire will automatically detect and assign column headers and data types, but you can change any of these settings. You can also tell Spotfire not to import specific columns or rows.

6. We want to open the file with all defaults, so we're just going to click on **OK**, but please do explore the dropdown options for columns and rows and experiment with the settings. The core philosophy of Spotfire is discovery, so start as you mean to continue and explore all the options.

7. Once you click on **OK**, Spotfire will import the spreadsheet, create a new page in your analysis, and display the data as a visualization. The type of visualization will depend on the default option you set under **Tools | Options | Document**.

8. If the data is not displayed in tabular form, then first close the visualization by clicking on **X** in the upper right-hand corner and then create a Table visualization by clicking on the New Table icon in the Spotfire toolbar.

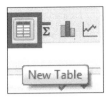

After you import the data and set up the Table visualization, you should see the following:

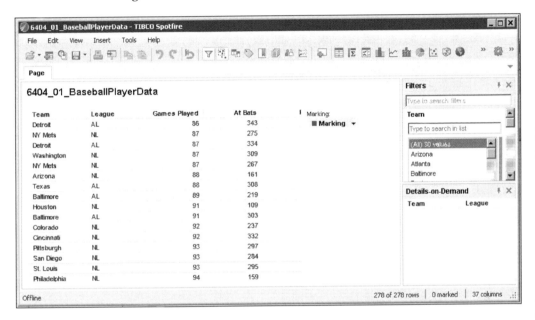

Take a look at the **General** tab in **Data Table Properties**, which you will find under the main **Edit** menu. The default **Store data** option for the table you loaded is **Linked to source**. This option means that the data always remains in the source file and is pulled into memory by Spotfire when the analysis file is opened or the data is refreshed (using the **Refresh Data** button next to the table list). To make the analysis file more portable, you can change the status to **Embedded in analysis**, which means that the data resides in the analysis independent of the original file. **Refresh Data** still works and updates the embedded data with any changes made in the source file.

9. Save your analysis file by clicking on the disk icon or by selecting **Save** or **Save As** in the **File** dropdown list. Name it *BaseballPlayerData*. We will be returning to this file in future examples.

Importing a text file into Spotfire

Ready for another example? This time, we're going to import a text file into Spotfire, which provides some useful options for structuring text files into a more analyzable form.

1. Follow the exact same procedure as for the Microsoft Excel spreadsheet, except this time we are going to open the data from a text file (BaseballPlayerData.txt, which you can download from http://www.insidespotfire.com).

2. Once again, you will be presented with an import dialog and data preview, but this time you will be able to customize how the file is delimited, which means how you want to separate the information into columns. You can also change properties related to text encoding.

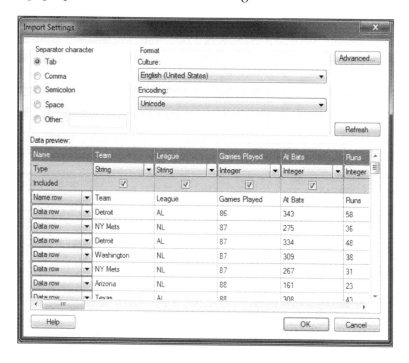

3. Spotfire has correctly detected the tab separator in the text. Simply accept the defaults and click on **OK** to import the text into Spotfire.

The data will display exactly as it did with the Excel import. Compare Spotfire's output with the raw file opened in Notepad.

Importing other file types into Spotfire

Spotfire can import data from other structured file types, such as Microsoft Access
(.mdb) and SAS (.sas). The basic process to open these files is no different than it is
for Microsoft Excel and text, except Spotfire uses the data structure embedded and
defined in these files and gives you control over which parts of the data to import.

Below is an example dialog for a SAS file. The three columns we don't want to
import are highlighted. The next step is to click on the **< Remove** button, after which
the columns will flip to the left-hand window. When we're happy with the selections,
we click on **OK**, and Spotfire will import a dataset based on the selections.

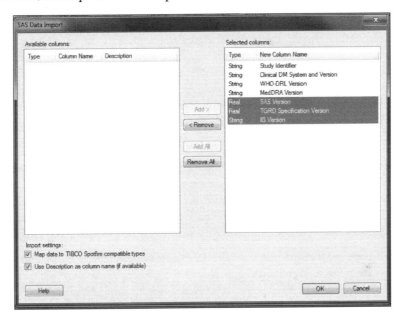

Key data concept – basic row/column structure of a data table

If you already understand the difference between *rows* and *columns*, great! You can
skip this section. If you are not sure, then read on because your understanding of this
concept is essential for data analysis and report authoring.

The columns in the dataset represent how the information has been categorized.
They exist even if there is no data. Most people these days are familiar with
Microsoft Excel. When you start a new spreadsheet, one of the first things you
probably do is decide what types of information you are going to add; for example,
First Name, **Last Name**, and **Department** in a simple human resources spreadsheet.

Once you have structured your spreadsheet in this way with column headings, you can begin to add the actual information, row by row. Your columns don't change in number or description, but your rows grow and shrink in number, and changes might be made to the information at any time.

One important distinction between **data tables** and spreadsheet workbooks is the way in which almost everyone manipulates the visual layout of the rows in a spreadsheet. You might, for instance, not repeat a department value until it changes; you might merge cells to improve the look and feel. You cannot do this with data tables. If the department column value for the first three rows is **Marketing**, then **Marketing** must be repeated in each row.

Invalid Data File				Valid Data File		
	A	B	C		A	B	C
1	Department	First Name	Last Name	1	Department	First Name	Last Name
2		John	Brown	2	Marketing	John	Brown
3	Marketing	Amit	Singh	3	Marketing	Amit	Singh
4		Sofia	Garcia	4	Marketing	Sofia	Garcia
5	Finance	Hina	Sato	5	Finance	Hina	Sato
6		Marie	Schmidt	6	Finance	Marie	Schmidt

Data content (the values in the cells) can change, but it is always filtered and selected through references to the column names. For example, the request, *show me all the records for Marketing*, might produce zero rows or several million rows, depending on how many records the query finds with the word **Marketing** in the **Department** column.

In a spreadsheet, it is easy to build calculations that reference any cell in the matrix. If you want to make a calculation in a data table, such as *sale amount - cost amount*, you can only do that across each row. You cannot subtract the *cost amount* in one row from the *sale amount* in another. This is a key distinction between data tables and spreadsheets. It might seem like a limitation in a data table, but the discipline of that structural integrity ultimately allows you to create very powerful analyses, and there are ways to change the structure of a data table into new forms to support a particular calculation requirement.

Reports and visualizations are built around column names. For example, you might want to create a simple *sales by region* visualization. What you are doing is putting the sales column against the region column and asking the visualization engine to populate the chart or graph with whatever row values are present beneath those columns in the given data set.

Key data concept – data types

Another key data concept that is important to mention at this point is that of **data type**. This concept is equally important in spreadsheets; it's just that spreadsheets don't generally force you to declare the data type, and they allow you to mix and match data types under individual columns. In data tables, each column must have a single data type for all the values in all rows.

So what does data type mean? There are, in essence, three types of data:

- Numbers
- Dates
- Text

They are defined as such because they have distinct properties. **Numbers** can be used in calculations, and the vast array of mathematical functions and operators can be brought to bear on them. **Text** can be parsed, concatenated, counted, and arranged into categorical hierarchies. **Dates** have a special meaning and can be used in time calculations and hierarchies (year>month>day, for example).

However, life is never simple, and there are several subtypes of these data types and a few other special data types that you need to understand.

Spotfire uses 12 data types, and all data columns imported into Spotfire must be put into one of these categories. The following table describes the ones you will use the most. Please consult the TIBCO Spotfire documentation for a more technical description.

Data Type	Definition
Integer	Numbers with no decimal places
Real	Numbers with decimal places
Date	Date with no time element
DateTime	Date and time combined
String	Text
Boolean	Logical True or False

Using the inbuilt filters in Spotfire

Spotfire's inbuilt filters offer a very powerful and immediate way to start analyzing your data. Every time you add a data table to an analysis file, Spotfire creates a filter for each column. Just reflect on this for a minute: if we are going to try to filter or screen our data in some way, we have to do so on the basis of the values in one or more of the data table's categories. That is why a filter always corresponds to a table column and its values to whatever data currently populates that column through the rows, or records, in the table.

Let's take a look at the baseball data we loaded earlier in this chapter.

1. Open the Spotfire analysis file you saved earlier (`BaseballPlayerData.dxp`) or reload the data if necessary.

2. Look at the Filters panel on the right-hand side of the analysis. If, for some reason, there is no **Filters** panel, simply go to the **View** menu and select **Filters**. Filters cannot be deleted in Spotfire. They can be hidden from view and configured in custom ways, but the underlying filters always remain.

3. Each of the filters has a header that describes the associated column. The values under each heading reflect the data found in the table's rows, so the filters can be a useful way to explore the scope of the data. For example, there are only two possible values under **League**—**AL** and **NL**—that's useful to know.

4. You'll notice that the filters take different forms for the different columns. That's because Spotfire chooses from a set of six **filter types** to best suit the data that is found under each column. Some columns have a small set of unique values, such as the **League** column, all the rows for which have either **AL** or **NL**; the check-box filter type is ideal for this scenario. In contrast, the **Games Played** column is numeric, with values ranging from **86** to **162**, so a slider filter is more appropriate.

5. Go to the filter for **At Bats** and move the left and right sliders until they define a range between **500** and **550**. If you double-click on the number, you can type in a value and then simply hit the return or enter key to move the slider precisely.

6. Go to the filter for **Runs** and move the left slider up to **80**.

7. What we're looking at now is records for players who were at bat between 500 and 550 times and who scored 80 runs or more. If you use the table's horizontal scrollbar, you can move through the columns until you find the **Player** column to see the players in question.

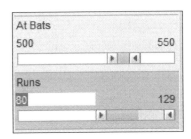

8. Notice how the other filters have adjusted to reflect the values available for the filtered dataset and how the row status at the bottom left of the analysis window has changed to **12** of **278** rows.

6404_01_BaseballPlayerData

Team	League	Games Played	At Bats	Runs
Chi Sox	AL	129	507	80
Cleveland	AL	141	504	82
LA Angels	AL	141	520	95
Florida	NL	144	521	81
Colorado	NL	144	509	92
Philadelphia	NL	147	543	93
Milwaukee	NL	148	538	87
Houston	NL	150	526	86
NY Mets	NL	150	550	85
Milwaukee	NL	158	537	80
San Diego	NL	158	545	92
Cincinnati	NL	160	543	107

9. Explore the filters yourself to get a feel of how they work and what is possible. To reset all filters back to their default state, simply click on the reset filter icon or select **Reset All Filters** from the **Edit** menu.

An important point to stress here is that we haven't removed any data from the underlying table. Our visualization — in this case, a basic table listing — has changed and *lost* some rows, but as you saw, when you reset the filtering, the visualization adjusted dynamically and displayed the refreshed results. We will cover additional aspects of filtering as the book progresses because it is central to the way Spotfire works.

Key data concept – data relationships

Let's quickly review what we learned so far:

- We covered how data tables are structured
- We discussed how data tables differ from spreadsheet workbooks
- We know how to load a datafile into Spotfire

Now, we're going to explore one of the most powerful aspects of data tables: linking or relating the information in two or more different tables. Building structural links between data tables is at the heart of the relational database model that underpins well-known databases, such as Oracle and Microsoft SQL Server. Spotfire is not a relational database as such, but it uses relational principles and provides some table relationship functionality.

If you think back to our discussion of rows and columns, you should be able to conclude that the relationships between tables are defined at the column level. In other words, if we have a table with a **Department** column, we might want to relate it to another table that also has a **Department** column. In plain English, we're going to say something like "relate these two tables based on the row values found under their respective Department columns; if you select **Marketing** records from one table, the relationship will be associated with any **Marketing** records in the other table."

Department	First Name	Last Name ▲
Marketing	John	Brown
Marketing	Sofia	Garcia
Finance	Hina	Sato
Finance	Marie	Schmidt
Marketing	Amit	Singh

Department ▲	Cost Center
Finance	253
IT	110
Marketing	123
Operations	532
Sales	221

An instructive corollary of this relationship—and this is a very important concept for you to grasp—is that the row values must match perfectly but the column names can be completely different. You can define a relationship between a "Department" column in one table and a "Dept" column in another. There is a limit, however, to how much you can tell the relationship *engine* how to interpret the values. For example, will Marketing, marketing, and MARKETING match? You have to explicitly define such match rules.

How to link data in Spotfire

Let's see how table relations work in practice. First, we have to add some new data.

The data used here is `BaseballPlayerData.xls` and `BaseballTeamData.xls`, which you can download from `http://www.insidespotfire.com`.

1. Open the baseball analysis file you've been working with.

2. We're now going to add a second data table to the analysis, so select **Add Data Tables...** from the **File** menu.

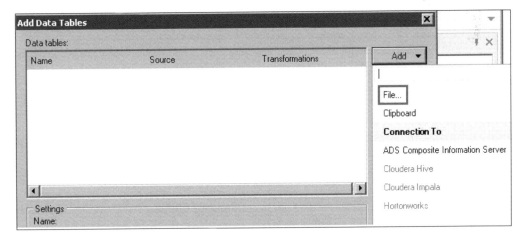

3. `BaseballTeamData.xls` is a Microsoft Excel spreadsheet derived from the baseball player dataset and contains team-level information only. We'll import it just like we did in the earlier examples, accepting the column definition defaults as before. The only difference is that, this time, you will add the table to an existing analysis. This datafile has one row for each team and provides aggregated values (mainly averages) for all the individual statistics provided by the player data table.

4. After you add the data table, Spotfire automatically adds a new page with a default visualization.

How to relate two tables

A core feature of Spotfire is the seamless way in which you can interact with multiple visualizations based on multiple data tables. Be patient, we will move on to the visualization part soon, in *Chapter 2, Visualize This!*. First, you must learn the key technique to link or relate different tables.

We are going to relate the player data table, where each row in the data represents an individual baseball player, with the team data table, where each row represents a baseball team. The obvious link is the team name, so that is how we will relate the two tables. Once related, the single row for, say, team Detroit in table 2 will be linked to the nine rows for team Detroit in table 1.

Data **granularity** is an important concept. One table here has a finer granularity (player) than the other (team). Such tables can be related through the lowest level of granularity that they share—team, in this case.

Table relations are defined in the analysis file's **Data Table Properties**.

1. From the **Edit** menu, select **Data Table Properties**. The dialog that opens shows you all the tables currently loaded into your analysis file.

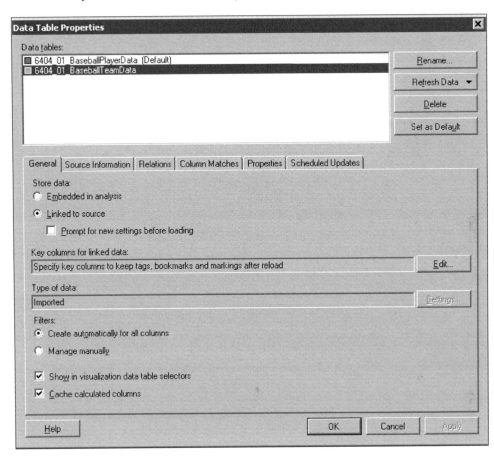

2. Navigate to the **Relations** tab and click on the **Manage Relations** button and then the **New** button to get to the table relations dialog.

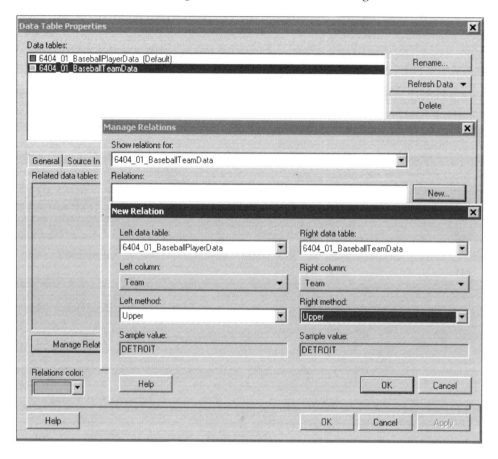

3. Select one table as the left data table and the other as the right table; it doesn't matter which is which. Now you need to decide how these tables are related by selecting the columns through which to connect them. Use the dropdown lists in each case to select **Team** because that is the common link between these two data tables.

4. If you want to define a more flexible matching rule, use the **Left Method** and **Right method** dropdown. For example, you could select **Upper** in both cases. This setting will ensure that the match is case insensitive. The data will not change, and one table might still have **Detroit** and **DETROIT** in any given row, but they will match the relationship because they will be converted to all uppercase for matching purposes.

5. Finally, click on **OK** in the **New Relation** dialog, click on **OK** in the **Manage Relations** dialog, and click on **OK** in the **Data Table Properties** dialog, noting as you do that both tables have been assigned the same color index, indicating a defined relation.

6. You can edit a relation at any time by going back to the **Manage Relations** dialog, selecting the relation of interest, and clicking on **Edit**.

7. If you need to relate two tables on the basis of more than one column, simply add each relation pair one by one.

Column matching

Another way to relate data in Spotfire is column matching, which is used to determine how multiple tables should be treated when used alongside each other in the same visualization. Spotfire will automatically match columns with the same name, regardless of whether you defined any relationship between the two tables.

You can override Spotfire or add new column matches by performing the following steps.

1. Navigate to the **Column Matches** tab.

2. You will notice the three columns already matched by Spotfire.

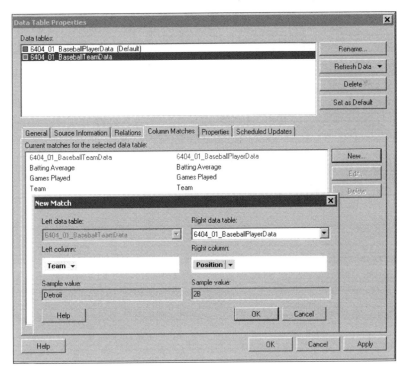

3. You can select and delete any of these columns using the **Delete** button.

4. You can edit any of the matches or you can add a new match. Spotfire will allow you to match any pair as long as they have the same data type. In the screenshot, **Team** and **Position** have been selected as a potential match, which doesn't actually make any sense. It does illustrate how important it is to understand all aspects of your data, not just its structure but also the values.

Connecting to a database

Working with text files and spreadsheets can be very convenient but, sooner or later you are going to want to work with databases, which offer many advantages such as scale and centralization. If you want to build scalable, enterprise analytical solutions, you will have to maintain your source data in a database or even distributed across multiple databases. Spotfire provides many ways to connect to databases, and you can retrieve data simultaneously from multiple databases and files.

Up to Version 3 of Spotfire, we had the option to connect to databases such as Oracle, Microsoft SQL Server, and Microsoft Access using standard data connectors such as ODBC, OleDB, Oracle client, and SqlClient. Explaining how these types of connectors work is beyond the scope of this book. You will find detailed explanations on the Internet.

They all require database-specific drivers, which you can think of as like an operating system plugin. Many of these drivers come bundled with operating systems; some you will have to download and install. Again, you will find lots of help on the Internet. The best place to look is on the websites of the various database vendors.

They all require some form of **connection string**, which is just a way to tell the driver the address of your database and the credentials you are using to connect. Most databases will require authentication before you can connect and access their data. The website `http://www.connectionstrings.com` is a good starting place. Sometimes the entire connection string is pasted as a literal string into a single configuration box; sometimes the individual elements of the connection string are entered into fields in configuration form; it just depends on the connector.

Using ODBC

Open Database Connectivity (ODBC) is one of the easiest drivers to use. It might not be perfect for all applications, but it's usually a reliable way to get started. As you gain experience, you will use other options. It might also depend on the database(s) you wish to connect to.

There are three important prerequisites before you start:

- The relevant ODBC driver must be installed on your machine.
- You must have local administrator rights to set up the ODBC connection.
- You must have connection details for the target database, including a username and password to authenticate.

How to set up an ODBC connection in Microsoft Windows 7

1. Open **Control Panel** and then **Administrative Tools**. If your control panel is organized by theme, you'll have to go into **System and Security** and then into **Administrative Tools**.

2. In **Administrative Tools**, open **Data Sources (ODBC)** and click on the **System DSN** tab.

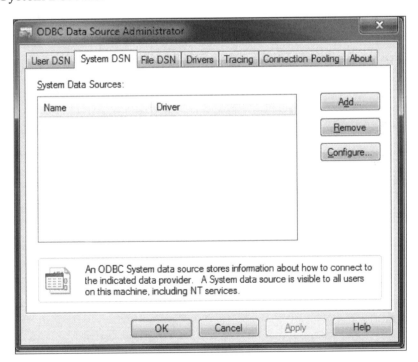

3. Click on the **Add** button to configure the connector, scrolling down the list of drivers until you find the one you need. For this example, we're interested in the Oracle driver.

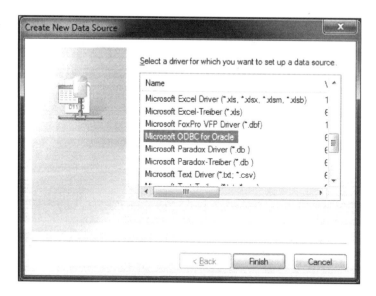

4. Click on **Finish** to get to the business end of the configuration.

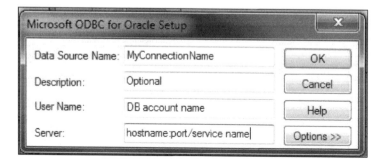

5. **Data Source Name** is entirely arbitrary; it is the reference you will use in Spotfire. The **Server** configuration includes a hostname, which is simply the name of the server hosting the database; a port, usually *1521*; and a DB service name, which you can get from the database administrator. Click on **OK** to finish and return to the **System DSN** tab, where you will see your entry. Make sure you click on **OK** to exit the ODBC administration tool.

Now you are ready to use this ODBC connection to retrieve data into Spotfire.

Using an ODBC connection in Spotfire

Use the **File** menu or the **Add Data Table** icon to navigate to the add data table dialog just as you did to add data from a file, except this time you are going to select **Database** rather than **File**.

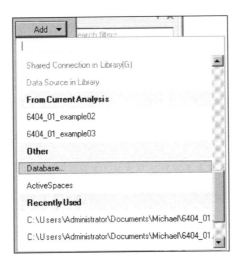

1. Click on **Database** to get the **Open Database** dialog. We're interested in **Odbc Data Provider**, so select it and click on the **Configure** button.

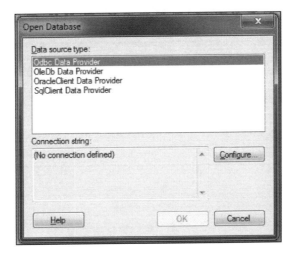

2. Select the connection name you configured in the ODBC administrator. You'll notice that a number of connectors are defined in the next screenshot, including one called **SpotfireDev**. You will need to create one of your own for a database to which you have access.

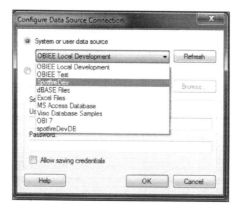

3. Click on **OK** to get back to the **Open Database** window; notice that Spotfire has created a connection string. Click on **OK** to open the database. The database will eventually open; it may take a little time if your network connection is slow or the database is complex. You will see a hierarchical organization of high-level containers, in each of which you should see data tables and their constituent columns. It's not unlike navigating a folder system on your computer.

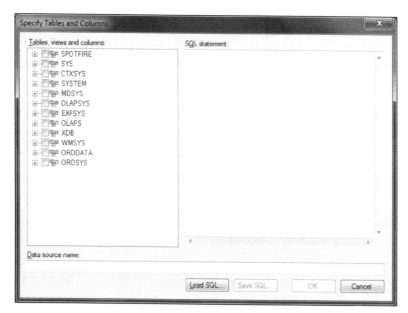

4. You will need to have some knowledge of the database and some idea of the data you are looking for, but Spotfire will allow you to navigate the database objects and select whole or partial tables to import. Spotfire will also generate the **SQL** automatically, but you can customize and fine-tune the SQL, adding a where clause, for example.

5. If you click on + next to one of the main objects, such as **SPOTFIRE** in the example, the entry will expand to list all the tables in that schema. You can then scroll down to a table of interest and expand further to view the individual columns in the table.

6. When you are happy with the selections, give the import a name. This will be the name of the table in Spotfire. The data will load just as the files did, except the structure of the data (column headers and data types) will be determined by the source database.

Key data concept – data queries

Our final data concept in this chapter is the idea of a data query, which is usually achieved using some flavor of SQL, a standard language to interact with databases. Although SQL varies a little from database to database, the basic syntax is fairly consistent. If you don't already have experience using SQL and you want to develop your data analysis skills, you will have to learn more about this key analytics tool.

When you work with text files and spreadsheets, the only practical way you can manipulate large amounts of data is at the column level, removing entire columns that you don't want. What if you want to manipulate the rows in a large dataset? In a spreadsheet, you could of course, use filters to remove rows.

Overall, however, manipulating data in this way is more tedious and potentially more error prone than using a single SQL statement. What if you want to involve more than one table in your "filter"? You can also take advantage of the enormous power of databases to handle large amounts of data and process complex queries.

Anatomy of a SQL statement

A basic SQL statement has just three elements, highlighted in the following code in all caps:

```
SELECT column_name_1, column_name_2, …, column_name_n
FROM schema_name.data_table_name
WHERE condition
```

You need to provide a schema_name. Remember when we connected to a database, we saw a set of logical containers into which the tables were organized. These are examples of schemas. The terminology **schema** may mean slightly different things in different databases, but most organize the tables into a set of logical containers, and you need to prefix table names in your query with the container name using a dot to separate the two elements.

Often, a database administrator will create what is known as a *view*. These are pre-written, often quite complex, queries spanning multiple tables that define a particular dataset. As an end user, you can use them just like tables.

 If you have a complex data requirement that you feel is beyond your SQL skills, talk to a database administrator or developer and get them to create a view for you. You can then select from the view as though it were a single table.

The SELECT and FROM clauses are mandatory, but the WHERE condition is optional and is just a logical expression to limit the data that is returned. For example:

```
WHERE column_name_1 = 'some text' AND column_name_2 > 4
```

If you want to include more than one table in your query, you will have to use what is known as a **join**.

```
SELECT a.column_name_1, b.column_name_2, …, etc
FROM schema_name.data_table_name_1 a
JOIN schema_name.data_table_name_2 b on a.column_name_x = b.column_
name_y
WHERE condition
```

Note how the aliases *a* and *b* have been used for the two tables. Aliases can be anything you like, but are usually short and make the statement easier to write and read.

The JOIN statement ensures that you only return rows where the join condition is true, as well as any other condition you defined. There are other types of joins. The following link of the w3schools website provides a helpful tutorial:
http://www.w3schools.com/sql/sql_join.asp

Summary

You have a come a long way in this chapter, and you should be pleased with the progress you have made. By now you should know how to add data to Spotfire from text, spreadsheet, and data files; link data in Spotfire; and connect Spotfire to a database.

We also covered Spotfire concepts like the inbuilt filters, data table properties, and table relations and column matches in Spotfire

Finally, you picked up a lot of essential data concepts like the basic row/column structure of a data table, different date types, data relationships, how to use ODBC, and data queries using SQL.

I hope this chapter has not been too dull. It is very important that you understand data sources, how to import data into Spotfire, and how to manipulate data. Even the most ingenious visualization or collection of visualizations is only as good as the underlying data. If you get the data part wrong or you can't get the data you want, you are wasting your time, at best, and grossly misleading your analytics consumers, at worst.

This chapter is just a basic foundation in data analysis, but it is sufficient and will serve you well to explore the more visually compelling aspects of Spotfire. Let's go straight to *Chapter 2, Visualize This!* and start visualizing!

2
Visualize This!

Human beings are fundamentally visual in the way they process information. I think the invention of writing was as much about visually representing our thoughts to others as it was about record keeping and accountancy. In the modern world, we are bombarded with formalized visual representations of information, from the ubiquitous opinion poll pie chart to clever and sophisticated infographics. The website `http://data-art.net/resources/history_of_vis.php` provides an informative and entertaining quick history of data visualization. If you want a truly breathtaking demonstration of the power of data visualization, seek out Hans Rosling's *The best stats you've ever seen* at `http://ted.com`.

In the last chapter, we spent time getting to know some of Spotfire's data capabilities. It's important that you continue to think about data; how it's structured, how it's related, and where it comes from. Building good visualizations requires visual imagination, but it also requires data literacy.

This chapter is all about getting you to think about the visualization of information and empowering you to use Spotfire to do so. Apart from learning the basic features and properties of the various Spotfire visualization types, there is much more to learn about the seamless interactivity that Spotfire allows you to build in to your analyses.

We will be taking a close look at 7 of the 16 visualization types provided by Spotfire, but these 7 visualization types are the most commonly used.

In this chapter, we will cover the following topics:

- Displaying information quickly in tabular form
- Enriching your visualizations with color categorization
- Visualizing categorical information using bar charts
- Dividing a visualization across a trellis grid
- Key Spotfire concept—marking

- Visualizing trends using line charts
- Visualizing proportions using pie charts
- Visualizing relationships using scatter plots
- Visualizing hierarchical relationships using treemaps
- Key Spotfire concept — filters
- Enhancing tabular presentations using graphical tables

Now let's have some fun!

Displaying information quickly in tabular form

While working through the data examples in the last chapter, we used the Spotfire **Table visualization**, but now we're going to take a closer look. People will nearly always want to see the "underlying data", the details behind any visualization you create. The Table visualization meets this need.

> It's very important not to confuse a table in the general data sense with the Spotfire Table visualization; the underlying data table remains immutable and complete in the background. The Table visualization is a highly manipulatable view of the underlying data table and should be treated as a visualization, not a data table.

The data used here is `BaseballPlayerData.xls`

Open the baseball analysis file from *Chapter 1, Show Me the Data*. If you didn't save it, just open a new analysis file and import the baseball player data.

I wrote at the very beginning of *Chapter 1, Show Me the Data*, that there is always more than one way to do the same thing in Spotfire, and this is particularly true for the manipulation of visualizations. Let's start with some very quick manipulations:

1. First, insert a table visualization by going to the **Insert** menu, selecting **New Visualization**, and then **Table**.
2. To move a column, left-click on the column name, hold, and drag it.
3. To sort by a column, left-click on the column name. To sort by more than one column, left-click on the first column name and then press *Shift* + left-click on the subsequent columns in order of sort precedence.
4. To widen or narrow a column, hover the mouse over the right-hand edge of the column title until you see the cursor change to a two-way arrow, and then click and drag it.

These and other properties of the Table visualization are also accessed via visualization properties. As you work through the various Spotfire visualizations, you'll notice that some types have more options than others, but there are common trends and an overall consistency in conventions.

Visualization properties can be opened in a number of ways:

- By right-clicking on the visualization, a table in this case, and selecting **Properties**.
- By going to the **Edit** menu and selecting **Visualization Properties**.
- By clicking on the Visualization Properties icon, as shown in the following screenshot, in the icon tray below the main menu bar.

It's beyond the scope of this book to explore every property and option. The context-sensitive help provided by Spotfire is excellent and explains all the options in glorious detail.

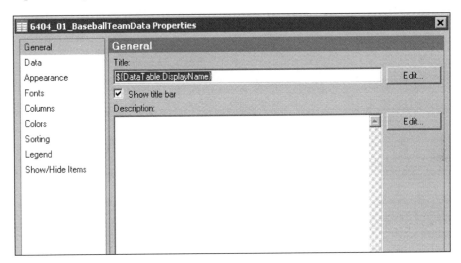

I'd like to highlight four important properties of the Table visualization:

- The **General** property allows you to change the table visualization title, not the name of the underlying data table. It also allows you to hide the title altogether.

- The **Data** property allows you to switch the underlying data table, if you have more than one table loaded into your analysis.

- The **Columns** property allows you to hide columns and order the columns you do want to show.

- The **Show/Hide Items** property allows you to limit what is shown by a rule you define, such as top five hitters. After clicking on the **Add** button, you select the relevant column from a dropdown list, choose **Rule type** (Top), and finally, choose **Value** for the rule (5). The resulting visualization will only show the rows of data that meet the rule you defined.

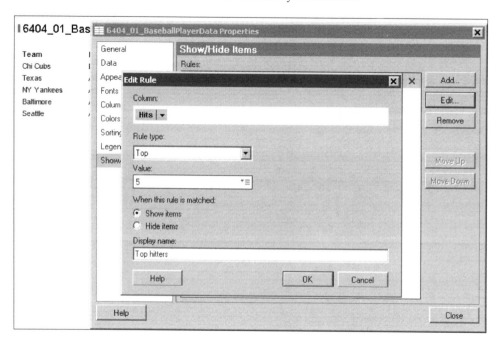

Enriching your visualizations with color categorization

Color is a strong feature in Spotfire and an important visualization tool, often underestimated by report creators. It can be seen as merely a nice-to-have customization, but paying attention to color can be the difference between creating a stimulating and intuitive data visualization rather than an uninspiring and even confusing corporate report. Take some pride and care in the visual aesthetics of your analytics creations!

Let's take a look at the color properties of the Table visualization.

1. Open the Table visualization properties again, select **Colors**, and then **Add** the column **Runs**.

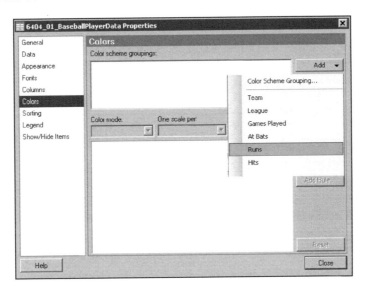

2. Now, you can play with a color gradient, adding points by clicking on the **Add Point** button and customizing the colors. It's as easy as left-clicking on any color box and then selecting from a prebuilt palette or going into a full RGB selection dialog by choosing **More Colors...**.

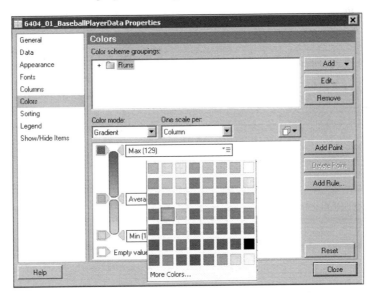

3. The result is a heatmap type effect for runs scored, with yellow representing low run totals, transitioning to green as the run total approaches the average value in the data, and becoming blue for the highest run totals.

‖6404_01_BaseballPlayerData				
Team ▲	League	Games Played	At Bats	Runs
NY Yankees	AL	154	584	104
NY Yankees	AL	159	654	122
NY Yankees	AL	162	629	103
NY Yankees	AL	162	605	124
Oakland	AL	116	377	55
Oakland	AL	118	381	48
Oakland	AL	122	434	76
Oakland	AL	131	462	66
Oakland	AL	134	464	52
Oakland	AL	139	582	75
Oakland	AL	150	601	70
Oakland	AL	160	625	92
Philadelphia	NL	94	159	17

Visualizing categorical information using bar charts

We saw how the Table visualization is perfect for showing and ordering detailed information. It's quite similar to a spreadsheet. The **Bar Chart** visualization is very good for visualizing categorical information, that is, where you have categories with supporting hard numbers—sales by region, for example. The region is the category, whereas the sales is the hard number or fact.

Bar charts are typically used to show a **distribution**. Depending on your data or your analytic requirement, the bars can be ordered by value, placed side by side, stacked on top of each other, or arranged vertically or horizontally.

There is a special case of the category and value combination and that is where you want to plot the frequencies of a set of numerical values. This type of bar chart is referred to as a **histogram**, and although it is number against number, it is still, in essence, a distribution plot. It is very common in fact to transform the continuous number range in such cases into a set of discrete *bins* or categories for the plot. For example, you could take some demographic data and plot age as the *category* and the number of people at that age as the value (the frequency) on a bar chart. The result, for a general population, would approach a bell-shaped curve.

Let's create a bar chart using the baseball data. The data we will use is
`BaseballPlayerData.xls`, which you can download from `http://www.`
`insidespotfire.com`.

1. Create a new page by right-clicking on any page tab and selecting **New Page**.
   You can also select **New Page** from the **Insert** menu or click on the new page
   icon in the icon bar below the main menu.

2. Create a Bar Chart visualization by left-clicking on the bar chart icon or by
   selecting **New Visualization** and then **Bar Chart** from the **Insert** menu.

3. Spotfire will automatically create a default chart, that is, rarely exactly what
   you want, so the next step is to configure the chart.

4. Two distributions might be interesting to look at: the distribution of home
   runs across all the teams and the distribution of player salaries across all
   the teams.

5. The axes are easy to change; simply use the axes selectors.

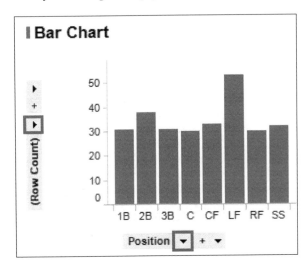

6. If the bars are vertical, it means that the category — **Team**, in our case — should be on the horizontal axis, with the value — **Home Runs** or **Salary** — on the vertical axis, representing the height of the bars.

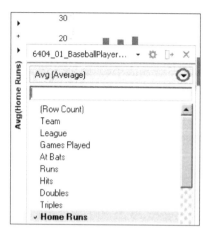

7. We're going to pick **Home Runs** from the vertical axis selector and then an appropriate aggregation dropdown, which is highlighted in red in the screenshot. **Sum** would be a valid option, but let's go with **Avg (Average)**. Similarly, select **Team** from the horizontal axis dropdown selector.

 The vertical, or value, axis must be an aggregation because there is more than one home run value for each category. You must decide if you want a sum, an average, a minimum, and so on.

8. You can modify the visualization properties just as you did for the Table visualization. Some of the options are the same; some are specific to the bar chart. We're going to select the **Sort bars by value** option in the **Appearance** property. This will order the bars in descending order of value. We're also going to check the option **Vertically** under **Scale labels | Show labels** for the **Category Axis** property.

9. There are two more actions to perform: create an identical bar chart except with average salary as the value axis, and give each bar chart an appropriate title (**Visualization Properties | General | Title:**).

 To copy an existing visualization, simply right-click on it and select **Duplicate Visualization.**

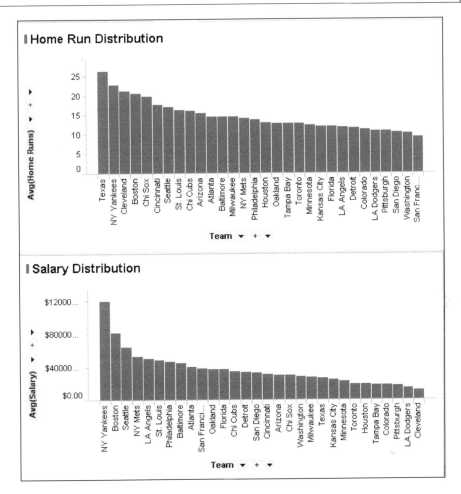

We can now compare the distribution of home run average and salary average across all the baseball teams, but there's a better way to do this in a single visualization using color.

1. Close the salary distribution bar chart by left-clicking on **X** in the upper right-hand corner of the visualization (**X** appears when you hover the mouse) or right-clicking on the visualization and selecting **Close**.

2. Now, open the home run bar chart visualization properties, go to the **Colors** property, and color by **Avg(Salary)**.

3. Select a **Gradient** color mode, and add a median point by clicking on the **Add Point** button and selecting **Median** from the dropdown list of options on the added point.

4. Finally, choose a suitable *heat map* range of colors; something like blue (min) through pale yellow (median) through red (max).

You will still see the distribution of home runs across the baseball teams, but now you will have a superimposed salary heat map. Texas and Cleveland appear to be getting much more *bang for their buck* than the NY Yankees.

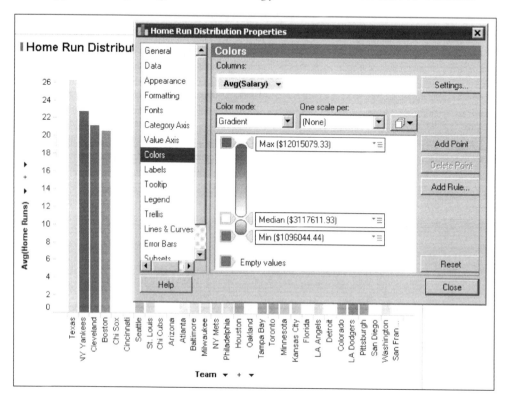

Dividing a visualization across a trellis grid

Trellising, whereby you divide a series of visualizations into individual panels, is a useful technique when you want to subdivide your analysis. In the example we've been working with, we might, for instance, want to split the visualization by league.

1. Open the visualization properties for the home runs distribution bar chart colored by salary and select the **Trellis** property.

2. Go to **Panels** and split by **League** (use the dropdown column selector).

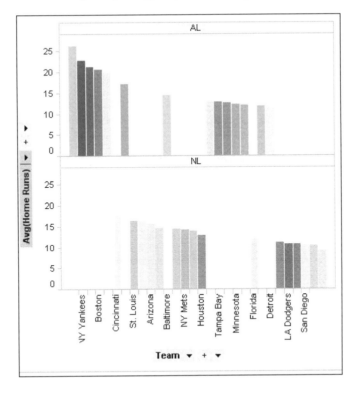

 Spotfire allows you to build layers of information with even basic visualizations such as the bar chart. In one chart, we see the home run distribution by team, salary distribution by team, and breakdown by league.

Key Spotfire concept – marking

It's time to introduce one of the most important Spotfire concepts, called **marking**, which is central to the interactivity that makes Spotfire such a powerful analysis tool. Marking refers to the action of selecting data in a visualization. Every element you see is selectable, or markable, that is, a single row or multiple rows in a table, a single bar or multiple bars in a bar chart.

You need to understand two aspects to marking. First, there is the visual effect, or color(s) you see, when you mark (select) visualization elements. Second, there is the behavior that follows marking: what happens to data and the display of data when you mark something.

How to change the marking color

From Spotfire v5.5 onward, you can choose, on a visualization-by-visualization basis, two distinct visual effects for marking:

- Use a separate color for marked items: all marked items are uniformly colored with the marking color, and all unmarked items retain their existing color.

- Keep existing color attributes and fade out unmarked items: all marked items keep their existing color, and all unmarked items also keep their existing color but with a high degree of color fade applied, leaving the marked items strongly highlighted.

The second option is not available in versions older than v5.5 but is the default option in Versions 5.5 onward.

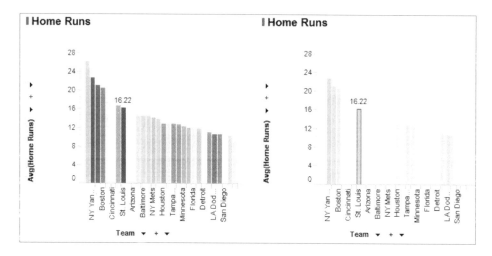

The setting is made in the visualization's **Appearance** property by checking or unchecking the option **Use separate color for marked items**. The default color when using a separate color for marked items is dark green, but this can be changed by going to **Edit | Document Properties | Markings | Edit**. The new option has the advantage of retaining any underlying coloring you defined, but you might not like how the rest of the chart is washed out. Which approach you choose depends on what information you think is critical for your particular situation.

When you create a new analysis, a default marking is created and applied to every visualization you create by default. You can change the color of the marking in **Document Properties**, which is found in the **Edit** menu. Just open **Document Properties**, click on the **Markings** tab, select the marking, click on the **Edit** button, and change the color.

You can also create as many markings as you need, giving them convenient names for reference purposes, but we'll just focus on using one for now.

How to set the marking behavior of a visualization

Marking behavior depends fundamentally on data relationships. The data within a single data table is intrinsically related; the data in separate data tables must be explicitly related before you configure marking behavior for visualizations based on separate datasets.

When you mark something in a visualization, five things can happen depending on the data involved and how you configured your visualizations:

Conditions	Behavior
Two visualizations with the same underlying data table (they can be on different pages in the analysis file) and the same marking scheme applied.	Marking data on one visualization will automatically mark the same data on the other.
Two visualizations with *related* underlying data tables and the same marking scheme applied.	The same as the previous condition's behavior, but subject to differences in data granularity. For example, marking a baseball team in one visualization will mark all the team's players in another visualization that is based on a more detailed table related by team.
Two visualizations with the same or related data tables where one has been configured with data dependency on the marking in the other.	Nothing will display in the marking-dependent visualization other than what is marked in the reference visualization.
Visualizations with *unrelated* underlying data tables.	No marking interaction will occur, and the visualizations will mark completely independently of one another.
Two visualizations with the same underlying data table or related data tables and with different marking schemes applied.	Marking data on one visualization will not show on the other because the marking schemes are different.

Here's how we set these behaviors:

1. Open the visualization properties of the bar chart we have been working
   with and navigate to the **Data** property.

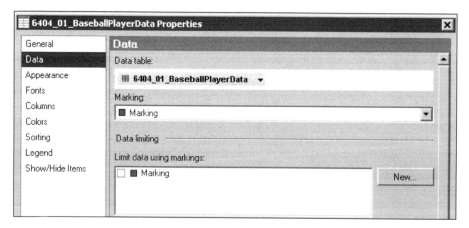

2. You'll notice that two settings refer to marking: **Marking** and **Limit data
   using markings**.

3. Use the dropdown under **Marking** to select the marking to be used for the
   visualization. Having no marking is an option. Visualizations with the same
   marking will display synchronous selection, subject to the data relation
   conditions described earlier.

4. The options under **Limit data using markings** determine how the
   visualization will be limited to marking elsewhere in the analysis.
   The default here is no dependency. If you select a marking, then the
   visualization will only display data selected elsewhere with that marking.

It's not good to have the same marking for **Marking** and **Limit data
using markings**. If you are using the limit data setting, select no
marking, or create a second marking and select it under **Marking**.

You're possibly a bit confused by now. Fortunately, marking is much harder to describe than to use! Let's build a tangible example.

1. We'll start a new analysis, so close any analysis you have open and create a new one, loading the player-level baseball data (`BaseballPlayerData.xls`).

2. Add two bar charts and a table. You can rearrange the layout by left-clicking on the title bar of a visualization, holding, and dragging it. Position the visualizations any way you wish, but I would suggest placing the two bar charts side by side, with the table below them spanning both.

Save your analysis file at this point and at regular intervals. It's good behavior to save regularly as you build an analysis. It will save you a lot of grief if your PC fails in any way. There is no autosave function in Spotfire.

3. For the first bar chart, set the following visualization properties:

Property	Value
**General	Title**	Home Runs
**Data	Marking**	**Marking**
**Data	Limit data using markings**	Nothing checked
**Appearance	Orientation**	**Vertical bars**
**Appearance	Sort bars by value**	Check
**Category Axis	Columns**	**Team**
**Value Axis	Columns**	**Avg(Home Runs)**
**Colors	Columns**	**Avg(Salary)**
**Colors	Color mode**	**Gradient** **Add Point** for median **Max** = strong red; **Median** = pale yellow; **Min** = strong blue
**Labels	Show labels for**	**Marked Rows**
**Labels	Types of labels	Complete bar**	Check

4. For the second bar chart, set the following visualization properties:

Property	Value
General | Title	Roster
Data | Marking	Marking
Data | Limit data using markings	Nothing checked
Appearance | Orientation	Horizontal bars
Appearance | Sort bars by value	Check
Category Axis | Columns	Team
Value Axis | Columns	Count(Player Name)
Colors | Columns	Position
Colors | Color mode	Categorical

5. For the table, set the following visualization properties:

Property	Value
General | Title	Details
Data | Marking	(None)
Data | Limit data using markings	Check **Marking**
Columns	**Team**, **Player Name**, **Games Played**, **Home Runs**, **Salary**, **Position**

Now start selecting visualization elements with your mouse. You can click on elements such as bars or segments of bars, or you can click and drag a rectangular block around multiple elements.

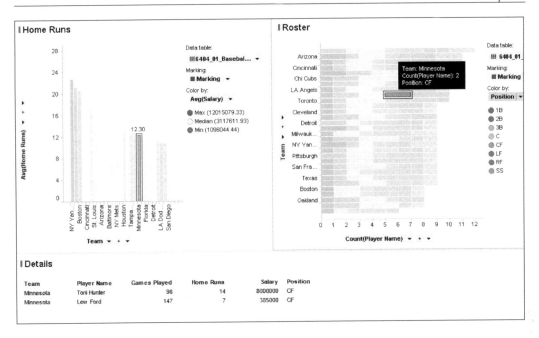

When you select a bar on the **Home Runs** bar chart, the corresponding team bar automatically selects the **Roster** bar chart, and details for all the players in that team display in the **Details** table. When you select a bar segment on the **Roster** bar chart, the corresponding team bar automatically selects on the **Home Runs** bar chart and only players in the selected position for the team selected appear in the details.

There are some very useful additional functions associated with marking, and you can access these by right-clicking on a marked item. They are **Unmark**, **Invert**, **Delete**, **Filter To**, and **Filer Out**. You can also unmark by left-clicking on any blank space in the visualization.

Play with this analysis file until you are comfortable with the marking concept and functionality.

Visualizing trends using line charts

The **Line Chart** visualization is typically used to show trends, usually trends over time, but any functional relationship will work; infant mortality rate versus GDP per capita, for example. In many ways, the line chart is just what we would have called a *graph* in science class, plotting y against x and connecting the dots.

We need some new data to create a classic temporal line chart. I pulled some market interest rate data for the Czech Republic, Sweden, and the United Kingdom from the European Commission's Eurostat website. The plots illustrate the banking crisis that hit Sweden in 1992 and the Czech currency crisis of May 1997.

1. Open the analysis file you've been working on or start a new analysis file, and import the Excel file containing the data (`MoneyMarketInterestRates. xls`, which you can download from `http://www.insidespotfire.com`).

2. Now create a new page in the analysis, and add a Line Chart visualization, using either the **Insert** menu or the line chart icon in the icon tray.

3. You have a choice now. You can open the visualization properties and make the necessary settings there, or you can use the dropdowns available directly in the visualization. If you added the market interest rate data to an existing analysis file containing baseball data, Spotfire would pick the baseball data by default, and you would have to change the data table assigned to the visualization. Depending on your visualization settings, you may have a data table selector in the legend. If you don't, you can change the data table through the visualization properties.

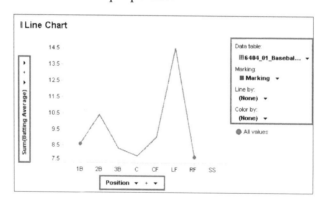

4. In either case, here are the settings you need to make:

Property	Value
Date table	MoneyMarketInterestRates
X-axis	Time
Y-axis	One-Month Rate
Line By	Country
Color By	Country

5. Explore some of the other properties, such as displaying markers. The data has a monthly granularity, so you'll see a lot of markers. If you like the look, you can also modify the width of the line and the size of the markers. The settings in the visualization properties are all pretty obvious.

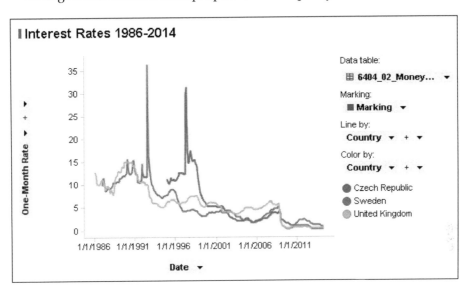

As an exercise, try creating a bar chart with the same data to show the trend. The best I could do was to a trellis. I think line charts are simply much better at showing trends, but sometimes the data or the purpose of your analysis can make a difference, so always keep an open mind.

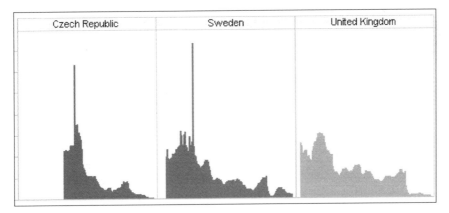

Visualizing proportions using pie charts

The Pie Chart visualization is useful for showing simple proportions for a limited number of variables. If you have four values to compare, then the familiar pie slices can be a powerful visual aid. Increase to ten values of near-equal proportion, and you lose the audience. The slices must also be mutually exclusive and add up to a meaningful whole, such as 100 percent. The popular media are guilty of presenting opinion poll pie charts that add up to more than 100 percent.

Also, because the proportions are determined by angles and triangular section areas, people have difficulty accurately estimating the proportions, especially when they are close. Therefore, pie charts are almost always labeled with numbers. There is an excellent article at `http://eagereyes.org/techniques/pie-charts` on the advantages and limitations of the pie chart.

Let's look at the pie chart in Spotfire.

The data we'll use here is `BaseballPlayerData.xls`, which you can download from `http://www.insidespotfire.com`.

1. Create a new page in your analysis and add a Pie Chart visualization using the **Insert** menu or the pie chart icon (I'll leave you to pick it out).

2. Use the baseball player data table, color the pie chart by position, and select **Sum(Runs)** for the **Size** property. Sector percentage labels are shown by default, but do explore the other label options.

3. Duplicate the pie chart, and change the **Size** property to **Sum(Stolen Bases)**.

4. Finally, create two bar charts that replicate the two pie charts you just created.

Which charts do you think provide the best visual insight into the data? Pay particular attention to the total runs for Third Base (**3B**), Right Field (**RF**), Center Field (**CF**), Left Field (**LF**), and Short Stop (**SS**), particularly if you remove the labels from the pie chart. Is the stolen bases pie chart the better of the two pie charts? Why?

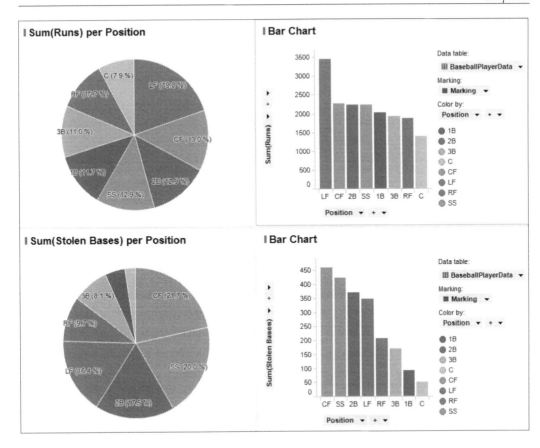

Visualizing relationships using scatter plots

The **Scatter Plot** visualization, for me, is one of the most powerful and versatile analytic tools in your visualization tool kit. The scatter plot's main strength is in the exploration of relationships between variables, height and weight, for example. Using just the x- and y-axes, you can conduct a simple two-dimensional analysis. However, the color, shape, size, and trellis properties provided by Spotfire offer the potential to increase the dimensionality of your analysis when it makes sense to do so.

As well as visualizing the correlation (or lack of correlation) between two variables, a scatter plot can reveal unusual and nonlinear trends, clusters, gaps, and, crucially, outliers in the data.

Let's take another look at the baseball data. Remember we looked at run totals and salary levels for the different teams using a bar chart, and we were able to get a sense of how much value for money the different teams appeared to be getting. The scatter plot allows you to take a more analytical look at such questions: Is there any correlation between the salary paid and home runs achieved?

1. Return to the analysis file you've been working on or create a new analysis file and import the player data.

2. Create a new page and insert a scatter plot, using either the **New Visualization** option from the **Insert** menu or the scatter plot icon in the toolbar just below the main menu. Spotfire will create a default visualization, but it won't be the one we want and you'll need to change a few settings.

3. Like the other visualization types we looked at, you can open up the full visualization properties dialog (**Edit | Visualization Properties**) for the scatter plot and work your way through the options you need to configure or you can work directly on the visualization for many of the properties, such as axes, data table, marking, color, and others.

4. Try the following settings to begin with:

Property	Value
Date table	BaseballPlayerData
X-axis	Salary
Y-axis	Home Runs

This is the basic plot we want — **Home Runs vs. Salary** — but it's not quite right because Spotfire has chosen a **Color by** setting (probably player position), and each dot (or bubble) represents a single row in the table. The granularity of the table is at the player level, so we are currently looking at the correlation between individual player salaries and individual home runs scored.

This initial plot is a perfectly valid analysis and shows a weak correlation between salary paid and home runs scored, but it is a little noisy. It might be better to remove the color for now and raise the granularity to the team level.

5. Make some further settings as follows:

Property	Value
Marker by	Team
X-axis	Sum(Salary)
Y-axis	Sum(Home Runs)
Color by	None (select **Remove**)
Labels	Label By | UniqueConcatenate(Team)
	Show labels for | Marked rows

6. In addition, to make the x-axis salary figures more readable, make the
    following change to the **Formatting** property:

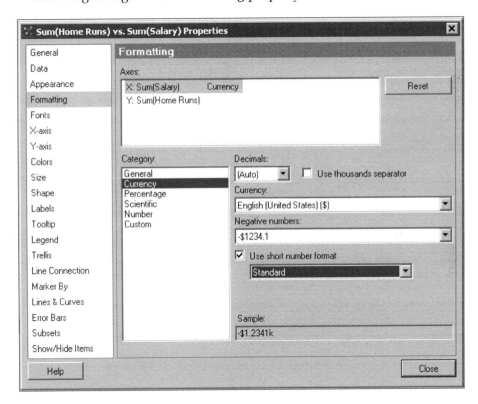

The plot resulting from these changes is a bit more coherent. Each spot now
represents a team, and the analysis looks at the total home run count for
each team against the total salaries paid by each team. There is a potential
nonlinear but positive correlation between salary and home runs, especially
if we discount a number of outlier teams (marked).

Outliers can and should ultimately be identified using statistical methods, but the scatter plot provides a quick, if subjective, way to look for trends and outliers. You can make your own mind up as to whether too many teams are discounted in the screenshot to highlight a perceived trend in the data. The next step would be to perform a statistically robust analysis.

Marker by is an important property of scatter plots and allows you to aggregate up to broader levels of granularity, assuming the reference points are in the data. In our baseball example, we have player, team, and league references. Note that the granularity of the visualization is determined by the **Marker by** setting, whereas the actual number of bubbles is affected by any **Color by** and **Shape by** settings. If there are seven player positions, and you mark by team and color by position, you will see up to seven bubbles per team.

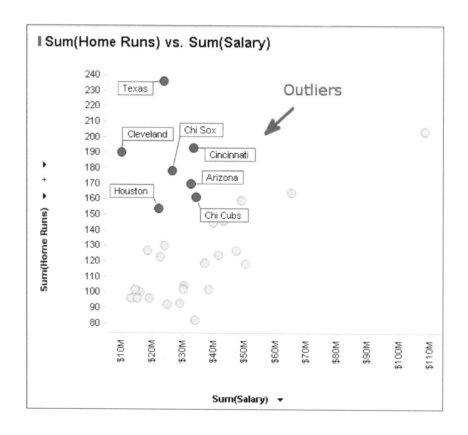

Let's increase the dimensionality of the analysis by configuring some more settings: bubble size and color.

7. Make some further settings as follows:

Property	Value
Size by	Count(Player Name)
Color by	League
Appearance	Use separate color for marked items

 After making the **Size by** setting, you might need to manually adjust the size of the bubbles to create a pleasing visual range. The relative sizes will always remain proportionate to the **Size by** setting.

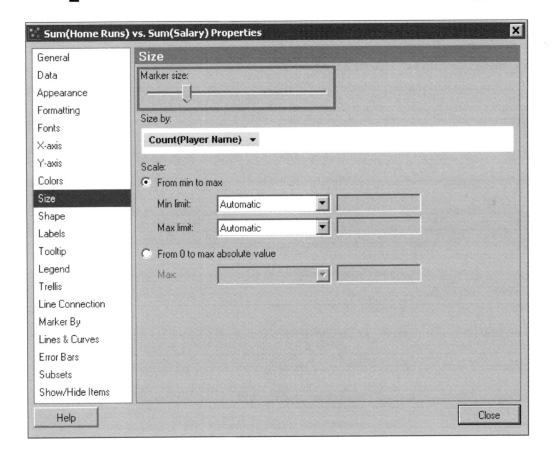

The scatter plot now shows us two further pieces of information: how the salary–home run correlation varies by league and by number of players in a team. It's clear that the four highest salary rosters belong to American League teams, three of them are achieving a reasonable return of home runs, and one of them–**LA Angels**–is below the overall trend of home runs per dollar spent. In this regard, the LA Angels could be considered an outlier, illustrating how the definition and identification of outliers often depends on context and data selection.

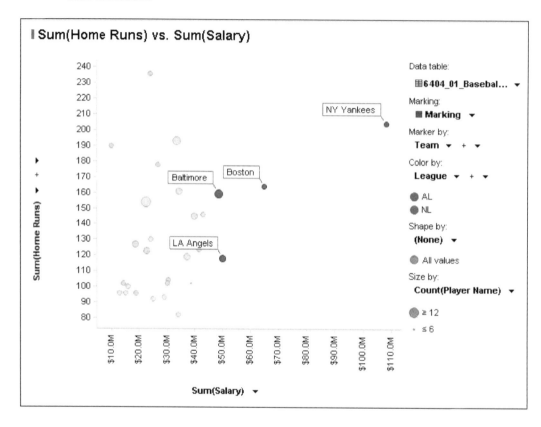

8. Configure the **Shape by** property to shape by **Position**. You can customize the shapes assigned to each position if you wish.

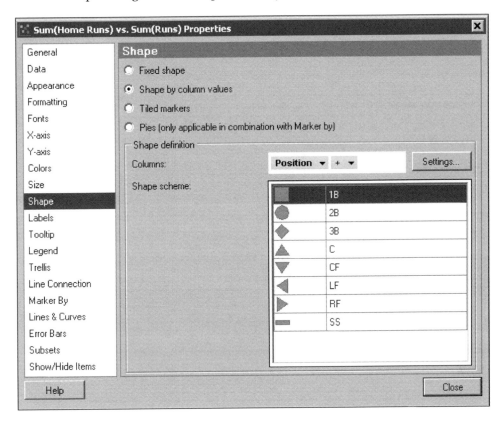

The visualization resulting from these changes is very information dense, but it does give you a picture of the potential correlation between team payroll and home runs scored, broken down by position and player roster numbers. You can also continue to identify individual teams by marking a point of interest and reviewing the label displayed.

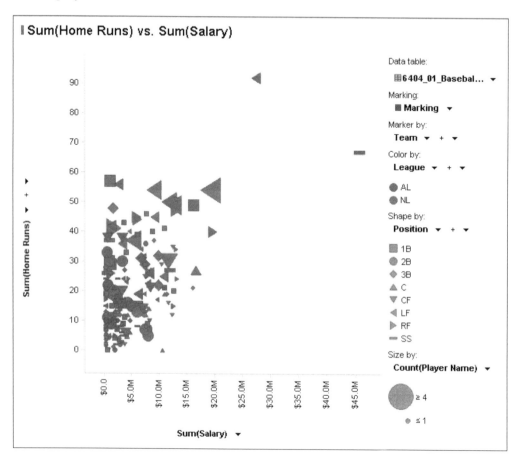

To make the picture a little clearer, configure the **Trellis** property to split panels by **Position**.

Visualizing hierarchical relationships using treemaps

The **treemap** is a relatively recent invention (early 1990s) to visualize hierarchical data in an easily perceptible proportionate way, making efficient use of space. Ben Shneiderman's account of the development of the tree map (`http://www.cs.umd.edu/hcil/treemap-history/`) shows how worthwhile it is to always look for new ways to visualize data.

In just a few quick steps, you can create a Treemap visualization with Spotfire and add the additional dimension of color to the visualization. A good example of the use of a treemap is the visualization of international **gross domestic product** (GDP) figures. We're going to take figures published by the World Bank for 2013 (`http://data.worldbank.org/data-catalog/GDP-ranking-table`), with some added regional classification, and plot them as a treemap. You can download the data file you need, `GDP_Data.csv`, from `http://www.insidespotfire.com`.

1. Import the GDP data into your analysis.
2. Create a new page and insert a Treemap visualization using either the **New Visualization** option from the **Insert** menu or the treemap icon in the toolbar just below the main menu.

Spotfire will create a default visualization, but as usual, you'll need to change a few settings to get the configuration you want.

3. The Treemap visualization has three key properties: **Hierarchy**, **Size**, and **Color**. The hierarchy determines the main structure of the treemap and is defined as a series of columns with some hierarchical relationship. The levels in the hierarchy of the treemap are represented as rectangles containing other rectangles. We're going to add region and country as our hierarchy for the GDP example:

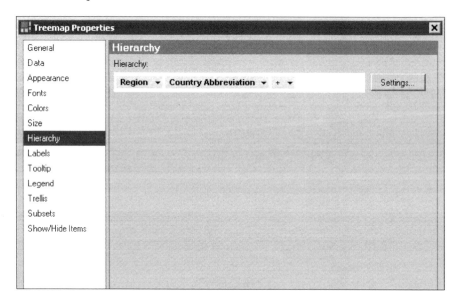

The order in which you add the columns will determine the order of the hierarchy. You can add more levels, if they exist in the data, by simply clicking on the dropdown arrow to the far right of the **Hierarchy** column selection.

The next step is to define how the rectangles in the hierarchy should be sized. The **Size** property is the factor or quantity you are interested in visualizing; in our example, this is the GDP values for each country, contained in the column **GDP USD Million**. You must also select an aggregation function. In our example, there is only one GDP value for each country, so the aggregation method is irrelevant; but you still have to pick a method. We'll just go with **Sum(GDP USD Million)**. If there was more than one GDP value per country — different years, for example — then the aggregation method becomes more important: would we want to look at the total or average GDP over the time period, for example?

The final property is **Colors**, which is optional but can add either a more visually compelling representation of the treemap hierarchy or an extra dimension of information. Simply select the column to color in the **Colors** property. We're going to use region. Again, an aggregation method is required; the standard aggregation to handle a string variable such as Region is **UniqueConcatenate**, which essentially extracts a unique list of values from the column to which it is applied. Select **Unique values** as the **Color mode**, which assigns one color to each region.

The result is, I hope you agree, a very striking and compact comparison of GDP across the world. The relative proportions of the rectangles provide a clear comparison of economic activity, and the hierarchical arrangement organizes the information in a geographically relevant way. Compare the results with what you could achieve (or not as the case may be) with a pie or bar chart. I'll leave that as an exercise for you to try.

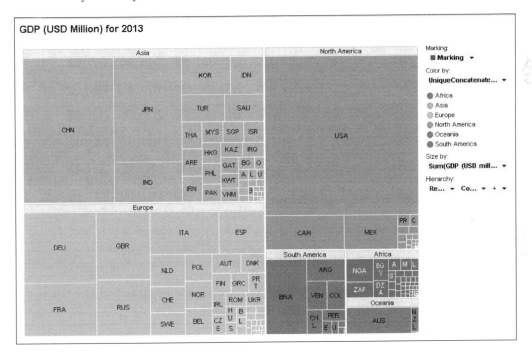

If you click on a hierarchy descriptor, such as South America, the treemap will zoom in to that region for a closer look:

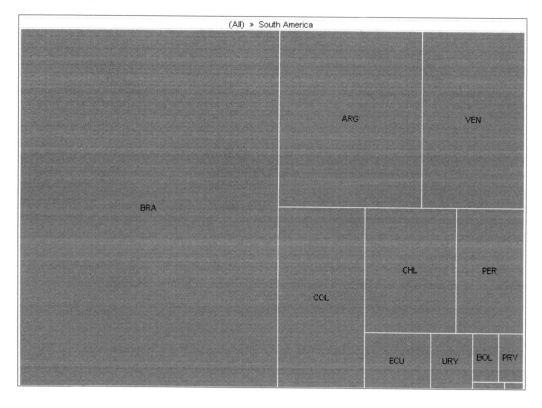

Key Spotfire concept – filters

You should have noticed by now the filter panel on the right-hand side of each page. By default, every column, or variable, in the data tables in the analysis file is represented in the filter panel by a filter. Each of those filters contains every value in the data for the respective column.

There are six filter types to cover the range and extent of the data that can be encountered.

Filter Type	Good for
Range filter	Allows you to filter a range of values. Very good for columns with large, continuous sets of numerical data or dates.
Item filter	Like the range filter, it uses a slider, allowing you to select one value at a time, including All and None. Can be used for small and medium lists of text values or discrete number sets (integers rather than decimals).
Check box filter	Allows you to select one or multiple values by checking or unchecking a box. Good for relatively small sets of text values or integer number sets.
Radio button filter	Similar to the check box filter, but restricts the selection to a single value. Good for relatively small sets of text values or integer number sets.
Text filter	Allows you to enter a string of text and finds matches in the data as you type. Good for large sets of text values.
List box filter	A bit like a text filter except you see a full list of all possible values, which you can select (one or multiple) or limit using a search string. Good for small or large sets of text values.

When you filter something on one page in Spotfire, the filter is applied to all pages in your analysis because, as we saw with marking, Spotfire is designed to be consistently interactive across your analysis, not just on individual pages.

Like marking, however, you can define multiple **filtering schemes** to isolate filter behavior on individual pages or across groups of pages if you so wish. To use multiple filtering schemes, first go to **Document Properties** and create a new filtering scheme, giving it any name you like. Then, check the **Show filtering scheme menu in Filters panel** option. You will now be able to choose which filtering scheme to use on each page from a dropdown at the top of the filter panel.

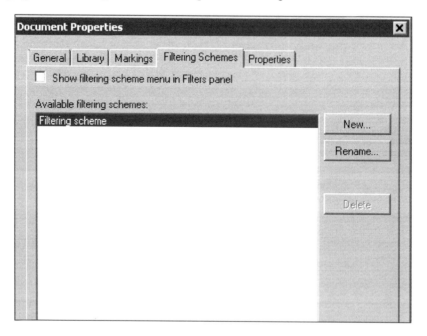

You can apply filters by going to the filter panel and making the desired selection(s), but you can also filter directly on visualizations through the marking functionality. The filtering scheme principle still applies, with a given filter action applying across all pages with the same filtering scheme.

Let's look at the scatter plot we created to explore the possible correlation between the salary bill and the home run count of American baseball teams.

Mark the outlier teams we identified before, and then right-click on the marked section and select **Filter Out**.

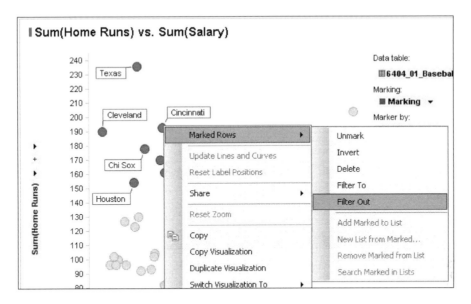

The result is to filter out all rows in the underlying data for the marked teams:

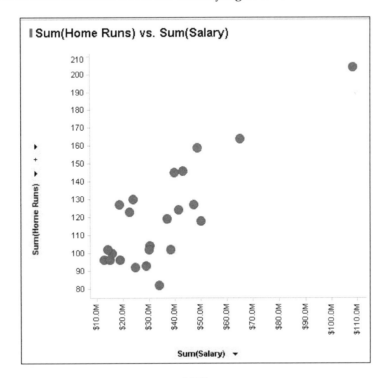

The visualization has readjusted. The key principle to grasp, however, is that any other visualizations in your analysis based on or related to the same data will also now be similarly filtered.

To reset all filters, click on the reset filter icon or select **Reset All Filters** from the **Edit** menu.

You can, of course, also manually set any combination of filters using the filter panel. Try filtering out each of the two leagues in turn by unchecking them in the filter panel. Does one show a stronger correlation between salary and home run count than the other?

Enhancing tabular presentations using graphical tables

The **Graphical Table** visualization is an enhanced version of the Table visualization that allows you to pack a lot more visual information into the presentation. Alongside regular table columns, you can add *sparklines*, *calculated values*, *conditional icons*, and *bullet graphs*.

Sparklines are miniature line charts. You could, for example, create a graphical table of countries with a sparkline showing the interest rate in each country over time.

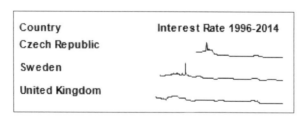

Calculated values are simply calculations, usually involving aggregation of the data. For example, we could list our baseball teams and provide a column for total runs scored.

Conditional icons such as upward and downward arrows can be associated with a rule such as above or below average.

Team	Stolen Bases	Above/Below Average
LA Angels	146	⬆
LA Dodgers	42	⬇
Milwaukee	45	⬇
Minnesota	85	⬆

Bullet graphs are a miniature representation of how one variable compares to another. The vertical bar represents variable 1, a target perhaps; the horizontal line represents variable 2; and the color shading can be configured to represent points of interest, such as percentages.

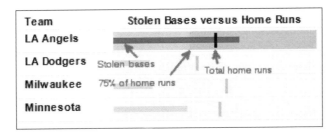

Let's work through an example to see how a graphical table is configured.

The data we use here is `BaseballPlayerData.xls`, which you can download from `http://www.insidespotfire.com`.

1. Open an analysis file with the baseball data already loaded or create a new analysis file and load the data.

2. Create a new page, and insert a Graphical Table visualization (use the **Insert** menu or click on the graphical table icon below the main menu).

3. Although a graphical table is presented in table form, it has axes. For the **Rows** axis, you select the data columns you want to include, and for the **Columns** axis, you define the graphical table elements you want to use. If you include multiple rows, Spotfire will nest the columns you select and apply the graphical table elements to the deepest level.

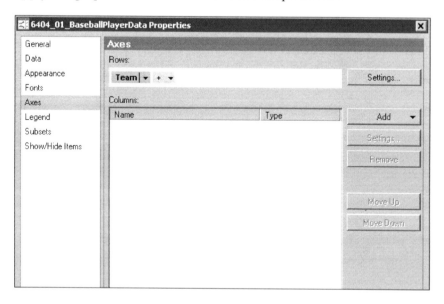

4. Select **Team** for the rows axis.

5. We're now going to define four columns, or graphical elements, by selecting from the **Add** dropdown in the **Columns** section of the **Axes** property.

6. We're going to use the graphical table to analyze the ratio of stolen bases to home runs across all the teams. Let's start with a simple calculated value to aggregate the number of stolen bases for each team (remember that the rows in our data are at the player level). Select **Calculated Value** from the dropdown selection.

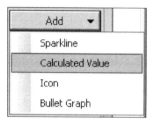

7. You will now be presented with **Calculated Value Settings**. The **Values** property should be selected by default. Under **Calculate values using**, select the **Stolen Bases** column and the aggregation method, **Sum**. There is an option to add color rules to the calculated value, but we're not going to define any.

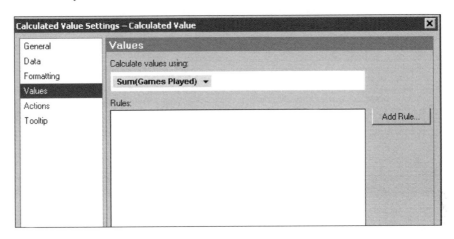

8. Before you click on **Close**, select the **General** property and give the calculated value an appropriate name, such as Stolen Bases. Now click on **Close**.

9. Next, we're going to add a conditional icon, so select **Icon** from the **Add** dropdown list. This time, the conditional icon settings will open.

10. We're interested in the **Icons** property, and we're going to add some rules. First, under **Calculate icons using**, select **Sum(Stolen Bases)**. Second, delete any existing default rules. Third, add rules for less than average and greater than or equal to average, selecting a down and up arrow, respectively. Finally, give the graphical element a suitable name, such as Above/Below Average.

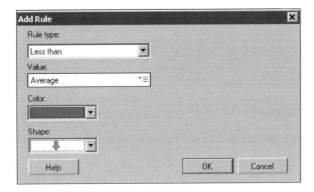

11. We'll complete the graphical table with a bullet graph, so select **Bullet Graph** from the **Add** dropdown selection. When the bullet graph settings dialog opens, we're going to configure the **Bullet Graphs** and **Color Ranges** properties.

12. Under the **Bullet Graphs** property, select **Sum(Stolen Bases)** for the **Calculate values using** setting, and **Sum(Home Runs)** for the **Calculate comparative values using** setting. The former defines the horizontal bar of the bullet graph, the latter defines the vertical line.

13. Under the **Color Ranges** property, check the box next to **Show color ranges**, select a suitable color for the default **Current ranges and their limits** setting, and add a second color range by clicking on the **Add** button. Right-click on the column selection dropdown that appears, select **Custom Expression...** and enter the expression Sum(Stolen Bases) * 0.75. Experiment with the colors to get a pleasing combination.

14. Give the bullet graph a suitable name, such as Stolen Bases versus Home Runs.

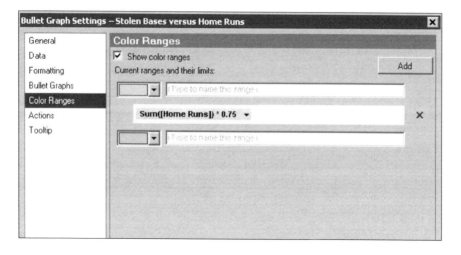

15. If you wish, you can add a further calculated value for home runs. The final result is an information-rich and visually appealing table.

‖6404_01_BaseballPlayerData

Team	Stolen Bases	Above/Below Average	Home Runs	Stolen Bases versus Home Runs
Arizona	66	⬇	170	
Atlanta	84	⬆	145	
Baltimore	70	⬇	159	
Boston	33	⬇	164	
Chi Cubs	60	⬇	161	
Chi Sox	110	⬆	178	
Cincinnati	61	⬇	193	
Cleveland	54	⬇	190	
Colorado	40	⬇	100	
Detroit	61	⬇	104	
Florida	93	⬆	119	
Houston	111	⬆	154	
Kansas City	38	⬇	96	
LA Angels	146	⬆	118	

I'll leave you to explore the sparkline element. It's just a matter of selecting a suitable x- and y-axis for the sparkline from the data table.

Summary

This chapter has taught you how to use a good cross-section of Spotfire visualizations and highlighted where their analytical strengths lie. You should now be able to build and configure the various visualization types but also, if you haven't already thought about such things, gained some insight into the science and art of data visualization.

You saw how the Table visualization is an easy and traditional way to display detailed information in tabular form; how the Bar Chart visualization is excellent for visualizing categorical information, such as distributions; how the Line Chart visualization is ideal for analyzing trends; usually, in time, but not necessarily; and how the Pie Chart visualization is good for visualizing simple proportions, but how it does have its limitations.

The versatility and power of the Scatter Plot visualization for analyzing relationships and providing multiple levels of presentation through its color, shape, size, and trellis properties should be clear to you. You should appreciate the Tree Map visualization's ability to compare the relative proportions of the elements in a hierarchy in a very compact and visually intuitive way. You should already be thinking of how to apply the Graphical Table visualization to create information-rich and visually appealing tabular presentations.

You learned how to enrich your visualizations with color categorization and divide a visualization across a trellis grid. This chapter introduced you to the key Spotfire concepts of marking and filters.

With the previous chapter and the current one under your belt, you should now be ready to begin using Spotfire to build your own analyses. Import some data that means something to you into a Spotfire analysis file, and experiment with the visualizations covered in this chapter. Explore the properties we haven't covered, and use the inline help to guide you. It is an excellent reference library.

In the next chapter, you will learn how to enhance the visualizations you build with controls, context, and collaboration tools. These additional techniques and functionality will allow you to develop rough, ad hoc analyses, and visualizations into professional analytic dashboards and applications for use by a wider audience.

3
Analyze That!

The first two chapters showed you how to work with data and create visualizations. This chapter is all about adding context and input controls to your Spotfire analyses. It will show you how to quickly transform even simple analyses into professional and powerful analytical toolkits that you can share with others or even develop for large enterprise audiences. You will learn how to annotate your analyses and add input controls that allow you and others to do "what if" explorations.

You can spend a lot of time shaping and modeling your data, and building cool, insightful visualizations. To realize the full benefit of all your hard work, especially if you intend to share your analysis with anyone, it's really worth spending some extra time considering how the analysis is presented and how easy it is for you and others to change options and parameters.

Even the most static dashboard-style report will usually benefit from the inclusion of some form of user-definable parameters, and a visually appealing and well annotated analysis will draw people in and encourage engagement. Visualization titles, information and instructions, and good overall layout and organization are essential design principles.

There are two quotations from the late Steve Jobs, the former CEO of Apple, that I particularly like, and they are very relevant to the philosophy of this chapter:

Design is not just what it looks like and feels like. Design is how it works.

Details matter, it's worth waiting to get it right.

In this chapter, we will cover the following topics:

- Framing your analysis using text areas
- Key Spotfire concept—document properties.
- Increasing interactivity using property controls

- Providing summary information at a glance
- Customizing the filter panel
- Getting details of marked items
- Annotating data using tags and lists
- Creating analysis snapshots using bookmarks

At the end of this chapter you will be ready to share your work and collaborate.

Framing your analysis using text areas

Spotfire's Text Area, though not strictly speaking a visualization, is as important as any of the visualizations on your analysis page. In terms of insertion on the page and maneuvering within the layout, the text area behaves in exactly the same way as a visualization, so treat it as one.

In its simplest form, the text area can be used to add some text to support your analysis: a title and brief description or some usage instructions. You can enter text plainly or take advantage of the text area's underlying HTML base for more sophisticated presentations. If you don't know much about HTML, the W3Schools website (`http://www.w3schools.com/html/`) is an excellent starting point. It's not that difficult to pick up some basic techniques.

However, the text area is much more than just a *text* area. In it, you can embed input fields, dropdown menu controls, images, URLs to external content, action buttons, filters, and even those visualization elements that are available to graphical tables such as conditional icons, calculated values, bullet graphs, and sparklines.

Let's start with a simple example using data from `BaseballPlayerData.xls`, which you can download from `http://www.insidespotfire.com`.

1. If you saved the scatter plot analysis of the baseball data, open it now or else just reload the baseball player data into a new analysis file and rebuild the scatter plot. You want to plot **Sum(Runs)** against **Sum(Salary)** and set the **marker by** property to **Team**.

2. Now, insert a new text area in exactly the same way as inserting a visualization. In the **Insert** menu, there is a separate entry for **New Text Area**, or you can click on the text area icon in the tool bar just below the main menu.

3. When you insert the text area, Spotfire will place it on top of the scatter plot across the width of the page. We want to move it to the side, so left-click the text area title bar, hold and drag into position. Resize by moving the cursor over the vertical line between the text area and the scatter plot until it changes to a vertical line with two arrows. Then simply click and drag to narrow the text area and widen the scatter plot.

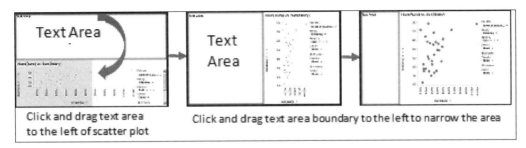

Click and drag text area to the left of scatter plot   Click and drag text area boundary to the left to narrow the area

4. Right-click anywhere inside the text area and select **Edit Text Area**. You can simply begin to type text using the dropdown formatting options to change the font or general styling.

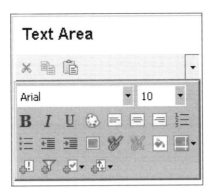

5. If you like, you can change the title of the text area or hide it by right-clicking anywhere in the text area, selecting **Properties**, and unchecking the **Show title bar** option.

6. If you're interested in exploring the HTML functionality, right-click on the text area and select **Edit HTML**. You'll see how Spotfire has already formatted your text using HTML tags.

7. You might like to include a major league baseball logo. Simply click on the insert image icon and navigate to a suitable saved image.

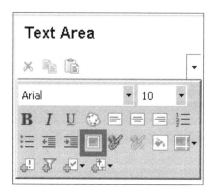

8. To size the image for the text area, you can use a graphics editor before you put the image into Spotfire, but it's probably easier to just edit the HTML tag once the image is in Spotfire. Just right-click on the text area, select **Edit HTML**, and change the size of the image.

The HTML code generated by Spotfire after you embed the image will look something like this:

```
<P><STRONG><FONT color=#3a6c9a><IMG border=0 src="ba17552a139f4ab1
9780f67db1e0dd6c.png"></FONT></STRONG></P>
<P><STRONG><FONT color=#3a6c9a>Major League Baseball Stats</
FONT></STRONG></P>
<P>Analysis of correlation between runs achieved and salaries
paid</P>
```

Change the IMG tag to include height and width values (in pixels). You might need to experiment to get the size and proportions right:

```
<P><STRONG><FONT color=#3a6c9a><IMG border=0 src="ba17552a139f4ab1
9780f67db1e0dd6c.png" height="100" width="150"></FONT></STRONG></
P>
```

```
<P><STRONG><FONT color=#3a6c9a>Major League Baseball Stats</
FONT></STRONG></P>
<P>Analysis of correlation between runs achieved and salaries
paid</P>
```

When you add the height and width dimensions to the IMG tag, use the save icon at the top of Spotfire's HTML editor to see the effect of your changes and continue editing if necessary. When you're happy with the result, close the editor.

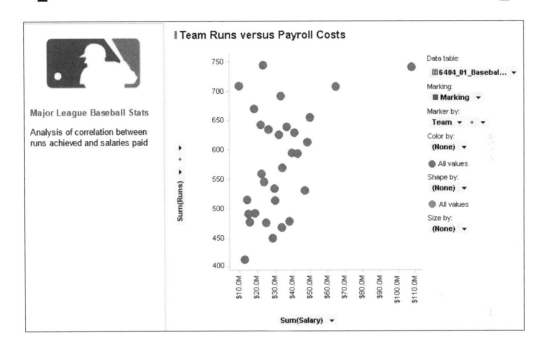

Key Spotfire concept – document properties

Before we continue exploring the text area, you need to understand an important Spotfire concept—the **document property**. Document properties are key to the use of user inputs and other controls. As we'll see shortly, you can create new document properties in the course of creating controls, but you can also access all document properties directly, creating new ones and editing existing ones through the main document properties dialog.

You'll find document properties under the **Edit** menu options. Select **Document Properties** and then the **Properties** tab.

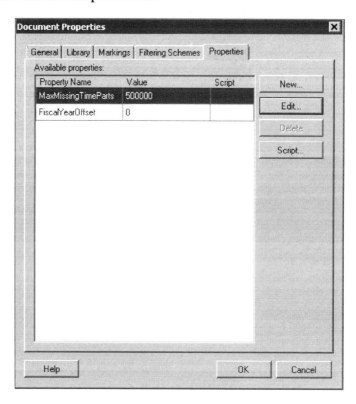

Don't worry about the **Script** button for now and stick to the **New** and **Edit** buttons. When creating a new property, you need to enter the following details:

- **Property name**: You must give the property a unique name with no spaces. You cannot change this once the property has been created, but you can delete the property and start again.

- **Data type**: You must choose a data type from the dropdown list. You cannot change this once the property has been created.

- **Description**: This is optional and only required for information purposes. You can change it later.

- **Value**: This is optional for strings, but you'll need to enter an initial value for numbers. It can be changed as often as you like after the property has been created. This is kind of central to how you use document properties in your analysis.

Once a document property exists, you can use it as the basis for an input control or reference it directly in a visualization. A dollar sign and braces are used when referencing a document property, for example, $\{ExampleDocumentProperty\}$. This is a very useful functionality, as we are about to see.

Increasing interactivity using property controls

There will be many occasions when you will want to give yourself or a wider audience the ability to quickly change the parameters affecting a visualization. The main filter panel and the marking functionality of Spotfire provide quick and powerful routes for interactivity and analysis, but they don't facilitate the same level of customization you can achieve with a text area control. Lets look at how useful property controls can be:

1. There are seven different property controls, ranging from simple labels to more complex multiline list boxes. You insert them by first entering the edit mode in a text area, as we did when writing simple text and embedding the image, and then using the dropdown list under the **Insert Property Control** icon. This control will insert wherever you have placed the cursor. You can also embed controls directly in the HTML editor.

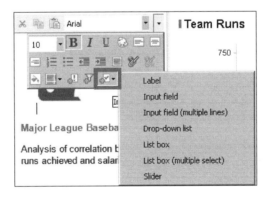

2. Let's start by creating a simple control to allow you to quickly select color by options for your scatter plot. Choose **Drop-down list** from the **Insert Property Control** options. After you select the control type, you will be presented with a standard document property dialog.

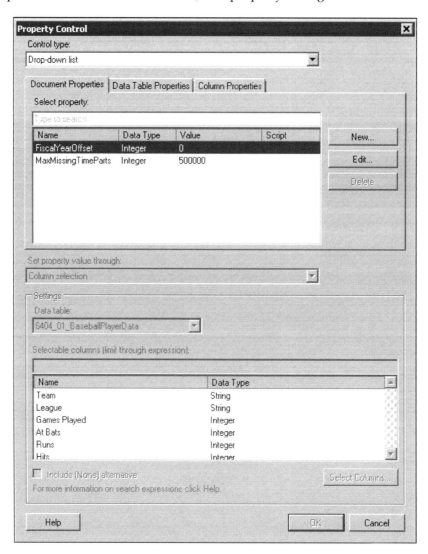

3. Create a new property, give it a meaningful name, and make it a string data type. Let's call the property SalaryAnalysisColorBy.

Document properties cannot have spaces or special characters such as underscores. When naming properties, it's good practice to use what's known as UpperCamelCase, concatenating the words you want to use and starting each with a capital letter. Try to cultivate a logical and consistent approach to naming properties such that the name is self-explanatory.

4. Now we need to configure the control, and there are two fundamental ways to do this: provide the control with fixed values or use some form of lookup in the data. These options are found under the **Set property value through:** dropdown list. We're just going to define some fixed values.

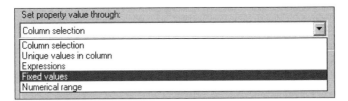

5. When you select **Fixed values**, a **Settings** panel will open to allow you to define the **Display Names** and **Values** you want to include. The display name is the text you want the user to see in the text area; it can be anything you like. The value you define will be assigned to the property control when the user selects the corresponding display name text. Ensure that you keep the data type consistent: if the document property is defined as an integer, the value must be an integer. Simply double-click on the display name or value box to begin entering details. Also, check the box next to **Include (None) alternative** if you want to include a **None** option.

You should now understand the dynamic nature of document property values and see their potential for facilitating custom user inputs.

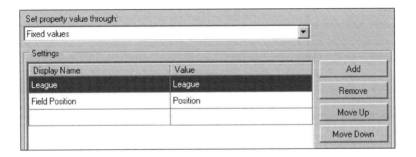

6. Click on **OK** to save your changes and return to the text area. You can always edit the control by right-clicking on it and selecting **Edit Control**; you must first be in edit mode in the text area.

7. Click outside the text area to exit the edit mode, and explore the control you have created. Apart from changing through the options you have selected, you won't see any obvious effects because we still have one more thing to do to link the control to the visualization. Before we do this, try making some selections in the new dropdown control and then opening the document properties to see how the value changes.

8. To link the control to your visualization, you need to apply the property you have set up in the text area to the relevant visualization property. First, select a value other than **None** in the control dropdown. Then open the visualization properties for the scatter plot, and navigate to the **Colors** panel.

9. Under the **Columns** item, right-click on the dropdown selector, select the **Set from property...** option, and choose **SalaryAnalysisColorBy**. Spotfire will assume that the value you defined in the control is a valid column name, and it will automatically wrap that value in square brackets. It will also pick what it thinks is the most appropriate color mode and assign some colors randomly. You can change any of these settings.

10. Right-click on the dropdown selector under **Columns** again but this time select **Custom Expression...**. You will see exactly how Spotfire has configured the visualization element—color in this case—to the property you have defined and exposed as an input control in the text area, essentially binding the property to the visualization element.

    ```
    <$esc(${SalaryAnalysisColorBy})>
    ```

    Spotfire uses `$esc(...)` to enclose a value with square brackets, but you can actually use a square bracket directly if you find it easier. For example, you could change the earlier expression to

    ```
    <[${SalaryAnalysisColorBy}]>
    ```

    The angle brackets designate the value as *categorical*, as distinct from *continuous*.

> Text values are treated as categorical information by Spotfire. They are always enclosed by angle brackets in expressions and have different visualization behavior characteristics to numbers, which are treated as continuous information and are not enclosed by angle brackets. For example, you cannot define a gradient of color for a categorical variable.

11. Click on **Close** to exit the color configuration, and try changing the options in the text area control now. You should see the visualizations change according to your selections.

As a final exercise, insert some descriptive text above the control and think about how you would allow the user to dynamically change the trellis configuration. Almost everything in the visualization can be bound to a property control, so give this some thought too.

You could create an independent **trellis by** control or bind the color by the property you've already created by navigating to **Trellis | Panels | Split by setting**.

When you have finished the exercise, you should have something like the following screenshot:

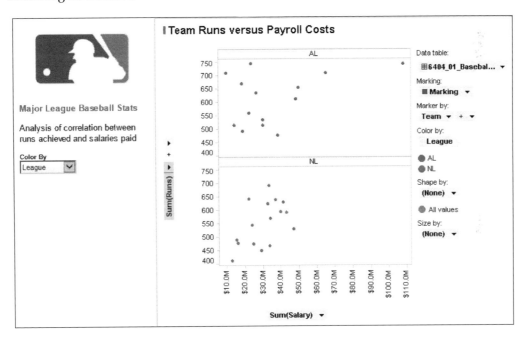

You can format the appearance of the control by right-clicking on the control in the text area edit mode and selecting **Format Control**.

Providing summary information at a glance

You might want to provide summary information but not in a full-blown visualization. The text area allows you to mix calculated values, conditional icons, bullet graphs, and sparklines with other text area elements. Furthermore, you can use the full range of formatting options, including HTML.

The use of these summary elements in the text area is not much different from their use in the Graphical Table visualization. You insert them using the **Insert Dynamic Item** dropdown list.

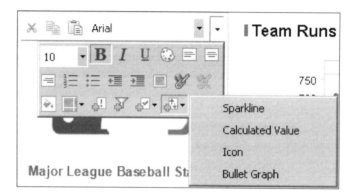

Once inserted, you configure the dynamic graphical elements in exactly the same way as in a graphical table, specifying the source data table, columns, and any rules you want to define. You can additionally do some visual formatting through the **Format Control...** dialog.

It's important to understand that any summary visualizations used in a text area represent all data in the source you specify. This is unlike the graphical table, where they can be combined with aggregated categories, such as team in our baseball examples. Therefore, the application of rules is limited. For example, a top 5 rule doesn't make sense when there are no elements to rank, just a total.

Let's take a closer look using a couple of calculated values in our baseball salary analysis:

1. Add two calculated value dynamic graphical elements to the text area. Insert the following text above the first one: Average cost per run. Insert the following text above the second element: Cost per run for selected teams.

2. Configure the first calculated value by right-clicking on the **Calculate values using:** dropdown in the **Values** setting and selecting **Custom Expression...**.

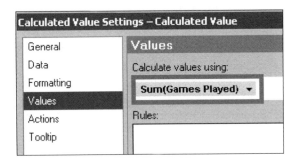

3. In the dialog that opens, enter the following expression under **Expression:**

   ```
   Sum([Salary]) / Sum([Runs])
   ```

   Optionally, enter `Cost Per Run` for **Display name:** (it's not that important in this instance, but it does mean that **Cost Per Run** will be displayed when the mouse hovers on the calculated value). Click on **OK** to save the expression and click on **OK** again to save the settings to the calculated value.

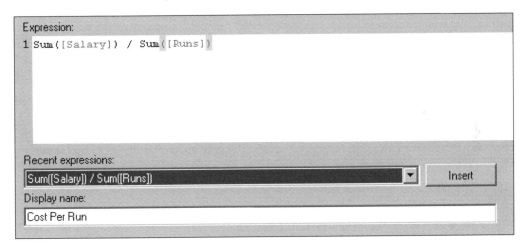

4. Now, format the output for currency display (just as we did for the scatter plot configuration in *Chapter 2, Visualize This!*).

5. Configure the second calculated value in exactly the same way except make one additional setting under **Data** to make the display dependent on marking in the main visualization. You need to check **Marking** under the **Limit data using markings:** setting. This means that the calculation will only be performed on teams you mark in the visualization.

You now have two totals: a static average cost per run across all teams in major league baseball and a dynamic cost per run linked to marking in the main visualization.

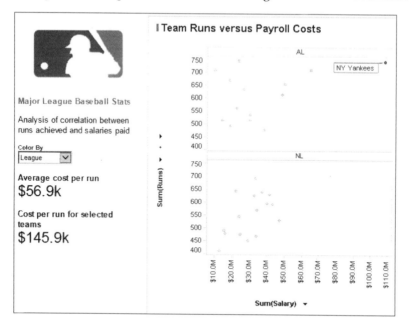

Customizing the filter panel

We had a look at filtering in *Chapter 2, Visualize This!*, where we covered the use of multiple filtering schemes. There are additional configurations you can make to customize the filter panel on each page.

The first is fairly simple. If you haven't worked it out already, you can change the filter type by right-clicking on any filter and selecting from the options available. Depending on the values in the column, some filter types might not be available.

You can hide any filter by right-clicking on the filter and selecting **Hide Filter**. Each data table has its own set of filters, and you can hide the entire set by right-clicking on the data table name at the top of the filter set and selecting **Hide Data Table**.

You can do more detailed customizations by right-clicking anywhere on the filter panel and selecting **Organize Filters....** When you do so, a new window opens allowing you to hide, rearrange, and group the filters any way you want.

If you create a filter group, you can move individual filters into the group by selecting and then moving them up or down the list until they fall into the group. In the following example, five groups have been created and three unwanted filters have been hidden:

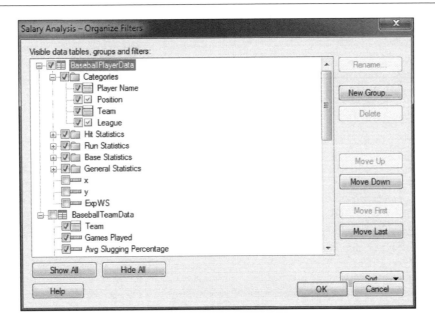

The result in the filter panel is a more coherent and logical organization. You can now apply that exact organization to any other page by right-clicking anywhere on the filter panel, selecting **Apply Filter Organization...**, and then selecting the desired pages.

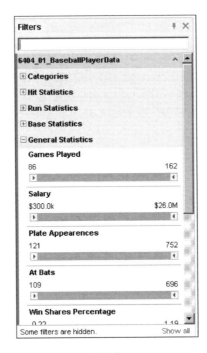

Getting details of marked items

In *Chapter 2, Visualize This!*, you learned how to create a detailed visualization that was dependent on the marking in other visualizations. Spotfire also provides a standard Details-on-Demand panel that does something similar. This panel might appear by default on every page, depending on settings. You can always add it by selecting **Details-on-Demand** from the **View** menu or clicking on the details-on-demand icon in the icon tray.

You configure the details-on-demand panel very much like a Table visualization, selecting the columns you want to display and their order. The one significant difference is the ability to switch the column orientation between horizontal and vertical. A vertical orientation is the traditional table layout of columns and rows and is the best option when multiple rows are selected. A horizontal orientation can work well for single-row selections.

Annotating data using tags and lists

You should now be comfortable with Spotfire's dynamic and interactive marking and filtering functionality, which allows you to mark and filter items of interest and look for relationships, signals, and trends in your analysis on the fly. What if you want to create more long-lasting selections or share your findings with others? Lists and Tags can help you to capture detailed analysis scenarios.

Using lists

Lists provide a mechanism for saving marking selections that persist from session to session in *any* analysis file you open or create. You can mark some points in your visualizations, save the markings to a list, and then recall the marking in a future session at the click of a button. You can maintain multiple lists and you can add new marking selections to your lists. Obviously, if you try to use a list created for one data table on a completely different table, nothing will happen: you can't mark an apple variety in a table of orange varieties.

Let's try using lists with our salary analysis page using the following steps:

1. First, you have to make lists visible by selecting **Lists** from the **View** menu or clicking on the lists icon in the icon tray.

 You can move panels such as the filter panel, the details-on-demand panel, and the lists panel around the page like any visualization or you can float them on top of the page by clicking on the pin in the top right-hand corner of the panel.

2. Now it's just a matter of marking the points of interest, right-clicking on the marked items, selecting **Marked Rows**, and then selecting **New List from Marked....** You'll be prompted to give the list a name, and then you'll see it appear in the lists panel with a number in brackets to indicate the number of items in the list.

3. You can add further items to the list by selecting it in the lists panel, marking some new items, right-clicking on them, selecting **Marked Rows**, and then selecting **Add Marked to List**.

4. To remove an item from a list, you have to select the list, remark the item in question, select **Marked Rows**, and then select **Remove Marked from List**.

5. There is one other way to create a list and that is through Venn logic on two or more existing lists. Click on the Venn diagram icon in the lists panel header, select the lists you want to use, and then choose the logic you want to use from the three options provided.

6. You could create a list of teams with high run cost by identifying all teams with a run cost greater than $75,000, marking them, and adding them to a new list. You could then block select all the NL teams and create a list for them. Now, if you want a new list of high run-cost NL teams, choose an intersecting Venn logic. The result is a list with the only NL team with a run cost greater than $75,000.

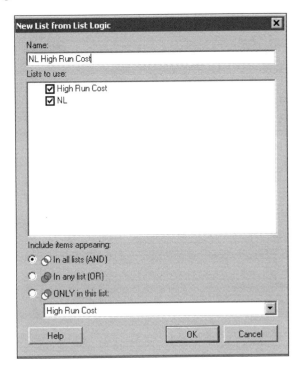

We can see the list of teams in the next screenshot:

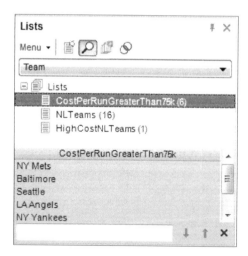

So you've created some lists, now what? First, they will still be there the next time you open any analysis file or start a new analysis. Second, you can double-click on a list item or select it and choose **Mark Items** and you're right back to the marking selection you found interesting.

For example, if you had to do an extended analysis over time, you could identify and save a shortlist of notable data points to a list through multiple sessions, or you could reappraise your analysis following a data update to see if any new items need to be added to the list.

 When you are finished using the lists panel, you can safely hide it without losing any of the lists you have created. Simply reclick on **Lists** in the **View** menu or reclick on the lists icon. Reselect it when you want to use it again.

It's important to note that lists are personal to your client installation, and you cannot share them with others. That's where tags come in.

Using tags

Tags are similar in concept to lists but differ in two important respects. First, they do not persist from session to session and may only be used in the analysis file in which they are created. Second, the main use of tags is that they create new columns to represent the selections you have defined, and you can filter on those columns just like any other column. In this way, you can share tags with others. They become part of the analysis file once it is saved.

Let's take a look at the salary analysis page to see how we might use tags:

1. First, you have to make the tags panel visible by selecting **Tags** from the **View** menu or clicking on the tags icon in the icon tray.

2. In the tags panel, you will see a list of all the tables present in your analysis file. Select the baseball player data table and either right-click and select **New Tag Collection...** or simply click on the corresponding icon just below the tag panel header. Give the collection a name (`Salary Analysis`, for example). This is the name Spotfire will assign to the new column in your data.

3. Now, select the tag collection you have just created and either right-click and select **New Tag...** or click on the corresponding icon. Give the tag a name (`High run cost`, for example). This will be the object we populate with our selections. You should notice that Spotfire automatically created an **Untagged** tag in the collection you created. This is a default tag to represent all untagged rows in the data table. It starts with all rows and then decreases as you tag items, which are naturally removed from the untagged group.

4. Return to your visualization and select the items that are of interest to you. This is where you can begin to use tags and lists together. Instead of reselecting all the teams with high run cost, use the list you have already created to select them.

5. When the items are marked, return to the tags panel and either right-click on the tag you created and select **Attach Tag to Marked Rows...** or click on the corresponding icon at the top of the Tags panel.

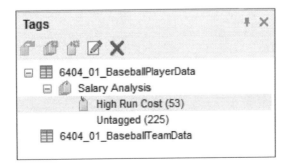

You have now created a new column in your table with values corresponding to the tags you have created within the respective tag collection. To help you understand better what you have created, take a look at the filter panel. You will see a new entry called **Salary Analysis** in which you will see the values **High Run Cost** and **Untagged**. You can now filter on those values. Try it.

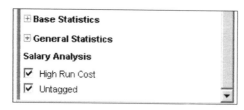

Now, create a Table visualization of the data table and take a look at the new column and how it relates to the teams. What do you think would happen if you created a new tag in **Salary Analysis** and tried to attach it to the **LA Angels**? Do the experiment.

Salary Analysis	Team
Untagged	Kansas City
Untagged	Kansas City
Untagged	Kansas City
Untagged	Kansas City
Untagged	Kansas City
Untagged	Kansas City
Untagged	Kansas City
High Run Cost	LA Angels
High Run Cost	LA Angels

You can delete individual tags or tag collections by simply right-clicking and selecting **Delete Tag** or **Delete Tag Collection**, respectively. To remove an item from a tag (to essentially untag that item), select it in a visualization, right-click on the tag, and select **Remove Tag from Marked Rows**.

There's one more thing we need to cover and that is the creation of tag collections directly from a list. In the exercise where we created the high run cost tag, we went through the process of creating the tag and selecting records using a list, but there is a much quicker way to create a tag collection if a list has already been created:

1. Delete the Salary Analysis tag collection.
2. Go to the lists panel, right-click on the **High Run Cost** list, and select **Create Tag Collection**.
3. Now return to the tags panel, and you should find a new tag collection and the tag you need. The only remaining task is to rename the collection (right-click and select **Edit Tag Collection...**, and give it a new name).

Creating analysis snapshots using bookmarks

We've seen how lists and tags can help you remember, or snapshot, particular analytical positions. What if the snapshot you want to save is more complex and entails a set of filters, markings, and other customizations? In short, you've spent some time exploring some data and arriving at a particular scenario and you either want to share it with others or simply save it for yourself to return to later.

Bookmarks allow you to do just this, capturing specific rows you have marked, the page and visualizations you are looking at, any filtering that you have applied, information about visualization properties (such as the column selected to color by), and any custom property values you have used on the active page.

Let's look at an example.

1. We'll stay on the **Salary Analysis** page, and we'll opt to color by **League**, filter by **High Run Cost**, and mark the **NY Yankees**.

2. Now make the bookmarks panel visible by selecting **Bookmarks** from the **View** menu or clicking on the bookmarks icon.

3. Click on the **Add Bookmark** icon in the bookmarks panel; Spotfire will create the bookmark and name it, date it, and assign your username to it. You can rename the bookmark using the drop-down options next to it.

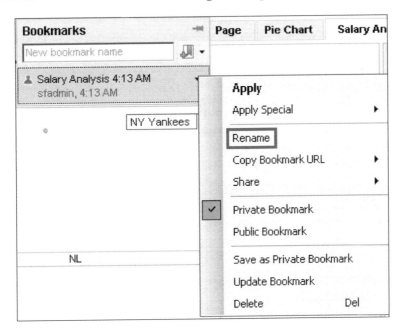

4. Now reset all your filters and markings, change the color by selection, and move to a different page.

5. Call up the bookmarks panel (if it's still not visible), and double-click on the bookmark you just created. The analysis you were looking at a few moments ago should reform in every detail.

By default, bookmarks are created as **Private Bookmarks** for your personal use only. Later in this book, when we take a look at the Spotfire library and web player, we will return to the topic of **Public Bookmarks**, which you can share with a wider audience.

By default, a bookmark will capture all possible attributes of your analysis, but you can customize the bookmark using **Apply Bookmark Special** from the bookmark dropdown selection. This functionality allows you to check for the inclusion of none or all of the following options: Page Layout and Visualizations, Active Page, Active Visualization, Filter Settings, Filter Organization, Markings, and Properties.

Summary

In this chapter, we've started to build some structure around our analyses. We've progressed from simple sets of visualizations to collections framed by descriptive information and property controls. Now, you and the potential consumers of your analysis can change key underlying parameters and even the detailed configuration of visualizations using some simple dropdowns.

You have learned how to use the versatile text area to embed descriptive information, user inputs, and dynamic, data-driven summary information. You have also learned how to customize the filter panel, get details of marked items on demand, annotate data using tags and lists, and create bookmarks of an analytic scenario you wish to capture.

You are well on your way to creating guided analyses and dashboards. These first three chapters have given you a solid understanding of how to get some relevant data into Spotfire, build some visualizations of that data, and enable end users to interact with and customize the analysis. Spotfire is fundamentally an exploration tool, and it's important that you keep exploring and expanding the concepts you are learning. Be curious!

There is still much to learn, and the next three chapters will take a deeper look at the concepts and techniques covered in the first three chapters. *Chapter 4, The Big Wide World of Spotfire*, will present an overview of the Spotfire system architecture and show you how Spotfire can be used as an enterprise as well as a personal analytics tool. We will return to analytics in *Chapter 5, Source Data is Never Enough*, with a look at some of Spotfire's advanced data manipulation tools. *Chapter 6, The World is Your Visualization*, will look at advanced visualization features and some visualization types we haven't encountered yet.

4

The Big Wide World
of Spotfire

It's time to take a break from the world of analysis and visualization and learn something about the Spotfire environment. So far, the focus has been on the detailed work of the analyst, or report author, but Spotfire is much more than an analysis tool for individuals; it is an enterprise application with multiple components. Although you can use the Spotfire Professional Client in an independent, offline mode, you need to log in to the Spotfire system to access the full enterprise functionality of the product. There is also a desktop-only version of Spotfire called TIBCO Spotfire Desktop, which has no enterprise or server-side component. This chapter has no direct relevance for users of TIBCO Spotfire Desktop.

You will find comprehensive architecture and administration documents online (`https://docs.tibco.com/`), but this chapter will introduce the main components of the Spotfire analytics framework. You will learn about the main Spotfire administration tasks, how to distribute dashboards and analytic toolkits to a wider audience, how to monitor the use and performance of the system, and how to automate repetitive tasks.

Although many readers of this book will not be Spotfire administrators, it's useful for you to have a good sense of how the platform is administered and, more importantly, how best to use the Spotfire architecture to deliver good analysis to your customers. Distributing your work to the enterprise is a logical stepping point from the last chapter, in which we began to explore mechanisms for guided analysis and collaboration.

In this chapter, we will cover the following topics:

- An overview of Spotfire components and architecture
- A quick guide to Administration Manager
- Using the Library Administration interface
- A quick tour of Information Designer
- An overview of Spotfire Analyst (formerly known as Professional Client)
- An overview of Spotfire Consumer (formerly known as Web Player)
- An overview of Spotfire Business Author (new with Version 6.5)
- Automating tasks using Automation Services
- An overview of system monitoring tools

An overview of Spotfire components and architecture

Spotfire has five core components:

- **Spotfire Server**: The spotfire Server is the hub of the Spotfire system. It handles user logins and the configuration of accounts, licenses, and other system preferences; it can connect users to external data sources; and it hosts and controls access to the Spotfire library, which is stored in the Spotfire Database.

- **Spotfire Database**: The Spotfire database stores all the account administration and configuration information needed to make Spotfire work. It also stores the Spotfire library, which looks to the user like a hierarchical file system for organizing and store analysis files but is in fact a set of database BLOBs (binary large objects). The Spotfire Database can be built in Oracle or Microsoft SQL Server.

- **Spotfire Web Player**: The Spotfire web player is a web application installed in the Microsoft **Internet Information Services (IIS)** web server. It delivers analysis files that are saved in the Spotfire library to users via a web browser, which is the general mechanism through which Spotfire users consume reports and analytics solutions. As of Spotfire Version 6.5, the web player has been renamed Spotfire Consumer. There is also a new web product called **Spotfire Business Author**, which offers limited report authoring via the web player.

- **Spotfire Automation Services:** Spotfire Automation Services is a tool for automating certain Spotfire tasks into jobs that can be run on demand or to a schedule.

- **Spotfire Client**: The Spotfire Client is a desktop installation that provides access to the report authoring functionality of the product according to the licenses granted to the user. Clients can be used in offline mode, but it is necessary to log in to the Spotfire server to save material to and retrieve material from the Spotfire library. An *enterprise* license provides nothing more than the equivalent of web player access and no report authoring is possible. A *professional* license provides full access to Spotfire's rich functionality, which now includes **TIBCO Enterprise Runtime for R (TERR)**, an enterprise-class implementation of the R statistical programming language. As of Spotfire Version 6.5, the professional client has been renamed Spotfire Analyst.

Three additional optional Spotfire components are worth mentioning:

- **Spotfire Advanced Data Services:** Spotfire Advanced Data Services delivers third-party data to Spotfire as prebuilt, reusable views.

- **Spotfire Statistics Services:** Spotfire Statistics Services delivers the results of S+ and R models to Spotfire for visualization from a central location.

- **Spotfire Desktop**: Spotfire Desktop is a completely standalone implementation of Spotfire that does not require any servers and is targeted at analysts who essentially work offline all the time. It has the full analytic power of the main product.

A quick guide to Administration Manager

Administration Manager is a tool available only to Spotfire administrators to control how each Spotfire user uses the system and its components. It is accessed through the **Tools** menu. The number of Spotfire administrators in an organization is normally very small. This section is included to give you some sense of how Spotfire is administered at an enterprise level.

Spotfire, like many other computer systems, allows you to organize users into groups and those groups into hierarchies of groups. Groups are used to organize users into categories of a common purpose, which could be to do with functionality or with access to particular data.

Spotfire uses the concept of a license to define functional granularity within the system. The term can be confusing. It is related at a high level to the product licenses purchased for a given Spotfire implementation, such as Spotfire Consumer and Spotfire Analyst licenses. However, it also refers to elements of functionality that fall under those product licenses. For example, a Spotfire administrator can restrict the visualization types available to a group of users who otherwise have full Spotfire Analyst licenses.

Using the **Users** tab of Administration Manager, an administrator can perform the following steps:

- View the group membership and licenses of an individual user
- Change the group membership of an individual user

 The management of user accounts and passwords and the authentication of login events can be enabled in a variety of ways in Spotfire. Account management can be handled solely within Spotfire or delegated to another authority such as Microsoft Active Directory, which is used to manage and authenticate users in an enterprise Windows environment. It's beyond the scope of this book to explore this aspect of user administration.

Using the **Groups and Licenses** tab, an administrator can perform the following steps:

- Create groups
- Assign users to groups
- Assign licenses to groups

Using the **Preferences** tab, an administrator can:

- assign configuration preferences to groups

Users

To look up the current assignment of groups and licenses to an individual user, you need to do the following (assuming you are logged in as an administrator):

1. Open the **Users** tab in **Administration Manager**, enter a search string for the user of interest using the asterisk symbol as a wildcard, and click on **Search**. All users matching the search string will appear in the left-hand window; select the one of interest.

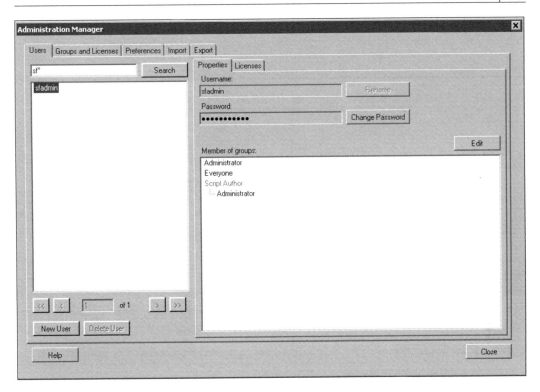

2. The **Properties** tab shows the user's group membership. To make a change, click on the **Edit** button. You will be presented with a simple dialog that allows you to add available groups to or remove groups from the user's profile.

3. The **New User** and **Delete User** options may not be available, depending on how user authentication has been set up in your system.

4. The **Licenses** tab shows the user's licenses, which cannot be changed from this dialog; you need to move to the **Groups and Licenses** tab to do that.

Groups and Licenses

As an exercise in creating new groups, assigning users to groups, and assigning licenses to groups, let's work through the following scenario:

1. Open the **Groups and Licenses** tab in **Administration Manager**, and click on the **New Group** button. Create the groups Marketing Department and Finance Department. You want to create these groups as top-level groups, not as part of a hierarchy.

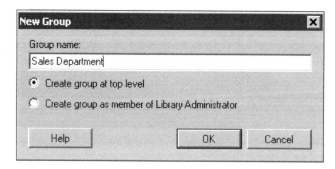

2. Now select the group **Marketing Department**, and create a new group as a member of this group. Name it Marketing Librarians. Create a second group called Marketing Spotfire Consumers. Do the same for the **Finance Department** group. The screenshot shows what you should have when you are finished.

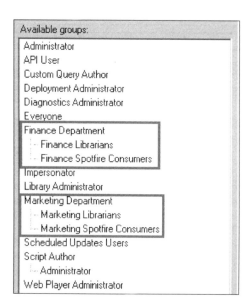

3. Select the group **Finance Department**, switch to the **Licenses** tab, and click on the **Edit** button.

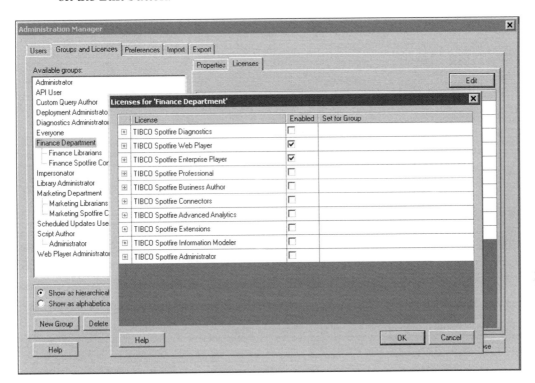

4. Check the **TIBCO Spotfire Web Player** and **TIBCO Spotfire Enterprise Player** checkboxes under the **Enabled** column. Click on **OK** to save the changes. Repeat for the group **Marketing Department**.

 All groups within Finance Department and Marketing Department will inherit the licenses you have granted.

5. Now select the group, **Finance Librarians**, click on the licenses tab **Edit** button, expand the **TIBCO Spotfire Administrator** license by clicking on the plus symbol next to it and check the **Library Administration** option, but *not* the **Administration** option. Click on **OK** to save the changes, and repeat for **Marketing Librarians**.

6. Select the subgroups you created, and in turn, select the **Properties** tab and click on **Edit Members** to add users to each group.

We created containers for two different departments, each with a report consumer group and a more privileged library administration group. We will use these groups to assign privileges at the user level.

Preferences

The preferences tab allows a Spotfire administrator to assign default settings and preferences for visualizations to any or all user groups. Examples would be the default font for labels and the marker shape for scatter plots. Users can, however, override these preferences.

Using the Library Administration interface

The **Library Administration** interface is a tool available only to full administrators or users who have been granted the **TIBCO Spotfire Library Administration** license. It is accessed through the **Tools** menu.

The Spotfire library is a repository of analysis files arranged in a folder-like hierarchy for distribution to the enterprise. It can be accessed from both Spotfire desktop clients and the Spotfire web player. Although all the items in the library are actually stored in the Spotfire Database, the library works very much like a Windows file system.

The Library Administration interface allows a library administrator to create folders and hierarchies of folders; move and copy analysis files between folders; and, most importantly, control who has access to each folder.

There is a special, built-in group called Library Administrator, and members of this group have full control of the entire library. If you want to delegate control to only parts of the library, along departmental lines, for example, you must create a separate group and grant it a TIBCO Spotfire Library Administration license. This is what we did while exploring the Administration Manager tool. You can then restrict the access of this group to certain folders in the library, effectively making those users departmental-level library administrators.

Folder permissions

Let's continue with our finance and marketing department scenario.

1. Open **Library Administration** from the **Tools** menu (assuming you are logged in as a member of either the Administrator or Library Administrator groups).

2. Click on **New Folder** to create a new folder and call it `Finance`; do the same for `Marketing`. You can give the folders descriptions if you wish, but it's not essential.

3. Select the newly created Finance folder and click on the **Edit** link next to **Permissions for Selected Folder**. The dialog that opens allows you to decide which users or user groups can access the contents of the folder to various degrees of privilege.

 The built-in groups Administrator and Library Administrator implicitly have full control over all library folders, irrespective of any permissions set explicitly.

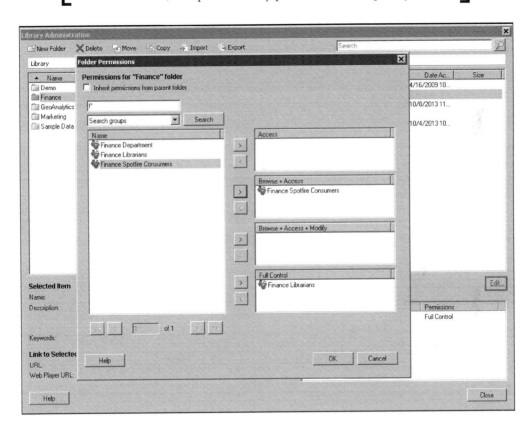

 Uncheck **Inherit permissions from parent folder** if you want to start a new inheritance hierarchy. Otherwise, you will not be able to remove, for example, the Everyone group, which is applied to the root of the library by default.

4. Search for the finance department groups, select **Finance Spotfire Consumers** and add it to the **Browse + Access** panel, and select **Finance Librarians** and add it to the **Full Control** panel. Remove all other groups from the permissions windows.

5. Do the same for the marketing department folders, and then remove the Everyone group from all other root folders.

 For security reasons, I would recommend removing the Everyone group from all root folder permissions and only adding the group back on a case-by-case basis, if ever.

With this setup, when finance department users log in, they will only see their departmental folder and any subfolders to which they have been granted permission. Although finance librarians have the elevated privilege of library administration, they too will only see the department folder. The difference is that they will be able to create new folders under that folder and control which groups and users have access and at which level. The control of user accounts and group membership remains with the Administrator group.

Import and Export

As a library administrator, you can also import and export individual files or entire folders with all their subfolders.

To export, select the folder or file of interest and click on the **Export** button. The selection will be exported as a zip file to a file directory location that is predetermined by a configuration setting on the Spotfire Server. The default location is the installation directory of the Spotfire Server, but it is possible to set up a network share and use that as a more communal area.

 All items in the library have an underlying unique identifier called a **globally unique identifier** (**GUID**), which is retained when exported.

To import, click on the **Import** button and browse to the exported package, which must be in the configured import/export directory. When importing a package back into the library, it's possible that either the name or the GUID (globally unique identifier) of an object in the import package is identical to an existing item at the target location. You must choose one of three following rules to resolve any conflicts:

- **Automatically assign a new name or GUID to imported item:** A "(2)" is appended to the name of the imported item, and it is given a new GUID.

- **Replace existing item:** The imported item assumes the name and/or GUID of the target item.
- **Keep existing item:** The item is not imported.

The same rules are used when simply copying or moving items around the library, except there is no potential GUID conflict in such cases, just a potential name conflict. When importing and exporting between multiple server environments, it's good practice to use **Replace existing item** because it ensures that any Spotfire analysis files that use the items imported to the library will continue to work without modification.

A quick tour of Information Designer

Information Designer is accessed from the **Tools** menu, but it is only available to users who have been granted a TIBCO Spotfire Information Modeler license. It is a tool for setting up data sources and building **information links,** which are essentially database queries that allow you to import a customized data view into Spotfire as a data table.

When you open Information Designer, you will be immediately struck by its similarity to the library you have just been looking at. That's because it is the library; it's just that Information Designer offers you specialized options to create data sources and information links. All of these objects are nevertheless stored in library folders.

It's important that you give some consideration to how you organize information link folders and how you determine access to them. The **Access** privilege you saw as a library folder permissions option gives users access to information links but does not allow the users to see the folder or its contents.

Information Designer allows you to create seven information modeling objects, as well as folders to contain those objects. A library administrator can move and reorganize these items in the library. These objects are interdependent, and some must be created in advance of others.

Data Source

Let's start with Data Source. You must clearly define a data source(s) before you start trying to define columns or information links. When you click on **Data Source**, Spotfire asks you for the database type and a connection URL. If you don't know how to define the connection URL, you will need to consult the database administrator or other relevant documentation for the database in question. You will also need a username and password for the database. The task is very similar to the one we covered in *Chapter 1, Show Me the Data*, to connect to databases.

Columns

The next thing you will want to do is click on **Column** or **Multiple Columns** to select the columns in the data source you need for an information link. This step is quite straightforward: you navigate through a connected data source, select the column(s) you want to use, and save it for later use. You should create folders to group the columns you select so you can find them easily for future information links. There's no need to create multiple copies of any column.

Join

If you need to select columns from multiple tables, you'll need to define the relationship between those tables by defining and saving the necessary join statement(s). When you select **Join** from the **New** dropdown, Spotfire will expect you to first select two columns, one from each of the tables you wish to relate. Then, you will have to decide what type of join is appropriate: an inner join (return rows only where both columns match) or an outer join (return all rows from one table, including nulls, and only the matching rows from the other).

If the tables are related uniquely through more than one pair of columns, define all the pairs necessary to define the relation. Once you've finished, save the joins to a suitable folder and give them logical names you will understand later.

Filter

You can use a filter element to predefine a filter on the data that is returned by an information link. Filter elements are defined similarly to column elements except you include a filter expression. You then add the filter as an element to an information link.

Procedure

A procedure is a piece of code that is defined in in the source database and runs there. You will find procedures in the data source schema represented as cog-wheel icons. Once you define a procedure as an information element, it can be added to an information link's **elements** section. Information links don't just return columns, therefore, they can be used to trigger procedures in the source database, the results of which may or may not be the return of data to Spotfire.

Information Links

Once you have defined and saved all the elements you require (most often columns and joins), you are ready to build the information link. This is the object you will invoke to, for example, import data into an analysis. The difference between an information link and the direct database connection we explored in *Chapter 1, Show Me the Data*, is that an information link is available for reuse by anyone who is given access to the library folder containing it.

Information links have nine sections, although only the main **elements** section is essential, and for basic information links, you will probably just define elements and joins.

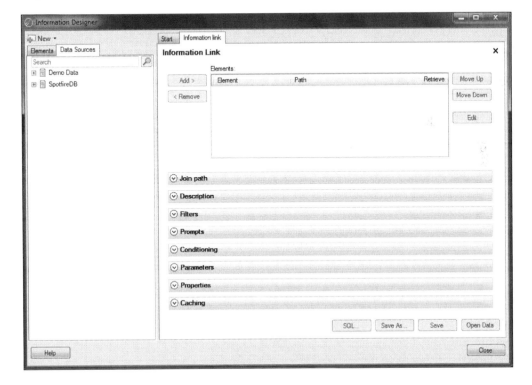

The purpose of each information link section is described in the following table:

Elements	The section where you add predefined columns, filters, or procedure elements.
Join path	The section where you add predefined join elements.
Description	Optional description of the information link.
Filters	An alternative to predefined filters but works in much the same way.
Prompts	Prompts can be added to allow the user to input a value or range for a column(s) in the information link.
Conditioning	Conditioning has two components: eliminating the return of duplicate rows by the information link (equivalent to a DISTINCT statement in SQL) and doing a pivot transformation.
Parameters	Parameters are very much like prompts, except they are defined directly in the information link SQL and are intended to be handled by scripts.
Properties	Allows you to add a custom property to the imported data table.
Caching	Caching options for the information link. The default is no caching.

When you define an information link using these information modeling tools, Spotfire creates the equivalent SQL statement, which you can read and modify by clicking on the **SQL** button.

An overview of Spotfire Analyst (formerly Professional Client)

Spotfire Professional Client, now referred to as Spotfire Analyst, is a desktop client installation that provides, depending on the licenses assigned to a user by a Spotfire administrator, the full functionality of the Spotfire platform. From the professional client, you can build analyses; access Administration Manager, Library Administration, and Information Designer; access advanced analytics functions; and complete other data management tasks. It is what we have been using to work through the examples in the book so far. TIBCO Spotfire Desktop provides similar functionality to the professional client, but without the administration and server tasks.

To use a Spotfire professional client, you need to log in at least once to a Spotfire server. This process authenticates you, determines the licenses that have been assigned to you, and provides any software updates that have been deployed to the server. Thereafter, you can choose to log in or work offline. Depending on the server configuration, you may have to log in periodically to reauthenticate. If you wish to open an analysis file from or save an analysis file to the Spotfire library, you will obviously have to log in to the server first.

You can configure a lot of default options through the **Options** item under the **Tools** menu. Any settings you make here will persist from session to session and override any preference settings assigned to your user group by the administrator. These options can save you a lot of time and frustration if you have strong preferences for certain details in your analyses and don't wish to make the changes every time you start a new file.

One very useful feature of the **Options** panel is the **Fonts** section. Any changes you make here can be applied across the current analysis by clicking on the **Apply to Document...** button, which can be particularly useful to refine the presentation of text areas.

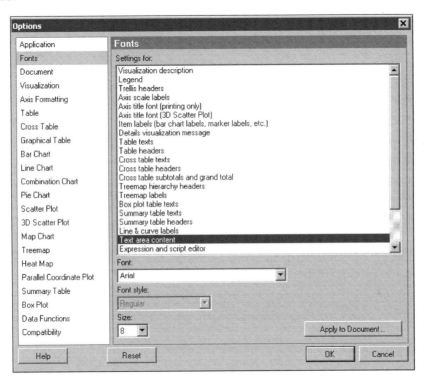

A special case of the professional client is the enterprise player. The installation is exactly the same, and you have the same software installed on your desktop. However, because the Spotfire administrator has only given you a TIBCO Spotfire Enterprise Player license, you cannot create any analyses or visualizations. You are restricted to opening files from the library and interacting with them as designed by the analysis author. It is equivalent in functionality to the web player, although it is possible to assign an administrator or library administrator license to an enterprise player for support personnel who do not need the full analytical functionality of the professional client.

An overview of Spotfire Consumer (formerly web player)

The web player is the standard platform to deliver Spotfire analyses to a wider audience. An analysis author can, in principle, share analyses with others using just the professional client and enterprise player, but it's not a very efficient delivery mechanism for a large audience.

The Spotfire web player server is installed in Microsoft IIS and is linked to the Spotfire server for user authentication purposes and, critically, for access to the Spotfire library. Analysts working with a professional client can save their analysis files to the library, where they can be controlled by a combination of user/group administration and library administration, and then served to consumers through the web player.

To access the web player, a user needs to open a standard web browser, enter the URL for the Spotfire web player, log in, navigate the library, and open the analysis file of interest. The standard URL for the web player is `http://<server name>/SpotfireWeb`. The web player interface looks and behaves very much like the professional client, but with some notable differences.

If a member of the finance department logs in to the web player, he or she can browse the library, but can only see finance department files.

If the user opens the Baseball Example file that has been saved to the `Finance` folder, he or she will see the familiar visualizations we have been working on. The main difference is the inability to select the visualization properties dialog or change any of the visualization properties directly on the page, as we could do in the client. However, all the other interactivity works exactly as in the client.

The icons in the top right-hand corner allow you to toggle the appearance of any collaboration panels created by the author, apply and add bookmarks, toggle the appearance of the filter details-on-demand panels, and access a menu of further items, including export to PDF and Microsoft PowerPoint. Bookmarks can be added as "private" for your own reference only or "public" for use by anyone with access to the analysis file in question.

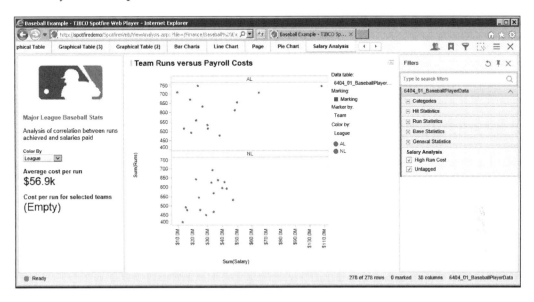

You should see now how useful those text area controls are. Without them, the user would not be able to change the **color by** properties of the plot.

An overview of Spotfire Business Author (new with Version 6.5)

Spotfire Business Author is an enhanced version of the web player that allows web users to make changes to visualizations and create new visualizations through a web browser. The functionality is not as extensive as it is in the professional client, but it does open up a more enterprise-friendly approach to report building.

This implementation is served from the standard Spotfire web player server, and it is made available to users through a new license called TIBCO Spotfire Business Author. If this license is assigned to the finance department group and a member of that group reopens the Baseball Example file in the web player, he or she will see a slightly different interface.

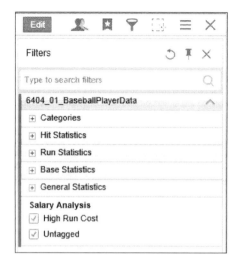

There is now an **Edit** button alongside the other icons in the top right-hand corner. If you click on this button, you get access to the properties of visualizations in the analysis and acquire the ability to create a limited number of new visualizations.

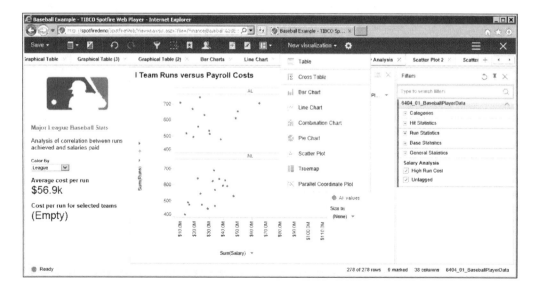

Automating tasks using Automation Services

Automation Services is a very useful tool for automating certain Spotfire tasks. The license to use Automation Services can be given to any user, but it's most likely to be used by someone responsible for the maintenance of a set of analysis files. It's probably not a tool that an analyst would use in the course of analysis creation or design.

The **Automation Services Job Builder** is found under the **Tools** menu, and you use this job builder to create an Automation Services job. Out of the box, 14 tasks are available to add to a job. Custom tasks can be created using the software developer kit (SDK), but this is an advanced topic for Spotfire developers with programming skills.

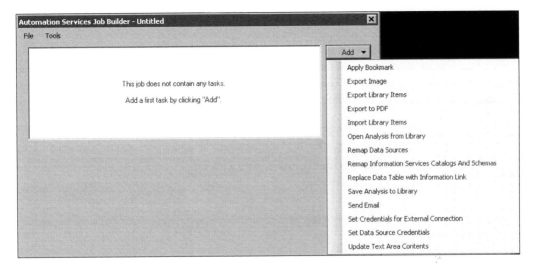

You can see from the list that the job builder offers a diverse range of tasks. Some are more backend administration tasks, such as importing and exporting library items or setting data source credentials; others help to provide updates to people, such as e-mailing them with a message and including images from an analysis file, a web player link to the file, or even an embedded analysis file.

When you select a task to add, a dialog window for that task opens to allow you to enter the relevant details. As you add tasks, they build up as a list in the job builder's window. You can remove individual tasks at any time, and you can move them up and down the order.

When your job is complete, you use the job builder's **File** menu to save the job as an XML file. This XML file can be edited directly, but it can also be opened in the job builder for editing, and that's an easier and safer way to make changes to a job.

Running Automation Services jobs

You can run a job directly from the job builder by selecting **Execute on Server** from the job builder's **Tools** menu, but to take full advantage of the power of Automation Services, you will want to run jobs on a schedule. To do this, you will have to use a third-party scheduler, such as Microsoft Windows Task Scheduler. To run your Spotfire jobs, you need an executable file called `Spotfire.Dxp.Automation.ClientJobSender.exe`. You'll find this file in the Automation Services installation directory on the Automation Services server. You can run it from there or copy it to a more convenient location.

Automation Services is a web application, and each instance is linked to a specific Spotfire server instance and, therefore, a specific Spotfire library. When running an Automation Services job, you must provide the URL for the Automation Services instance you want your job to run against. The final piece you need to run an Automation Services job is, of course, the XML file you saved from the job builder.

An example Automation Services job syntax is as follows:

```
Spotfire.Dxp.Automation.ClientJobSender.exe http://
myAutomationServerName/SpotfireAutomation/JobExecutor.asmx C:\myJobs\job.
xml
```

To schedule the job, simply add that instruction to a batch file and schedule the batch file to run.

An overview of system monitoring tools

All versions of Spotfire create logs that can be analyzed, but Version 6.5 provides some new visual system monitoring tools. We'll take a quick look at the traditional logs and then move on to look at the new functionality in Version 6.5.

Spotfire server administrators can view the system logs via the administration console (http://<Spotfire server name>/Spotfire); a server admin account is needed to log in to the console, which also provides software deployment tools, so it may be tightly controlled by your IT department. Under **Open Logs and Diagnostics**, you'll find a **Server Log Files** tab, where you can set debug levels, view the extensive system logs produced by Spotfire, and export details to a file. You can also copy the logs directly from their location in the Spotfire installation directory on the server.

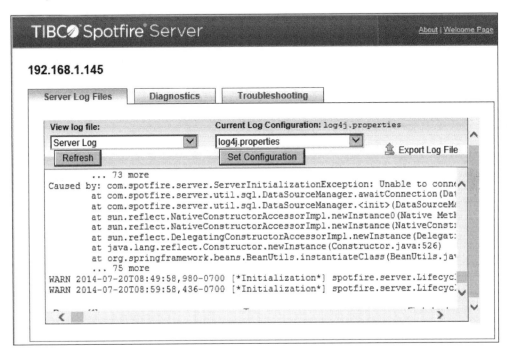

Spotfire logs import into analysis files with a well-formatted structure, and a simple Table visualization can be a very powerful way to interrogate a log file. Beyond that, you can develop further log visualizations and analysis tools using Spotfire Analyst.

Spotfire 6.5

In an enterprise setting, the Spotfire web player is a key component that administrators want to monitor. It is the place where most users access analysis files and interact with them. Spotfire 6.5 provides logs directly through the web player, and you can export the logs to a preconfigured Spotfire DXP file for a detailed analysis.

This functionality is accessed directly from the web player as **Diagnostics** under **Tools**, so a regular Spotfire administrator can access it without the need to gain access to the Spotfire servers.

The default **Web Player Monitoring** view is the **Open Analysis** subtab, which provides a summary of the current activity on the web player, showing active users and some useful status information. You can view some useful performance counters, and you can also view the raw web server log and get information on the status and specifications of the main Spotfire components.

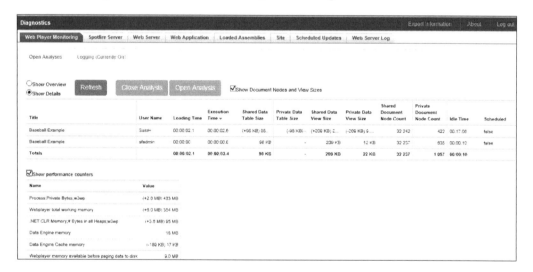

A really cool feature is the **Export Monitoring Logs and Analysis** tool, which you will find by switching to the **Logging** subtab on the **Web Player Monitoring** page. It exports a preconfigured dxp file with a snapshot of the log data. You can open this dxp file in a Spotfire client and access a rich suite of prebuilt visualizations. Also, because the export includes the log files, you can customize the dxp file for your own purposes and continue using the logs provided by the tool.

The dxp file includes very useful **Glossary and Columns** and **Help & Configuration** pages, which explain how to use the dxp file, including instructions on how to set up the analysis file to show real-time data from the server.

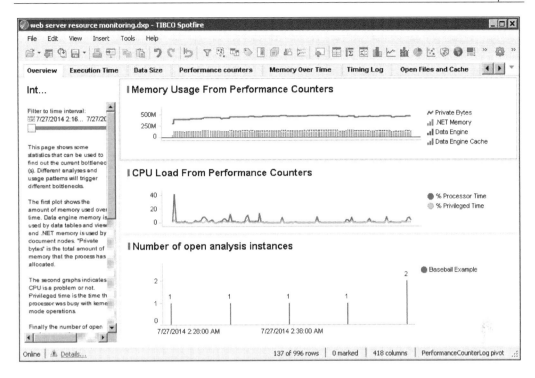

Summary

This chapter has provided a whistle-stop tour of the Spotfire landscape, giving you a sense of the different parts of the system and how they work together. We looked briefly at the main Spotfire components and took quick tours of Administration Manager, Library Administration, Information Designer, Spotfire Analyst (formerly known as Professional Client), Spotfire Consumer (formerly known as Web Player), Spotfire Business Author (new with Version 6.5), Automation Services, and system monitoring tools.

Many of the items we looked at require some level of admin or specialist access, and many of you will not be Spotfire administrators. Nevertheless, I think it's useful for you to have a good sense of how the platform is administered and, more importantly, how best to use the Spotfire architecture to deliver a good analysis to your customers. The inline help files in the Spotfire client are always the best starting place for information about the product's tools and features, and the TIBCO website (https://docs.tibco.com/) provides more detailed documents on all the topics covered in this chapter.

In the next two chapters, we are going to explore some more advanced data analysis and visualization techniques.

5
Source Data is Never Enough

Any analysis, no matter how clever or imaginative, is only as good as the underlying data. *Chapter 1*, *Show Me the Data*, got you started with data; this chapter will take you through some more advanced concepts and techniques. It will show you how to use Spotfire's data tools to transform your source data, when necessary, into a form that is more suitable for your analysis needs.

It's always good practice to do as much heavy lifting as possible in source systems and data warehouses before you import data into a front-end analysis tool such as Spotfire. If you need to combine data from multiple tables, ask a database administrator or modeler to create a view in the database and use that view as your data source. If you need to combine data from multiple data sources, ask an **extract transform load** (ETL) developer to create the necessary integration scripts and stage the data you need in a form convenient for your analysis needs. What's more, following Spotfire 5.0, it's possible to pass complex queries to a database to process at the source and then work with the results that come back. This is an efficient use of database resources.

All that said, however, as a creative analyst and data explorer, you will always have a need to modify and transform data after it arrives in Spotfire, and Spotfire is a great tool for doing so. It's actually pretty good at manipulating data, and it gives you lots of flexibility to reach the analytic insight you seek. If you can't wait for an IT development team to build the exact source specification you require, Spotfire provides a powerful suite of data tools that allow you to freely experiment with data transformation and manipulation to achieve more independently. It can also help you to develop a data specification for long-term and robust enterprise implementations that do require formal IT development.

In this chapter, we will cover the following topics:

- Creating metrics using calculated columns
- Using the Data Panel tool
- Key data concept—dimensional hierarchies

- Adding dimensionality to your data by defining hierarchies
- Categorizing continuous numerical data using binning functions
- Slicing and dicing data using hierarchy nodes
- Merging data from multiple sources
- Key data concept—narrow tables versus wide tables
- Transforming data structure through pivots and unpivots
- Using Spotfire's Information Designer
- Optimizing complex data manipulations using in-database analytics

Creating metrics using calculated columns

Probably the most fundamental and useful data manipulation tool provided by Spotfire is the ability to create calculated columns in imported data tables. A calculated column is created by writing an expression that references other columns in the table, documents property values, and values that you supply, or *hard code*. The expression can be a simple piece of arithmetic, such as dividing one column by another to get a proportion, or a more complex piece of conditional logic. Once created, a calculated column can be used exactly like any other column.

Basic metric

Let's work through an example by looking at two key metrics of batting performance in baseball: the **on base percentage** (**OBP**), which is essentially how often a batter reaches base, and the walk-to-strikeout ratio (BB/K), which is a measure of a hitter's plate discipline.

The data we will use here is `BaseballPlayerData.xls`, which you can download from `http://www.insidespotfire.com`.

1. Create a new analysis file and import the baseball player data.
2. The OBP for each player is already included in the data, but we're going to recalculate it from scratch. Go to **Column Properties** in the **Edit** menu. From here, you can select the data table you want to work with and you can see all the columns in the table. You'll notice that **Column Type** for each column is **Imported**, meaning it comes from the data source.

3. Select **Calculated Column...** from the **Insert** dropdown to open the calculated column dialog. Double-click on **Walks** from the **Available columns** window and notice how it appears in the **Expression** window. Type the division operator / after **[Walks]** and then double-click on **Strike Outs** in the **Available columns** window. Finish by providing a suitable name for the new column in the **Column name** input box.

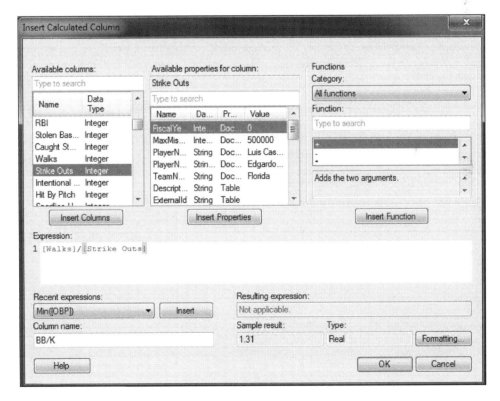

4. Follow the same process to create the OBP calculation, which is as follows:

```
([Hits] + [Walks] + [Hit By Pitch]) / ([At Bats] + [Walks] + [Hit
By Pitch] + [Sacrifice Flies])
```

 Be sure to click on **OK** to exit the **Insert Calculated Column** dialog and again to exit the **Column Properties** dialog.

You have now created two simple calculated columns, and they will appear in the column properties list as **Calculated** under **Column Type**, indicating that you created them and they are not from the source data.

Dynamic metric

Now we'll try something a little more complicated. You're going to create a calculated column that changes dynamically depending on what you select in a text area dropdown list.

1. Using the same process we followed in *Chapter 3, Analyze That!*, create a text area and then a dropdown control called `TeamName`. In the examples of *Chapter 3, Analyze That!*, you selected **Fixed values** under **Set property value through**; this time, select **Unique values in column** and then select **Team** as **Column**. This will create a dropdown of team names.

2. Reopen **Column Properties** and create a calculated column with the following expression:

```
If([Team]="${TeamName}",[Player Name])
```

This expression states that, if a row in the data has a team value corresponding to the team selected in the control property `TeamName`, then give this row in the calculated column the corresponding [Player Name] value; otherwise, leave it empty. Name the column `SelectedTeamPlayer`.

After you create the calculated column, create a Table visualization and explore how the calculated column values change as you select different teams in the dropdown box.

3. Create a list box control in the text area, call it `PlayerName`, and set it to populate through unique values in the column `[SelectedTeamPlayer]`.

4. Create a calculated column with the following expression:

```
If([Player Name]="${PlayerName}",[Player Name])
```

Name the column `Selected Player`.

What you have built now is a way to select a team from a list to get a list of players in that team, so you can select an individual player in the team and use that selection to drive a set of visualizations. We have three more columns to be created to bring the example together.

1. Create a calculated column called `On Base Percentage (OBP)` with the following expression:

```
If([Player Name]="${PlayerName}",[OBP])
```

2. Create a calculated column called `Walks per Strikeout (BB/K)` with the following expression:

```
If([Player Name]="${PlayerName}",[BB/K])
```

These two calculated columns will only return values for the player selected in the dropdown list. Again, I would recommend creating a table visualization to explore the dynamics.

3. Create a calculated column called `Quadrant` with the following expression:

```
case
when ([OBP]<=Percentile([OBP],50)) and ([BB/
K]<=Percentile([BB/K],50)) then "Banjo Hitter"
when ([OBP]<=Percentile([OBP],50)) and ([BB/
K]>Percentile([BB/K],50)) then "Patient Hitter"
when ([OBP]>Percentile([OBP],50)) and ([BB/
K]<=Percentile([BB/K],50)) then "Solid Hitter"
when ([OBP]>Percentile([OBP],50)) and ([BB/
K]>Percentile([BB/K],50)) then "Top Performer"
end
```

For the last column, we are using a **case** expression to build a more complex piece of logic than a simple **If** expression. You can nest "If" statements, but the syntax becomes very difficult to read, whereas a case statement is relatively easy to follow. We are also using the function **Percentile**, the value below which a defined percentage of the data values fall. The 50th percentile is the median.

With this expression, we are categorizing players into one of the four categories, based on which OBP–BB/K quadrant they fall into.

You will find excellent explanations and examples of all the expression elements you can use in Spotfire under the **Function** window in the **Insert Calculated Column** dialog. You can also search by typing some hint text.

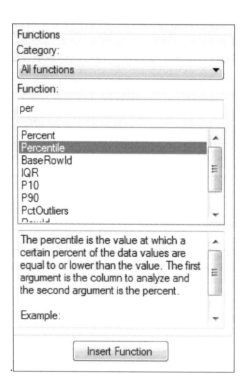

Now, create two visualizations:

- A bar chart with the calculated columns [On Base Percentage (OBP)] and [Walks per Strikeout (BB/K)] as the value axis columns and **(Column Names)** as the category axis and **trellis by** [Active Player] to provide a convenient title to the chart.

- A scatter plot with the calculated columns [OBP] and [BB/K] as the x- and y-axes, respectively; marker by **(Row Number):** color by the calculated column **[Quadrant]**, and label by **[Player Name]**.

When you select a player in the text area dropdown, the bar chart shows you only that player's OBP and BB/K stats. The scatter plot shows you the picture for all players, with the percentile quadrants color coded. When you select a bar in the bar chart, you can see how the selected player compares with the others. You could also add a details table below the bar chart.

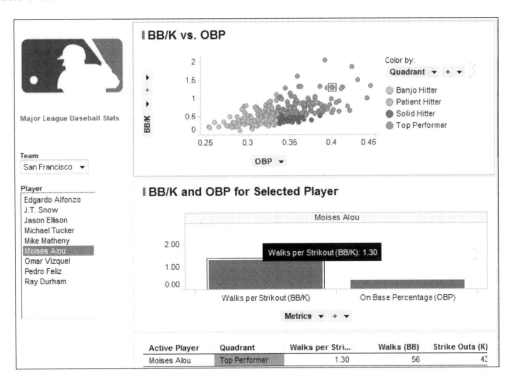

Using the Data Panel tool

The **Data Panel tool**, which you can toggle on and off by selecting **Data** in the **View** menu or clicking on the corresponding icon in the icon tray, is very useful to work with data on an analysis page. It gives you an overview of all the columns in all the tables currently loaded in the analysis file and the relationships between those tables. If you click and drag a column onto any visualization, you will get a set of context-sensitive options, such as **Color by** that column in the visualization.

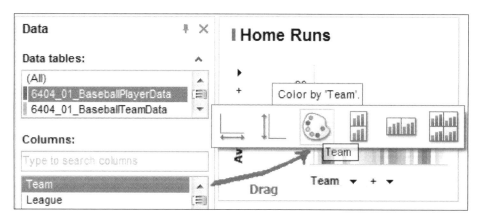

Key data concept – dimensional hierarchies

Data will often contain intrinsic dimensionality. The most common example is a date. Dates are usually entered as single values, such as *12-May-2005*, but if you think about it, there is an intrinsic dimensional hierarchy you might find useful when building visualizations: *year > month > day*, for example, but also *year > quarter > month > day*. Include time and you have additional dimensions.

Independent data attributes, or columns, can also be arranged in a hierarchy. A common example is geography (*region > country > province > city*). The order of the hierarchy can vary depending on your exact needs for a given situation. Do you want to arrange your music collection as *artist > year > album > song* or *year > artist > album > song*?

You won't always need to use dimensional hierarchies, but they can be a useful and powerful way to navigate your data.

Adding dimensionality to your data by defining hierarchies

Spotfire makes it easy for you to use hierarchies. First, whenever you select a date column for visualization, Spotfire offers you a set of prebuilt hierarchy options, including hierarchy sets and individual hierarchy elements.

If you select a hierarchy set for a visualization axis, the user is presented with a convenient slider to select which level of the hierarchy he or she wishes to view on that axis. The visualization adjusts dynamically.

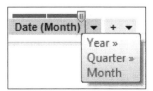

You can also build your own date hierarchies or any other hierarchy you need by selecting the columns that define the hierarchy. You do this from the same dialog **Column Properties** window, where you build calculated columns. The only difference is you select **Hierarchy...** from the **Insert** dropdown and then select the columns or date elements you want to add to the hierarchy in the desired order and give the hierarchy a name. Once created, the hierarchy can be used as a regular column in visualizations.

It's important to understand that although a hierarchy column will always give you a slider when applied to a visualization axis, allowing the user to change the granularity of the axis from, say, league to team to player in the case of the baseball data, you need to ensure that other visualization properties support the dynamic nature of the slider. The other axis must be an aggregation (such as sum, min, or avg) that rolls up the data, and, in the case of a scatter plot, the **Marker By** property must be set to **(Column Names)** or **(None)**.

Categorizing continuous numerical data using binning functions

The final way in which you can create custom columns in Spotfire is through binning. Just as for calculated and hierarchy columns, you create binned columns using the **Insert** drop-down in **Column Properties**, selecting the option **Binned Column...**. A binned column is just a way to turn a continuous set of values, usually numeric but not always, into a set of more discrete values or bins. Age would be a typical case. You might prefer, when using a bar chart to show an age distribution, to plot a series of boundaries, such as < 20, 20–30, 30–40, 40–50, 50–60, 60–70, and >70, rather than a continuous set of individual ages.

The **Binned Column...** dialog offers five methods for binning data, and each of these methods corresponds to a function that you can later edit using the expression editor:

- You can set specific limits by using the following expressions:

  ```
  BinBySpecificLimits([column name], value 1, value 2, …, value n)
  ```

  This method allows you to explicitly define each bin boundary; any values below or above your minimum and maximum values are placed automatically into bins as well.

- You can set a specific number of bins with even intervals by using the following expressions:

  ```
  BinByEvenIntervals([column name], number of bins)
  ```

  This method allows you to focus on the number of bins and not worry about the distribution of values.

- You can set a specific number of bins with an even distribution of unique values using the following expressions:

  ```
  BinByEvenDistribution([column name], number of bins)
  ```

  This method allows you to focus on the distribution of values, still dividing the values into bins, but telling Spotfire to create the bin boundaries to equalize the distribution.

- You can set the bins based on the standard deviation using the following expressions:

  ```
  BinByStdDev([column name], scaling factor 1 * SD, scaling factor 2
  * SD, …, scaling factor n * SD)
  ```

  This method is similar to the specific limits method except you refer to a scaled list of standard deviation values.

- You can set the bins based on substrings in text values using the following expressions:

  ```
  BinBySubstring([column name], number of characters from beginning
  or end of string)
  ```

  This method allows you to categorize string values into bins based on a defined number of characters from the beginning (positive number) or end (negative number) of a string.

Slicing and dicing data using hierarchy nodes

Spotfire provides a set of **OVER** functions to allow you to aggregate data over the nodes of a hierarchy, usually a date hierarchy but not necessarily. At its simplest level, the OVER function is a means to define at what granularity you wish to aggregate a value. For example, you could create the following calculated column in the baseball data:

```
Avg([Hits]) OVER [Team]
```

The result would be the average number of hits achieved by the players in each team. As each team has more than one row in the data, the lowest granularity of which is a player, you will end up with the following result:

Team ▲	Avg Hits
Arizona	114.18
Arizona	114.18
Arizona	114.18
Atlanta	108.40
Atlanta	108.40
Atlanta	108.40

The OVER function has some more advanced and challenging methods. On their own, these methods may not initially seem particularly useful to you and may even be a little hard to understand. However, they become very powerful when used in expressions.

In *Chapter 1, Show Me the Data*, when considering the key data concept of rows and columns, we saw that you cannot subtract a value in one row from a value in another. In other words, you cannot build expressions that cross the row boundary. The OVER function, with its suite of methods, allows you to overcome this limitation because it gives you a means to reference the values at different nodes in a hierarchy in the same expression. For example, it allows you to subtract the sales figure for this month from the sales figure for the same month last year. The sales figures are the nodes in a date-based hierarchy.

There are 14 OVER methods, and the in-line help in the Spotfire client provides details and examples for each. The **Functions** panel in the **Insert Calculated Column** dialog also provides basic descriptions and syntax. The help files in Spotfire for the OVER function tend to focus on **custom expressions**, rather than calculated columns. We will cover custom expressions in *Chapter 6, The World is Your Visualization*.

Here we will cover some of the more interesting and challenging OVER methods using the market interest rate data we used in *Chapter 2, Visualize This!*, for the line chart example, but this time using just the Sweden data. In the following sections, "Agg" refers to an aggregation method such as average or sum, "column" contains the value to be aggregated, and "hierarchy" is the hierarchy to navigate.

For these examples, we are using the **Year-Month** and **Year** hierarchies created on the Date column.

LastPeriods

```
Agg(column) OVER LastPeriods(n, hierarchy)
```

The `LastPeriods` method allows you to apply an aggregation over the current node and n – 1 previous node in the hierarchy. It can be used, for example, to calculate a three-month moving average:

```
[Moving Average]
Avg([One-Month Rate]) OVER (LastPeriods(3,[Hierarchy.Year-Month]))
```

MoneyMarketInterestRatesSweden

Date	One-Month Rate	Moving Average	Explanation
01-Jan-1987	9.85	9.85	
01-Feb-1987	11.42	10.64	Jan-Feb Average
01-Mar-1987	11.56	10.94	Jan-Feb-Mar Average
01-Apr-1987	9.85	10.94	Feb-Mar-Apr Average
01-May-1987	9.45	10.29	Mar-Apr-May Average
01-Jun-1987	8.71	9.34	May-Jun-Jul Average
01-Jul-1987	8.64	8.93	

Parent

```
Agg(column) OVER Parent(hierarchy)
```

The `Parent` method allows you to specify the parent of the current node in a hierarchy. If there is no parent, then all rows are included. In itself, it's not immediately useful, but we'll see how essential it is in the next section.

PreviousPeriod

```
Agg(column) OVER PreviousPeriod(hierarchy)
```

The `PreviousPeriod` method allows you to populate the rows for one node/period of the hierarchy with an aggregation on the previous node/period. In itself, this displacement is not particularly interesting, but if we use it in a calculation, we can determine changes in value from one period to another. For example, say we'd like to see the difference between the average interest rate for one year and the average interest rate for the previous year, we would use the following expression:

```
[Delta]
Avg([One-Month Rate]) OVER (Parent([Hierarchy.Year-Month])) -
Avg([One-Month Rate]) OVER (PreviousPeriod(Parent([Hierarchy.Year
-Month])))
```

We are calculating the average for the parent node (year in our hierarchy) of the current row and subtracting the average for the parent node in the previous period (year).

MoneyMarketInterestRatesSweden

Date	Delta	Current Year's Average	Previous Year's Average
01-Oct-1989	1.48	11.71	10.23
01-Nov-1989	1.48	11.71	10.23
01-Dec-1989	1.48	11.71	10.23
01-Jan-1990	2.08	13.79	11.71
01-Feb-1990	2.08	13.79	11.71
01-Mar-1990	2.08	13.79	11.71
01-Apr-1990	2.08	13.79	11.71
01-May-1990	2.08	13.79	11.71
01-Jun-1990	2.08	13.79	11.71
01-Jul-1990	2.08	13.79	11.71
01-Aug-1990	2.08	13.79	11.71
01-Sep-1990	2.08	13.79	11.71
01-Oct-1990	2.08	13.79	11.71
01-Nov-1990	2.08	13.79	11.71
01-Dec-1990	2.08	13.79	11.71
01-Jan-1991	-1.93	11.86	13.79
01-Feb-1991	-1.93	11.86	13.79

ParallelPeriod

```
Agg(column) OVER ParallelPeriod(hierarchy)
```

What if we want to compare values across parallel periods, such as a month-on-month analysis for this year's figures against last year's? For example, how does June this year compare with June last year. That's where the `ParallelPeriod` method can help. It allows us to get a value in a previous period at the same level in the current period. Note that it can only go up one level to define the period, for example:

```
[Month-On-Month Difference]
[One-Month Rate] - Sum([One-Month Rate]) OVER
(ParallelPeriod([Hierarchy.Year-Month]))
```

Here, we take the current interest rate value and subtract the interest rate value for the same month last year.

MoneyMarketInterestRatesSweden

Date	One-Month Rate	This Month Last Year	Month-On-Month Difference
01-Jan-1987	9.85		
01-Feb-1987	11.42		
01-Mar-1987	11.56		
01-Apr-1987	9.85		
01-May-1987	9.45		
01-Jun-1987	8.71		
01-Jul-1987	8.64		
01-Aug-1987	9.00		
01-Sep-1987	9.12		
01-Oct-1987	9.20		
01-Nov-1987	9.41		
01-Dec-1987	9.21		
01-Jan-1988	9.22	9.85	-0.63
01-Feb-1988	9.45	11.42	-1.97
01-Mar-1988	9.59	11.56	-1.97
01-Apr-1988	9.87	9.85	0.02

You're probably thinking, what exactly is the difference between PreviousPeriod and ParallelPeriod? PreviousPeriod is simply the previous period in the same node, whereas ParallelPeriod traverses the hierarchy to a parallel node.

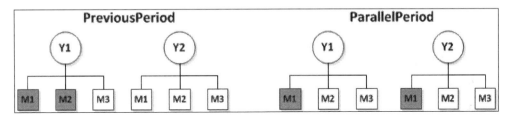

NavigatePeriod

```
Agg(column) OVER NavigatePeriod(hierarchy, node/period name, period
displacement, period level for aggregation)
```

The NavigatePeriod method allows you to specify the period level, or node, you want to use; how much, if any, you want to move forward or backward; and the level at which you want to aggregate, zero being the top level, incrementing by one for each level into the hierarchy. For example, in the following expression:

```
Avg([One-Month Rate]) OVER (NavigatePeriod([Hierarchy.Year
-Month],"Year",1,0))
```

Year specifies the period, the *1* calls for a displacement by one period forward, and the *0* specifies the year as the aggregation period. This expression is equivalent to the NextPeriod construction:

```
Avg([One-Month Rate]) OVER (NextPeriod([Hierarchy.Year-Month]))
```

Say we have daily interest rate figures, a `Year-Month-Day` hierarchy, and are looking at the row for Day 1, Month 1, Year 1. Then, the following results will be returned by a NavigatePeriod call for the average rate:

"Year",1,0	"Year",1,1	"Year",2,1
Average for Year 2	Average for Month 1, Year 2	Average for Month 1, Year 3

Intersect

```
Agg(column) OVER Intersect(hierarchy)
```

The `Intersect` method finds the intersection, or common values for two or more hierarchies. This method is best used in conjunction with other OVER methods. For example, imagine we have monthly market interest rate data for countries across multiple regions, and we defined region-country and year-month hierarchies. The following expression returns the lowest interest rate for each region for each year:

```
Min([One-Month Rate]) OVER (Intersect(Parent([Hierarchy.Region
-Country]),Parent([Hierarchy.Year-Month]))))
```

Merging data from multiple sources

It is best practice to transform your data, including merging from multiple sources, before it arrives in your analysis tool. However, you might not have this facility or access to good data integration tools, or perhaps you just want to explore something quickly to follow an analytical hunch. Spotfire provides some easy-to-use and powerful data merging tools.

When merging data into an existing data table, the first thing you have to decide is whether you are adding new columns or new rows. Then, you must define how the data sets are related. If you are adding new columns of data, you must define the key columns in each table that link the two data sets uniquely for the columns you add. If you are adding new rows of data, you must match or map the column names.

When defining key columns and mapping columns, the names used in the two tables can be different as long as you know that their values and data types are equivalent.

Let's work through some examples to make things a bit clearer.

Insert columns

For this example, we will use two copies of the baseball data: one with all the original columns minus the player position and one with just league, team, player name, and position.

The data used here is `BaseballPlayerDataNoPosition.xls` and `BaseballPlayerDataPositions.xls`, which you can download from `http://www.insidespotfire.com`.

1. Start by loading the first file, `BaseballPlayerDataNoPosition.xls`, into Spotfire.

2. Now select **Columns...** under the **Insert** menu, and when the insert columns dialog opens, use the **Select** button next to **Add columns from:** to select the **File...** option. Navigate to the file `BaseballPlayerPositions.xls`.

3. You'll get a preview of the table, just as you do when importing a table. Click on **OK** to accept the table structure.

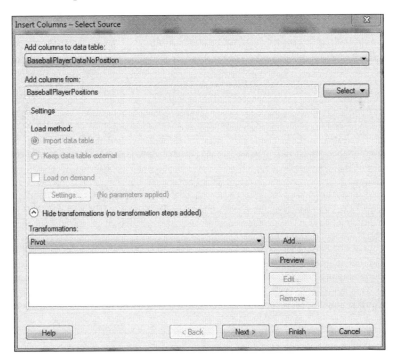

4. We don't need to do any transformations, so just click on **Next >**.

5. In the next dialog, you will define how the two tables are related by matching all relevant columns. Select **Player Name** in each panel, and click on **Match Selected**. The columns will move to the **Matched columns:** panel.

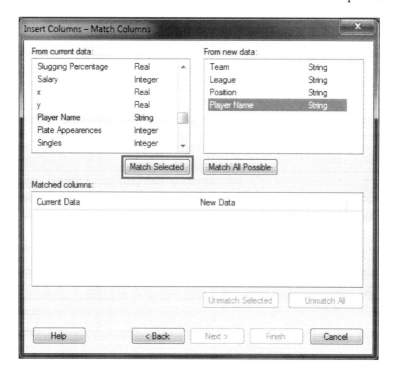

There is no need to match **Team** or **League** because **Player Name** uniquely relates both tables.

6. Click on **Next >**, and when the column selection dialog opens, check **Position** and select a join method (we're just going to use the default left outer join). Click on **Finish**.

Leave **Team** and **League** unchecked because they are already present in our current data table; if we checked them, we would create duplicate columns.

The [Position] column has been added to the "no positions" table, with values correctly matched to each player.

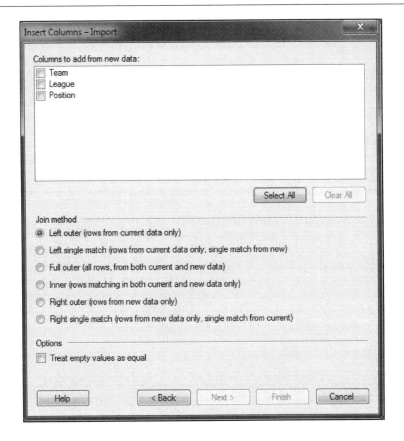

Insert rows

For this example, we will use a copy of the baseball player data with 80 rows removed and a file containing just those 80 rows. The data used here is BaseballPlayerDataTruncated.xls and BaseballPlayerDataNewRows.xls, which you can download from http://www.insidespotfire.com.

The process to insert rows is almost identical to that of inserting columns, except you start by selecting **Rows...** under the **Insert** menu. You go through the same dialogs, but, when you reach the column-matching section, this time you want to match *all* the columns belonging to the data you want to add. Spotfire gives you a **Match All Possible** button to automatically match columns with the same name, but you can match manually if you know two columns with different names are nevertheless the same attribute. For example, one table might have a column called "Player" and the other might have a column called "Player Name," but you know that both tables contain the same category of information: player name.

There is no join definition to add rows because we are not trying to match the table structures, just add more rows under the matched columns. If the new table has additional columns, you can add these, but obviously (at least I hope it's obvious), those columns will only contain values in the added rows, not in any existing rows in the data.

Key data concept – narrow tables versus wide tables

Data tables are row-by-column matrices, and obviously they can range in size from one row by one column to many rows by many columns. You might have come across the colloquial expressions **narrow table** and **wide table**, or even narrow long table and wide short table. These concepts refer to the number of columns in the table, but not in a literal sense.

They refer to the fundamental way in which the data is structured or categorized in a table. In a basic narrow table, a list of categories is contained under a single column and a second column lists values associated with each of those categories: just two columns, but potentially many rows. In reality, there may be other reference columns, but the basic concept holds: one column containing all values across categories. In a basic wide table, each category gets its own column and the associated values appear under it: potentially a lot of columns and as few as one row.

Consider the GDP data we used for the treemap example in *Chapter 2, Visualize This!*. The table we used was a narrow table:

Country Abbreviation	GDP (USD million)
USA	16800000
CHN	9240270
JPN	4901530
DEU	3634823

As a wide table, it would look very different:

CHN_GDP	DEU_GDP	FRA_GDP	JPN_GDP	USA_GDP
9240270	3634823	2734949	4901530	16800000

Each type of structure has its advantages. Narrow tables are good for associating attributes. For example, it's trivial to add full country name and region columns to the narrow table alongside the GDP data but not really possible in the wide table. On the other hand, if we want to do row-level calculations, such as a ratio, it's easier if our figures are in a single row in a wide format. If we want to be able to plot the GDP for one country against another over time, we need to have each GDP series under a separate column in a wide format.

Transforming data structure through pivots and unpivots

You can use **pivot** and **unpivot** transformations to change narrow tables into wide tables and vice versa. You can also use a pivot to permanently reduce the granularity of a data table by summing up to a higher level.

Take a look at the baseball player data. What sort of table do you think it is? It has columns for player name and team and then individual columns for a range of standard baseball statistics, with each statistic getting its own column. This was very convenient when we wanted to calculate the walk-to-strikeout ratio.

Unpivot

Let's see what happens when we unpivot the baseball player data table.

The data used here is `BaseballPlayerData.xls`, which you can download from `http://www.insidespotfire.com`.

1. Load the baseball data into an analysis file.
2. Open the **Add Data Tables** dialog and using the **Add** dropdown, select the baseball player data **From Current Analysis**. So far, we've been adding data from external sources, but it's also possible to copy an internal table and transform it in the process.

3. Don't click on **OK** yet. Give the table a new name in the **Name:** setting. Expand the **Show transformations** section if it's not visible, select **Unpivot** from the **Transformations:** dropdown, and click on **Add**.

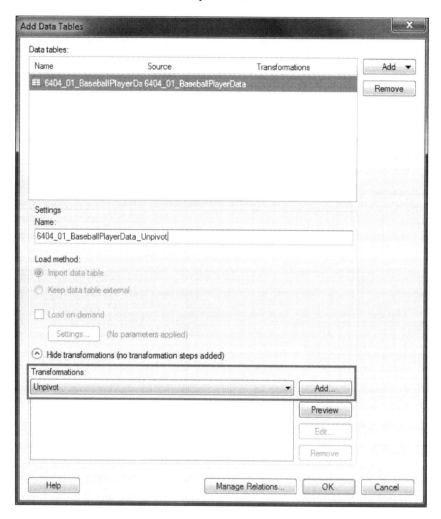

4. When the **Unpivot Data** dialog opens, add **Team, League**, and **Player Name** as **Columns to pass through**. Add **Games Played, At Bats, Runs, Doubles, Triples**, and **Home Runs** as **Columns to transform**. We could add all the statistics, but let's stick to those few to illustrate the principle.

5. Under **Category column name**, type Statistics Category; under **Value column name**, type Statistic. Notice how the preview window changes as you make changes.

6. When you are finished, click on **OK** and then again to complete the transformation.

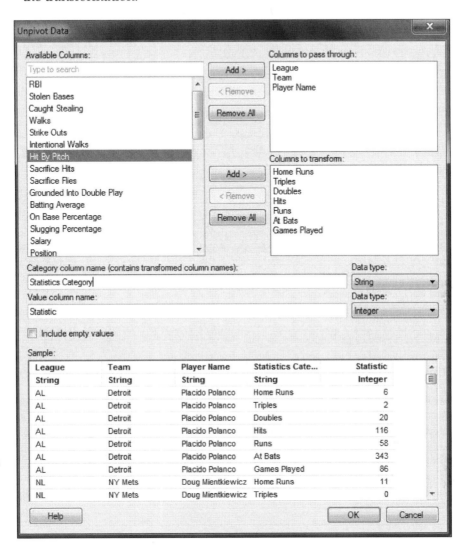

Inspect your new table. What form is it in now?

Pivot

Now, we'll try to reverse the unpivot and recreate the multiple statistics columns. We'll also reduce the granularity as an additional option.

1. Once again, open the **Add Data Tables...** dialog, but this time, choose the unpivot table you just created.

2. Give the new table a name, select **Pivot** from the **Transformations:** dropdown, and click on **Add**.

3. When the **Pivot Data** dialog opens, make the following settings:

   ° Add **League** and **Team** as row identifiers

   ° Add **Statistics Category** as a column title

   ° Add **Statistic** as a value and choose **Sum** as the aggregation method

   ° Change the column naming pattern to just %C

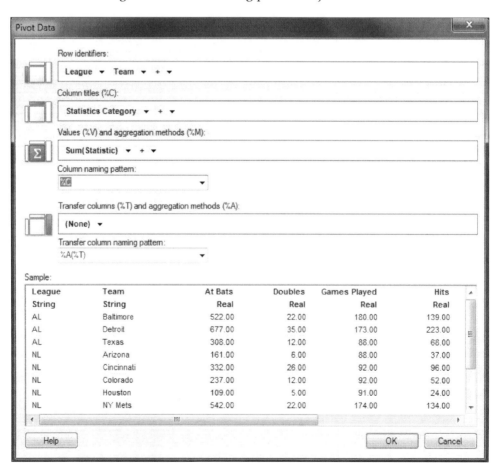

To familiarize yourself with the column naming setting, play around with the patterns and watch how the preview changes.

4. Click on **OK** and then again to complete the transformation.

Inspect the resulting table. You have added back in the individual statistics columns, as in the original table, and removed the player level of granularity, aggregating up to the team level by summing the statistics.

If we had included all the statistics in the pivot transformation, we would have had to look carefully at the aggregation method in each case. Sum is appropriate for some, but Avg would be required for others, such as Batting Average. Having selected different aggregation methods, we might have included the method in the column name pattern, such as %M(%C) to yield Aggregation Method(Statistic Category).

Using Spotfire's Information Designer

In *Chapter 4, The Big Wide World of Spotfire*, we started looking at **Information Designer** and the elements needed to create an information link. We're going to take a closer look now and build an example, not just of how an information link can be used to extract data, but also to write data from Spotfire to a database. To use Information Designer, you must have a reasonable command of SQL and relational database principles, although Spotfire will do a lot of the work for you and try to make the process user friendly by building the SQL query step by step.

Building an information link to multiple source data tables

For this example, we're going to build an information link to Spotfire's own database to extract information on the assignment of Spotfire licenses to users. You will need access to the Spotfire database to follow this example exactly. If you don't have access to the Spotfire database, try doing something similar with a database to which you do have access.

1. Launch Spotfire and open **Information Designer** from the **Tools** menu.

> Remember that you must log in to a Spotfire Server to access Information Designer because information links and their elements are always stored in the library for reuse by anyone who has access to them.

2. Start by creating a new folder to hold the elements you'll create. Select **Folder** from the **New** dropdown, and create a folder called `Information Links`. In this folder, create subfolders called `Columns` and `Joins`.

3. Define the columns you need by selecting **Multiple Columns** from the **New** dropdown. When the configuration window opens, select the **Data Sources** tab, expand the **SPOTFIRE** schema, and look for a table called **GROUPS**.

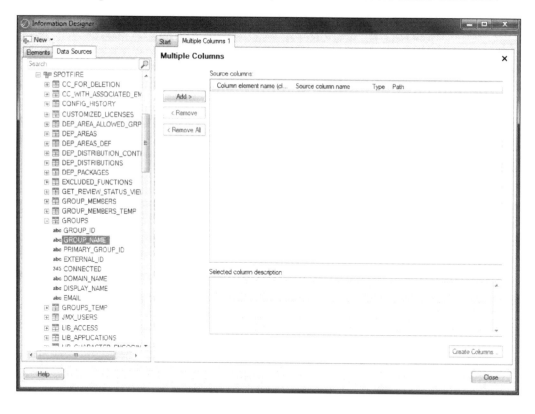

4. We just want the column **GROUP_NAME**, so select it and click on **Add** to add it to the list of column elements on the right.

5. Repeat the selection process for the following columns: `CUSTOMIZED_LICENSES.LICENSE_NAME` and `USERS.USER_NAME`.

In SQL queries, database objects such as tables are referenced in the database schema using a dot nomenclature in the same way you would use slashes to reference a folder or file in a Microsoft Windows environment.

6. Click on the **Create Columns** button to save your selections to the Columns folder you created in step 2.

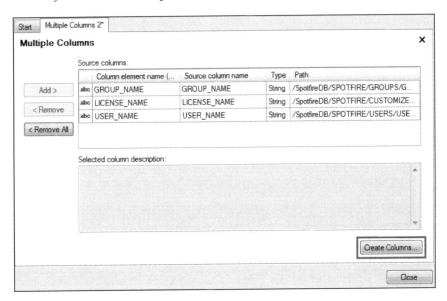

 Don't click on **Close** unless you want to exit Information Designer. To close individual element configurations, click on **X** in the top-right corner.

7. Because we want to use columns from multiple tables, we need to tell Spotfire how those tables are related or joined. From the **New** dropdown, select **Join**.

8. We're going to create three pairs of column joins, selecting columns from the database schema just like we did when creating column elements, except this time we only select two columns per join. We also need to specify the join type, and we will use a simple **inner join** in each case.

9. The first join is between GROUPS.GROUP_ID and CUSTOMIZED_LICENSES. GROUP_ID.

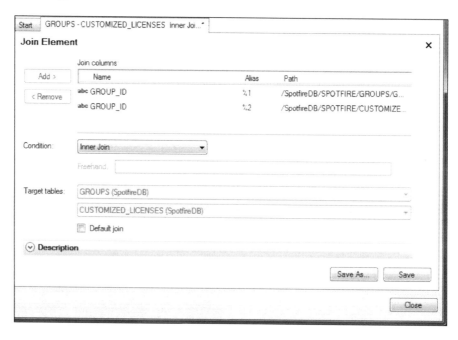

10. Complete each join by clicking on **Save** and saving the join definition to the **Joins** folder you created in step 2. Give the join an intuitive name such as GROUPS.GROUP_ID inner join CUSTOMIZED_LICENSES.GROUP_ID. The remaining joins you need to create are:

   ° GROUPS.GROUP_ID inner join GROUP_MEMBERS.GROUP_ID

   ° USERS.USER_ID inner join GROUP_MEMBERS.MEMBER_USER_ID

11. The final step is to build the information link. Select **Information Link** from the **New** dropdown, and add the columns folder you created to the **Elements** section and the three joins to the **Join path** section. Click on **Save** and give the information link a name such as License Assignments.

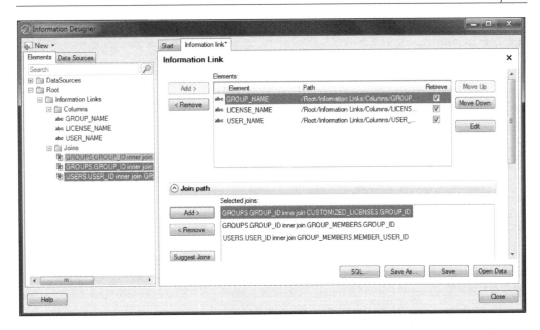

To view your results, add the information link you just created as a data table or click on the **Open Data** button to retrieve the data from the information link you just created.

Building an information link that writes data back to a database

You need to be very careful when writing data back to a database. I wouldn't advise writing any data to the Spotfire tables we used in that previous example; you could seriously damage the Spotfire installation. To illustrate write-back, we're going to use a table created specially for that purpose and populate it with some basic information. After first creating an information link to that table, just as we did in the previous example, we're ready to enable write-back through that information link.

You select the information link in Information Designer and click on **Edit**. When the familiar configuration window opens, click on **SQL** to open the SQL editor. In the screenshot, you will see the SQL select query that Spotfire built based on the column selections. We want to add a SQL insert statement, so we click on the **Pre-Updates** button and enter an insert statement.

It's best to use the syntax style used by Spotfire in the select statement, so copy and paste as needed.

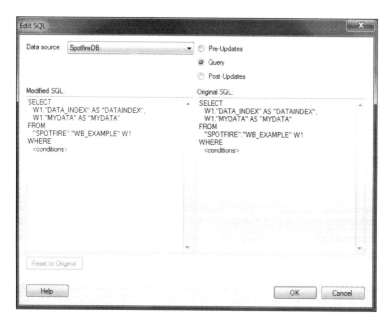

The screenshot shows the insert statement entered in the **Pre-Updates** window:

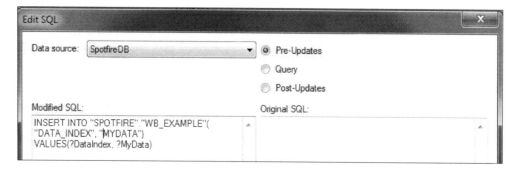

The question marks in front of **DataIndex** and **MyData** (those labels can be any text) tell Spotfire that these are prompt parameters that will be assigned values programmatically. To create an elegant write-back function, you would incorporate those parameters into a script, but for now, we can test the write-back by simply adding the information link as a data table. When you do this, Spotfire asks for values for the parameters, each in turn, and the values you enter are inserted into the data table. For example, you could enter 2 as the index and Second Entry as the data.

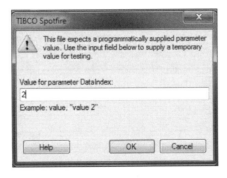

When the data table appears in Spotfire, the insert statement has already been executed, showing us the new row that has just been inserted.

WriteBack

DATA_INDEX ▲	MYDATA
1.00	First Entry
2.00	Second Entry

This is a very crude example, but it illustrates the principle. You can use the SQL update and delete statements to complete the range of write-back operations.

Optimizing complex data manipulations using in-database analytics

Following Spotfire 5.0, it has been possible to push data calculations and aggregations to the source system, facilitating the handling of data volumes too large to fit into the primary memory and take advantage of the power of the source database. When using this **in-database (in-db)** analytic functionality, you access only a selected or aggregated set of data.

When a visualization is configured to use an in-db connection, every time a change is made to the visualization's data-dependent properties, a new query is sent to the external data source and a new table of aggregated data is returned.

The use of in-db data, as opposed to in-memory data, does introduce limitations. For example, automatic date and time hierarchies are not available. Consult the in-line help on working with in-database data for a full list of constraints.

So, how do you use in-db analytics? You start by adding a data connection, as distinct from a data table. Spotfire 6.5 can connect to a wide range of data systems, including Microsoft SQL Server, Oracle, Cloudera Hive, HP Vertica, and Teradata. To open a data connection, you need the relevant data connector, which you must obtain from the provider and install on your client machine.

You can add a data connection from the **Add Data Tables** dialog by selecting an available item under **Connection To**. You can also open **Shared Connection in Library** that has been saved there using **Manage Data Connections** in the **Tool** menu.

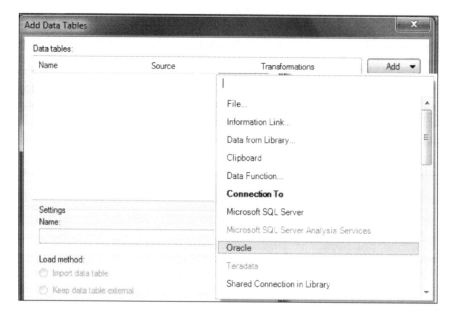

You can set up your connection in three basic ways:

- Simply add a collection of tables you want to use
- Create a view across a number of tables by defining the relations between them
- Create a view using a piece of custom code

Selecting data for a data connection

After connecting to a data source, you can navigate the schema and add the tables or views you want. However, there is an extremely useful function that allows you to select a table that interests you and then click on the button **Add Related Tables**, which will find all the related tables in the source and add them automatically for you.

This is particularly useful if you are connecting to a star schema, a popular data warehousing data mart organization consisting of a fact table referenced to a set of dimension tables (date, geography, and other descriptive attributes).

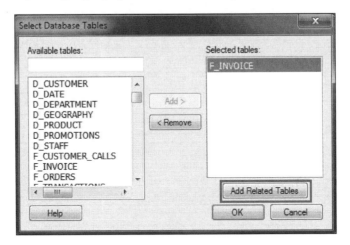

Creating in-database views

You can just work with a set of tables in a data connection and use them to build visualizations, but you can also create data views, which are essentially virtual tables. One way to do this is to select a table of interest and then define its relationships with other tables. The tables are then combined into a single view of the data. First, select a table.

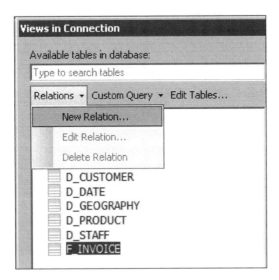

Then, select **New Relation...** to define how it is related to another table.

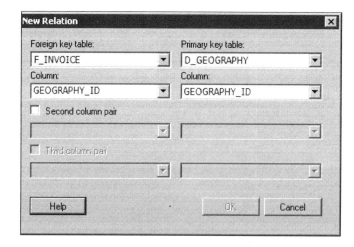

When you finish building the table relations, you can select which columns are to be made available to Spotfire in the view you created.

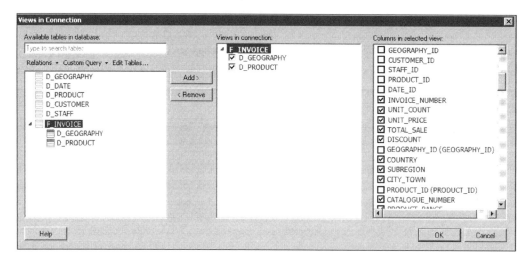

To fine-tune in-db views even more and get the source system to do data calculations and aggregations at source, you can write a custom query. Right next to the **Relations** dropdown in the **Views in Connection** window, where we defined table relations for a view, there is a **Custom Query** dropdown. When you select **New Query**, a dialog opens to allow you to write a query in a language that is supported by the target database. For Oracle or Microsoft SQL Server, this would be SQL. The query you write could be very simple, or it could use advanced functionality.

The point is that the query runs in the source database and returns the results, not the underlying data, to Spotfire for visualization.

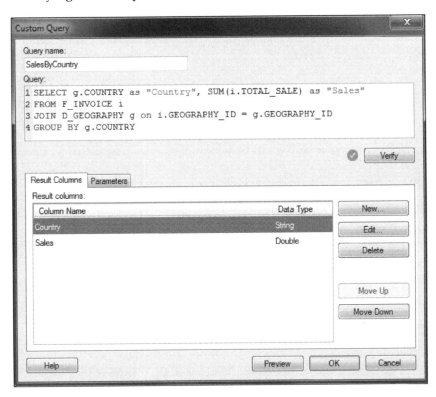

When you verify and save the query, the view is created with the name you gave the query, and you can add it to the list of objects to pass to Spotfire in that saved data connection. The view will appear in Spotfire as a table of sales by country. Any changes to values in the source system will be reflected in Spotfire. You can also customize the data caching settings.

 When working with in-db data, use the data panel. It will not only give you a good overview of the data, views, and underlying relationships, it will allow you to create filters by simply dragging columns to the filter panel.

Summary

In this chapter, we delved a bit deeper into the world of data analysis. Even if you are only using Spotfire as a conventional visualization tool with well-modeled and standardized data, you will inevitably need to do a little data manipulation to get the visualization analysis right.

You learned some essential techniques for shaping and fine-tuning the data you import into Spotfire for more creative and versatile analysis. You've learned how to create metrics using calculated columns and how to use calculated columns to condition your data. You should also have a good grounding in data hierarchies and the access they give you to more complex calculations on groups of rows.

Moving beyond basic visualization building, you have explored Spotfire's built-in ETL (extract, load, transform) techniques and learned how to merge data rows and columns from multiple sources and create and manipulate narrow and wide tables through pivot and unpivot operations. You have used Spotfire's Information Designer to build custom queries into a data source and write-back data to a data source.

Finally, you have had a quick peek at the potential of in-database analytics, through which calculations and aggregations on large volumes of data can be delegated to powerful source systems.

Spotfire's versatile and comprehensive suite of data modeling tools offers maximum flexibility. It can be used to support the data discovery needs of an individual analyst, it can also support an enterprise business intelligence deployment on top of a data warehouse, and it can help an experienced analyst create sophisticated guided analysis of large data collections for small and enterprise-wide audiences.

I hope you're ready for some more visualization techniques because that's where we're headed in the next chapter.

6

The World is Your Visualization

For the routine analysis you want to do, you might be content with tables, bar charts, and scatter plots, but we've already seen how more specialized types of visualizations can suit certain situations. A basic visualization, such as points on a graph, may adequately represent the core information you wish to convey, but there is a lot more to visualization than core properties such as x- and y-coordinates. The use of color is important, as is the addition of reference lines and points. Try to be a communicator, not just a data analyst, and ensure that you use (and know how to use) all the elements available to you to turn a visualization into a story that makes instant sense to the target audience you have in mind. That can be a challenging objective, but always aim for it.

In *Chapter 2, Visualize This!*, we looked at some of the most common visualization techniques. In this chapter, you will learn how to use additional visualization types provided by Spotfire to achieve specific types of analyses. You will also learn how to use some of the more advanced features of the visualization types you learned about in *Chapter 2*.

In *Chapter 5, Source Data is Never Enough*, we spent some time looking at calculated columns and hierarchy nodes at the data level. The same techniques can be used in a more dynamic way directly on visualization elements such as axes, and we're going to take a look at that functionality in this chapter.

In this chapter, we will cover the following topics:

- Applying custom expressions directly to visualization properties
- Key Spotfire concept—difference between calculated columns and custom expressions
- Annotating visualizations with reference lines, fitted curves, and error bars
- Defining color rules and organizing document color schemes
- Slicing and dicing visualizations using hierarchy nodes
- Mashing up data from different tables in a single visualization
- Creating dynamic pivots using cross tables
- Visualizing categorical information and trends together in combination charts
- Visualizing statistical measures using box and whisker plots
- Summarizing statistical measures using summary tables
- Visualizing complex multidimensional data using heat maps
- Profiling data using parallel coordinate plots
- Exporting and publishing data and visualizations

Applying custom expressions directly to visualization properties

The **Insert Calculated Column** dialog that you learned about in the last chapter can also be opened directly on any visualization property that references data. If you right-click on an axis or color **Columns** property, for example, you'll see the option **Custom Expression...**. If you select **Custom Expression...** a dialog called **Custom Expression** will open to give you access to the same expression builder you saw in the **Calculated Column** dialog.

Apart from allowing you to apply a **custom expression** for a visualization property, the custom expression dialog provides a very important aesthetic tool: the ability to change the display label of the property. For example, let's return to a scatter plot we created in *Chapter 2, Visualize This!*, where we plotted Sum([Home Runs]) against Sum([Salary]). Those axis labels, though accurate, might be off-putting or even hard to understand for your audience. It might seem trivial, but changing the y-axis label, or name, to Home Runs and the x-axis label to Salary Bill could make a big difference to the ease with which your audience assimilates the information.

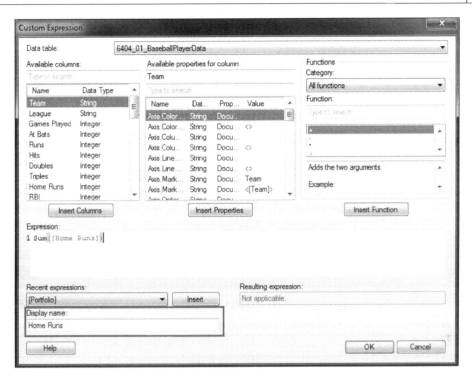

The more complex your expression becomes, the more important it is to pay attention to the label you use. Always be sure to choose a label that accurately describes the metric, and focus on the information you are trying to convey. This process can even help you devise the metric in the first place.

Key Spotfire concept – difference between calculated columns and custom expressions

When you enter an expression in the calculated column dialog, you create a new column in the data. This column behaves like any other column, and its values remain static, fixed by the expression you have defined. If you apply a filter to the columns used in the underlying expression, the calculated values will not change. For example, if you create a column in the baseball data for the sum of home runs by league, it will have two values, one for each league. If you now filter out some AL teams, the AL total will remain the total for *all* AL teams.

If you want the outcome of an expression to respond to filtering on its component columns, you need to use a custom expression directly on a visualization property. The outcome of custom expressions does change in response to filtering. For example, if you create a custom expression for the sum of home runs by league on an axis and then filter out some teams, the sum will change. In the next example, the data is filtered to include only three teams. The left-hand scatter plot is using a calculated column, **Sum([Home Runs]) OVER ([League])**. The right-hand scatter plot is using a custom expression, **Sum([Home Runs])**.

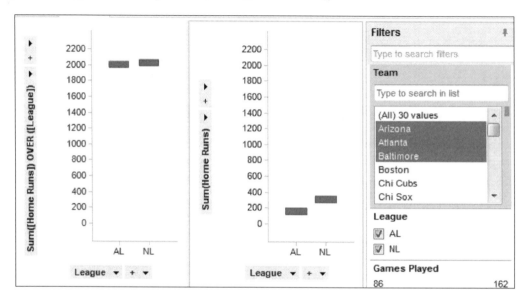

Another important consideration when using custom expressions is understanding the granularity of the visualization: the level of detail each marker or visual element represents. When you define "sum of home runs", is that per team or per league? The answer depends on how you configure the axes, markers, and other elements (such as color) on the visualization.

Annotating visualizations with reference lines, fitted curves, and error bars

Adding horizontal and vertical lines to a visualization to indicate limits or boundaries can significantly enhance the information you wish to convey. Take, for example, the batting performance visualization we created in *Chapter 5, Source Data is Never Enough*. We colored by quadrant, and we can further enhance that visualization by adding appropriate reference lines.

1. Open the scatter plot's visualization properties and select **Lines & Curves**. You can use any pre-existing vertical and horizontal lines or select from the drop-down list provided by the **Add** button.

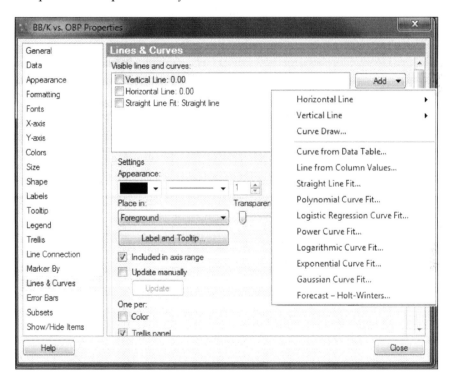

2. Check the boxes next to **Vertical Line: 0.00** and **Horizontal Line: 0.00**, and edit each to change the **Line position** to "**Median**." You can also change the color and thickness of the lines if you wish, using the **Appearance** settings.

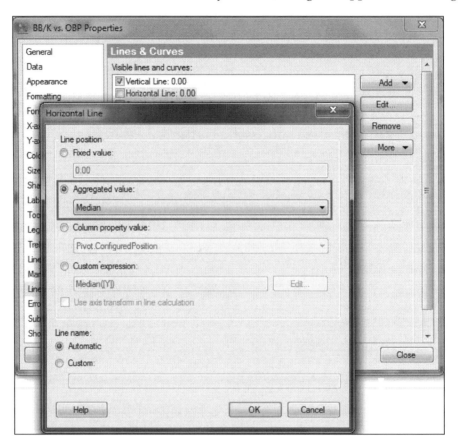

The result of this reference line configuration is the appearance of horizontal and vertical lines corresponding to the color boundaries of the four quadrants we defined for the plot. This example has important and instructive limitations. The median lines respond to filtering because they work just like custom expressions on the visualization, whereas the quadrant colors do not respond to filtering because they are derived from median values set in a calculated column. The configuration only works when no filters are applied.

You can add straight-line fits or more complex curve fits to a visualization using the same dialog. The only difference is that you select the fitted curve you require from the **Add** drop-down list.

To be meaningful, a fitted curve should be supported by some underlying hypothesis or model. Do you expect a linear relationship between the two variables you are plotting? Always challenge such assumptions by exploring real-world relationships as well as patterns in the data. Be particularly careful when using nonlinear fits: a high-order polynomial curve will closely fit the quirkiest data patterns, but the result will not really tell you anything meaningful about the real-world relationship between the variables concerned. For that you need a more specific equation that actually models something that can be tested.

Error bars

Error bars are used to illustrate the precision of a set of observations or measurements; and by precision, I mean the repeatability of a measurement. The tighter the precision, the more confidence you have that the average of your measurements is accurate to the true value.

For example, say you are a meteorological enthusiast who measures the temperature every hour, every day, and you want to plot the average daytime temperature over time. You could just plot the average or you could include error bars to indicate the range in your measurements.

Take, for example, hourly temperature data for a city over an entire year (one source of such data is the United States' National Climatic Data Center (http://www.ncdc.noaa.gov/cdo-web). You could do a straight plot of average monthly temperature against month and also use a calculated column to define a nominal daytime dataset and plot those temperatures against month.

You can use the DatePart function to define the daytime dataset. For example:
```
If((DatePart("hour",[Date Time])>7) and
(DatePart("hour",[Date Time])<18),[Date Time])
```

In each case, you could include error bars to represent the standard deviation in the data (all those hourly measurements). To configure the error bars, you need to:

- Open the visualization properties and select the **Error Bars** property
- Set the upper and lower errors by defining a suitable expression, such as StdDev([Temperature]) in each case

It's pretty typical to use some statistical function of the relevant axis variable to define an error bar. You can also choose the color of the error bar or just keep the color the same as the marker.

For the sake of argument, say we want a profile of the average *daytime* temperatures in New York City by month. Without knowing how the data is configured, the second plot might give you more confidence that it is a truer representation of daytime temperatures than the first due to the tighter error bars.

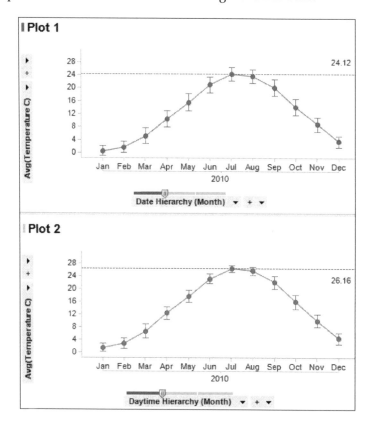

Defining color rules and organizing document color schemes

We've used color to good effect in the examples we've looked at so far in the book. Now, let's take a closer look at color rules and schemes. Let's use the batting performance analysis file we built in *Chapter 5, Source Data is Never Enough*, and add come color rules.

1. Open the scatter plot's visualization properties and select the **Colors** property. We've already assigned colors to the four quadrants. Save this color classification as **Document Color Scheme** using the drop-down button next to the setting **One Scale per:**. You can call it something meaningful, such as `Quadrants`.

2. Now open the table's visualization properties and select the **Colors** property. The **Color scheme groupings:** window will initially be empty, but you can add items using the **Add** drop-down, which will show only the columns actually being used in this particular table. Add the **Quadrant** and **Runs** columns, which you'll notice are added as color groups.

 You can edit a group to change its name and add more columns, where, for example, the rule you want to define applies to more than one column. All columns in a group must have the same data type.

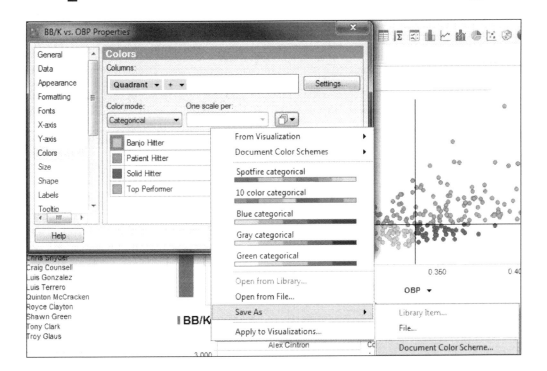

3. Select the **Quadrant** group, configure **Color mode** as **Unique values**, and use the same drop-down you used to save the Quadrants document color scheme to select that scheme. When asked, apply **Colors matched to values**. This action will ensure that the coloring in the scatter plot and table is consistent, and it will save you the task of reconfiguring the Quadrant colors individually in the table.

> The alternative apply color scheme option, **Colors only**, can be used to apply a saved color scheme to a completely different set of values. Spotfire will use the colors in the scheme and only those colors, applying them randomly to the new values.

4. Now, add some rules for the **Runs** group. I precalculated the 25th, 50th, 75th, and maximum run totals for the dataset, and we're going to use those intervals to divide the players into four groups: <46, 46–61, 62–78, and >78. Color the lowest interval the same as the bottom-left quadrant, the second interval the same as the upper-left quadrant, the third interval the same as the bottom-right quadrant, and the fourth interval the same as the upper-right quadrant. For completeness, save this color scheme as Runs.

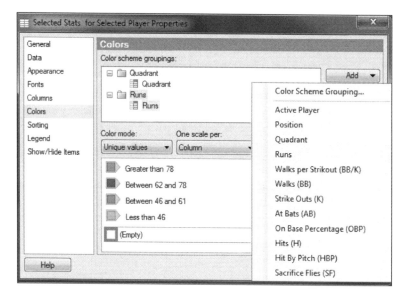

The table should now show you a fairly tight correlation in color between the quadrant classification of a player and his accumulated runs, although some players will buck the trend.

Active Player	Position	Quadrant	Runs
Rafael Palmeiro	1B	Top Performer	47

Active Player	Position	Quadrant	Runs
Brian Roberts	2B	Top Performer	92

For example, Rafael Palmeiro is in the **Top Performer** quadrant but has a mediocre run total, whereas Brian Roberts' run total matches his **Top Performer** rating.

Slicing and dicing visualizations using hierarchy nodes

We spent some time in the last chapter looking at hierarchy nodes and the use of the OVER function. We're now going to look at the use of the OVER function in custom expressions, where it becomes a more dynamic tool. There are also some additional syntax options.

To recap, a familiar hierarchy is implicit in every date, which we can break down into nodes, the most basic set of nodes being *Year>Month>Day*. The OVER methods allow us to reference nodes across the normal row structure of the data, such as comparing a value for 03-Feb-2013 with 03-Feb-2012, as shown in the following figure:

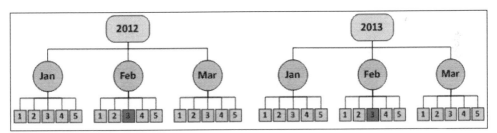

Also, just to remind you, the OVER function can always be used without an explicit method to simply aggregate a value over some hierarchical quality in the data, and you don't have to formally define the hierarchy in this case. An example in the baseball data would be AVG([Runs]) OVER [Team].

You can use OVER methods in a custom expression just as we did in calculated columns, except you need to reference a column-based visualization property directly, and the column must have categorical, not continuous, values. The exact syntax varies from visualization to visualization, but the general form is `Axis.Axis_Name`, where Axis Name could be "X" or "Color."

Visualization Property	Axis Name	Comment
X-Axis	Axis.X	Axis.Columns in Cross Tables
Y-Axis	Axis.Y	Axis.Rows in Cross Tables
Color	Axis.Color	
Trellis	Axis.Rows; Axis.Columns; Axis.Pages; Axis.Panels	
Line	Axis.Line	Visualizations with line by options
Shape	Axis.Shape	Scatter Plot only
Marker	Axis.Marker	Scatter Plot only
Hierarchy	Axis.Hierarchy	Treemap only

Let's look at some examples using the Market Interest Rate data for Sweden. We're going to build an analysis page that allows you to explore some of the key OVER methods.

Load up the Market Interest Rate data (`MarketInterestRatesSweden.xlsx`) for Sweden, and create the following elements:

Element	Property	Values
Tag	**Tag Collection**	Year Subset
	Tag	2010-14 Data for years 2010-14 only Remaining data is untagged
Text area 1	Drop-down **AggregationPeriod**	Integer values 1, 3, 6, 9, and 12
	Drop-down **AverageCumulative**	Display Name: Average Value: `Avg([One-Month Rate]) OVER (LastPeriods(${AggregationPeriod},[Axis.X])) as [${AggregationPeriod}-Month Moving Average]`
		Display Name: Cumulative Value: `Sum([One-Month Rate]) OVER (LastPeriods(${AggregationPeriod},[Axis.X])) as [${AggregationPeriod}-Month Cumulative Sum]`

Element	Property	Values
Text area 2	Drop-down **OverMethod**	Display Name: Next Value: `Next` Display Name: Previous Value: `Previous` Display Name: ParallelPeriod Value: `ParallelPeriod`
	Filter	Year Subset
Scatter Plot	**X-Axis**	[Year-Month] (hierarchy)
	Y-Axis	${AverageCumulative}
Bar Chart	**Category Axis**	[Year-Month] (hierarchy)
	Value Axis	`Sum([One-Month Rate]) - Sum([One-Month Rate]) OVER (${OverMethod}([Axis.X])) as [Difference ${OverMethod}]`

The layout should be scatter plot above bar chart, with text area 1 next to the scatter plot and text area 2 next to the bar chart.

Let's start with the selections **Average**, **1** (for months to aggregate over), and **Next**.

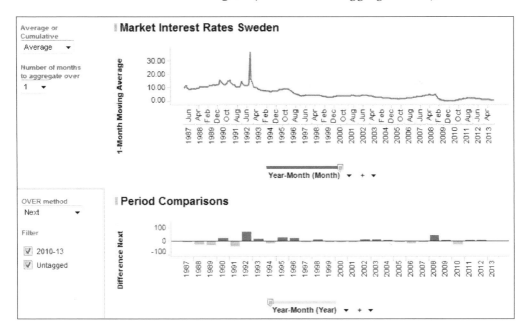

The scatter plot is showing the monthly interest timeline because we have chosen to take the average each month (aggregate setting = 1), which means taking every point. The effective expression in this case is:

```
Avg([One-Month Rate]) OVER (LastPeriods(1,[Axis.X])) as [1-Month
Moving Average]
```

Note how the "1" in the y-axis label is populated dynamically from the document property `AggregationPeriod`. Recall the expression we used:

```
Avg([One-Month Rate]) OVER (LastPeriods(${AggregationPeriod},[Axis
.X])) as [${AggregationPeriod}-Month Moving Average]
```

The bar chart category axis hierarchy slider is set to the year level to make the plot more readable. There is too much information at a monthly level. This plot is showing how the current period (year) compares with the next, plotting the relative ups and downs in the cumulative interest paid each year. The effective expression in this case is:

```
Sum([One-Month Rate]) - Sum([One-Month Rate]) OVER (Next([Axis.X])) as
[Difference Next]
```

Remember that, like the scatter plot expression, this expression is being built dynamically based on the selections made in the text area. Look closely at the expressions we used to build the visualizations.

Now let's change the aggregation level for the scatter plot to **12** and the bar chart OVER method to **Previous**.

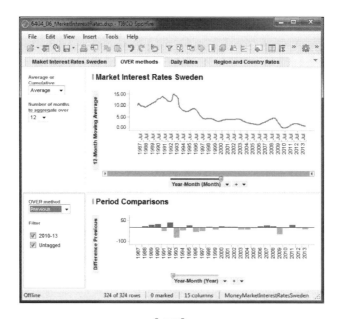

Notice how the interest timeline is much smoother now. That's because we are spreading the average interest rate over a running 12-month period. Notice too how the bar chart has changed to reflect a backward, rather than forward, comparison.

Finally, change the scatter plot aggregation mode to **Cumulative**, change the bar chart OVER method to **ParallelPeriod**, move the category axis hierarchy level to the month level, and uncheck the "**Untagged**" filter checkbox.

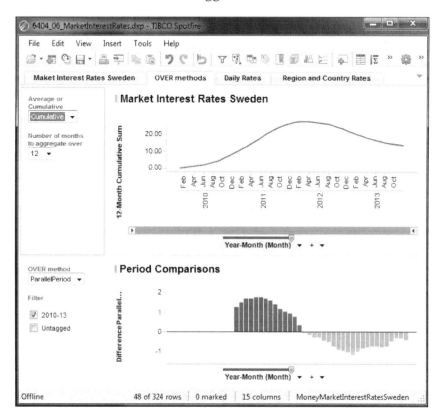

You're now looking at the running 12-month cumulative interest paid on the scatter plot for the years **2010–13**. Meanwhile, the bar chart is showing you how the interest paid in each month compares with the interest paid in the same month in the previous year:

```
Sum([One-Month Rate]) - Sum([One-Month Rate]) OVER
(ParallelPeriod([Axis.X])) as [Difference ParallelPeriod]
```

We've only touched the surface of the power and versatility of OVER methods, but I hope I've given you a good foundation for further exploration. Understanding this function and using it effectively can save you a lot of trouble trying to transform data to facilitate cross-row calculations.

To help you further, the aggregation selection drop-down for each axis provides prebuilt expression shortcuts. You first select a column, then, from the aggregation drop-down, the expression shortcut you require, and finally the parameters relevant to the chosen expression.

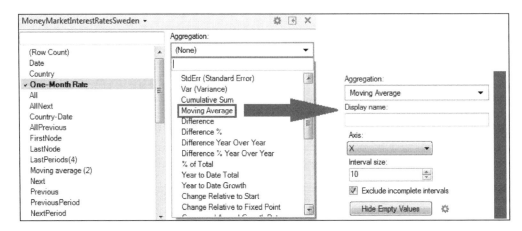

Mashing up data from different tables in a single visualization

Spotfire allows you to combine data from multiple tables in the same visualization and automatically matches any columns with the same name and data type. You can also manually match columns with different names or data types that you know to be equivalent.

If the columns that you want to use from the two data tables match, then the operation is very easy: you pick the columns you want from the table you want. For example, say you have an analysis file with two tables, one containing the column [Player Name] and some player statistics, the other containing the column [Player Name] and some background information such as team and salary. With [Player Name] set on the category axis of a bar chart, you can then mix any columns you want on the value axis.

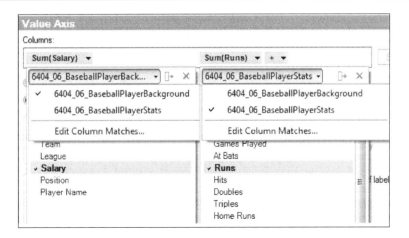

Even if there is no matching column but you know that a column is a unique category across two data tables, you can use it. For example, even though the column [Team] is present only in one table, it can be used to color a bar chart built on the other table. Be aware, however, that if a player has appeared for more than one team, he will show up twice, and the values will be inaccurate. Alex Gonzalez has played for Florida and Tampa Bay, scoring 45 and 47 runs, respectively. In a data mash-up, he shows up as scoring 92 runs for both sides. Be very careful when you mash up data.

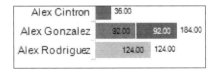

How to create dynamic pivots using cross tables

We're going to spend the rest of this chapter covering most of the remaining visualization types in Spotfire, starting with the **Cross Table**. In *Chapter 5*, *Source Data is Never Enough*, we looked at data pivoting, and we've also seen an example of pivoting in the graphical table, where we tabulated a high-level category—baseball team—and aggregated some values against it from the player level.

The Cross table is a dedicated and feature-rich visualization tool to do these types of pivots without the need to transform any data. The cross table does the transformation for you on the fly. There are two main reasons to use a cross table:

- Rolling up, or aggregating, data values to a category in tabular form (you could perhaps think of it as a tabular bar chart)

- Creating a cross tabulation, or matrix, of values to help you find interactions or relationships between variables

Pivot aggregations

Let's look at an example of the aggregation use case.

1. Load up the baseball data (`BaseballPlayerData.xls`), and create a new **Cross Table** visualization from the **Insert** menu or the icon tray. As usual, the initial visualization properties chosen by Spotfire are unlikely to suit us.

2. Open the cross table's visualization properties, and select the **Axes** property. You'll notice there are three possible axes: **Horizontal**, **Vertical**, and **Cell values**. We don't need the horizontal axis for this example, so remove all data columns from it by right-clicking on the axis selector and selecting **Remove**. The horizontal axis of a cross table represents columns in the display (not to be confused with columns in the data).

3. The vertical axis represents rows in the display (not to be confused with rows in the data), and we're going to select **League**, **Team**, and **Player Name**, in that order.

4. The cell values axis represents the aggregations or expressions you want to assign to the rows you selected in the vertical axis. We're going to define `Sum(Runs)` and `Avg(Batting Average)`.

> If you are entering multiple columns, right-click on the cell values column selector and click on **Select Columns**. You will be able to move multiple columns back and forth more easily and block-assign the different aggregation methods you want to use.

5. Now select the **Appearance** property, and check the **Grand total for columns** checkbox. Select the **Column Subtotals** property, and check **Show subtotals** for **League** and **Team**.

6. You now have a cross table that breaks down the total runs scored and the batting average by league, team, and player.

League	Team	Player Name	Sum(Runs)	Avg(Batting Average)
AL	Baltimore	B.J. Surhoff	30.00	0.257
		Brian Roberts	92.00	0.314
		Chris Gomez	27.00	0.279
		David Newhan	31.00	0.202
		Javy Lopez	47.00	0.278
		Jay Gibbons	72.00	0.277
		Luis Matos	53.00	0.280
		Melvin Mora	86.00	0.283
		Miguel Tejada	89.00	0.304
		Rafael Palmeiro	47.00	0.266
		Sammy Sosa	39.00	0.221
		Subtotal	**613.00**	**0.269**
	Boston	Bill Mueller	69.00	0.295
		David Ortiz	119.00	0.300
		Edgar Renteria	100.00	0.276

7. To improve the look of the table, remove the **Axis Selectors** by unchecking them in the visualization options panel (top-right corner).

The cross table **Appearance** property provides you with options to show row- and column-level "grand totals." It is important to understand that these are not so much "totals" as "aggregations." For example, if your column is an average, then the "grand total" for the column is actually a "grand average." Sometimes, the grand aggregation is meaningless. For example, it is simply not possible to express a correct grand aggregation across columns with different aggregation methods (sum, count, average, and so on). In such cases, you should always hide the grand total.

Cross tabulation

The other main use of a cross table is for, well, cross tabulation. For the batting performance analysis example we worked up in *Chapter 5, Source Data is Never Enough*, we created a column called Quadrant, which classified players into one of four categories. We're going to use a cross table to look at the breakdown of those categories and a few other statistics across each league.

1. Create a new cross table. This time assign **League** to the vertical axis, and assign **Quadrant** and **(Column Names)** to the horizontal axis.

2. Assign the following aggregations to the cell values axis:

    Count() and Sum([Win Shares])

    You can add as many additional aggregations as you wish.

     You can improve the display if you include an as clause. The entire custom expression is:
    ```
    Count() as [Players], Sum([Win Shares]) as
    [Win Shares]
    ```

3. Finally, uncheck **Grand total for columns** in the **Appearance** property.

The result is a cross tabulation of our quadrant category by league, combined with some supporting metrics.

League	Banjo Hitter		Patient Hitter		Solid Hitter		Top Performer	
	Players	Win Shares	Players	Win Shares	Players	Win Shares	Players	Win Shares
AL	52	600.00	15	185.00	15	247.00	42	853.00
NL	49	444.00	23	229.00	23	329.00	59	1206.00

You can also add color to a cross table through the use of color rules. As an exercise, apply a heat map coloring to the **Win Shares** metric, assigning dark blue to the lowest values, red to the highest values, and gray to intermediate values.

 Hint: Use the median as an inflexion point.

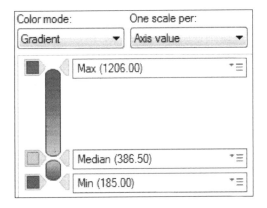

Visualizing categorical information and trends together in combination charts

The **Combination Chart** visualization combines bar and line charts in one plot, allowing you to visualize categorical information and trends alongside one another. It might be viable to plot multiple lines or multiple bars, side-by-side, and that is indeed possible to do with a combination chart, but the contrast in visualization type can often provide a more striking comparison.

The **Pareto** chart, named after Vilfredo Pareto, and used extensively in Lean Six Sigma, is a classic example of a combination chart, where individual values are represented in descending order by bars, and the cumulative total is represented by a line. Let's construct a Pareto chart using the data file ParetoData.xlsx, which you can download from http://www.insidespotfire.com.

We are going to use some fictitious results for a survey asking why a website would drop down on search engine rankings. The results consist of nine, ranked reasons and a corresponding citation count. After loading this data into Spotfire, we can create a Pareto chart in no time by following these steps:

1. As a prerequisite, create a Rank-Reason hierarchy to put the reasons in order of importance. We'll use this hierarchy to create a cumulative sum using an OVER function.

2. Now create a **Combination chart** through the **Insert** menu or by clicking on the combination chart icon. Open the chart's visualization properties, and set the x-axis to the hierarchy, Rank-Reason, and add two custom expressions to the y-axis: Sum([Citations]) as [Citations] and Sum([Citations]) OVER AllPrevious([Axis.X]) as [Cumulative Sum]. When you make this setting, you will get an error message to the effect that you need to use **(Column Names)** on the x-axis or to series or trellis by it.

3. Select the **Series** property, and configure the **Series by:** setting to **(Column Names)**. You'll notice that the two y-axis entries you have made are now represented as bar charts. Change the **Cumulative Sum** entry to a line type. You can also change the colors assigned to each series.

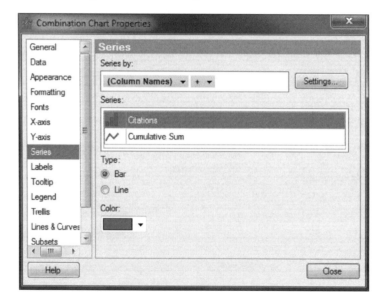

4. In the **Appearance** property, you can sort the x-axis by values (we don't need to because the rank value takes care of the sorting for us), the bar width, the line weight, whether you want to show markers on the line, and how large you want the markers to be.

5. The only thing left to do is insert a horizontal line equal to the 80 percent level of citations. Go to the **Lines & Curves** property, check the **Horizontal Line** entry, and edit it to be a custom expression: 0.8*Max([Y]). Give the line a custom name (80%) and make that label display on the chart by clicking the **Label & Tooltip...** button in the **Lines & Curves** property and checking **Label** for **Curve name**.

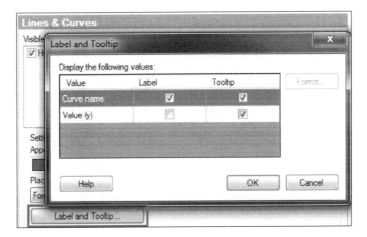

The chart visualizes the Pareto principle, or the 80/20 rule: ignore anything beyond the point at which the cumulative sum crosses the 80 percent line and focus on the things before that point. It's basically the law of diminishing returns.

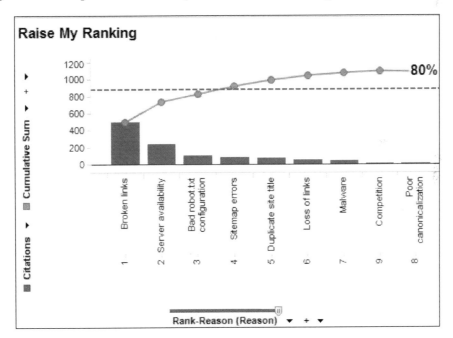

Visualizing statistical measures using box and whisker plots

The **Box Plot** visualization is a convenient graphical tool for displaying descriptive statistical measures such as median, mean, and quartile. We have to look at some statistical theory now because the main reason for using a box plot is to show statistical measures, and it's important that you understand the basic principles. In broad terms, statistical analysis may be divided between parametric and nonparametric approaches.

Parametric statistics are based on an assumption that the data falls into some known probability distribution, and they make inferences about the parameters of that distribution. They can provide good accuracy and precision and, therefore, good statistical power, but they are not robust because they depend on assumptions about distribution. The *mean* (what people commonly refer to as the *average*) and *standard deviation* are parametric statistical measures.

Nonparametric statistics make no assumptions about the probability distribution of the data and, therefore, have less intrinsic statistical power than parametric approaches, but they provide a very robust way of looking at data, especially when you work with new, unfamiliar data and want to find some pattern in it. "Median" and "quartile" are nonparametric statistical measures.

Check out the website *Math is Fun* to read more about **normal** and **skewed** data distributions (http://www.mathsisfun.com/data/standard-normal-distribution.html and http://www.mathsisfun.com/data/skewness.html).

The box plot provides a functional and visual representation of the distribution of values in a dataset, primarily along nonparametric lines. If the data is perfectly normally distributed under a bell curve, then the median equals the mean. Height distribution in the general population would be a classic example. If the data is skewed to the left or right with a long tail, then the median will be closer to the center of the distribution and may represent a better measure of central tendency than the mean, which will be more strongly influenced by that long tail. This introduces the idea of outlying data or data fences: we might be interested in the outliers or we might want to exclude them. This is what makes nonparametric analysis more robust than parametric analysis.

Let's look at the baseball data. In *Chapter 3, Analyze That!*, we attempted to analyze the runs achieved by a team against the salaries paid out, and we used a scatter plot to visually demarcate the data. Our eye was drawn to patterns in the data, and we arbitrarily chose a pattern and dismissed the remaining points as "outliers." Let's take a more statistically robust look at the same analysis using a box plot.

The data used here is `BaseballPlayerData.xls`.

1. Open the salary analysis page or recreate it, and add a box plot alongside the scatter plot using the **Insert** menu or icon tray.

2. Configure the box plot axes by right-clicking on the x-axis selector and selecting **Remove** (we could create separate bars for another variable such as League, but let's just look at the total picture) and adding the following custom expression to the y-axis:

   ```
   Sum([Runs]) OVER ([Team]) / Sum([Salary]) OVER ([Team])
   ```

   This expression reflects the scatter plot, which shows total runs against salary paid by team.

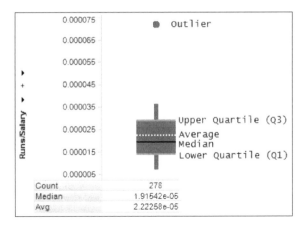

 There are four quartiles, which divide the data into groups of approximately equal observations. Q1, Q2, Q3, and Q4 are equivalent to the 25th, 50th, 75th and 100th percentiles, respectively. Q2 is also referred to as the median. A percentile is a reference point at which that percentage of the total values in the data falls. For example, 25 percent of the data fall at or below the 25th percentile.

The "box" of the plot is the interquartile range and represents the core 50 percent of the data. The whiskers fence the two tails according to established statistical conventions (Spotfire's inline help on the box plot and on statistical measures will give you more detail). The outliers are beyond those tail fences.

So what does all this mean for our analysis?

The outlier is a single team: Cleveland. You can see this by selecting the outlier and observing the corresponding marking on the scatter plot. If you select the box, you'll see a core group of teams highlighted on the scatter plot. Statistically, the remaining teams are the outlying data, which demonstrates very well the difference between statistical analysis and visual bias. Filter to the marked items to see how the "core" teams plot on their own.

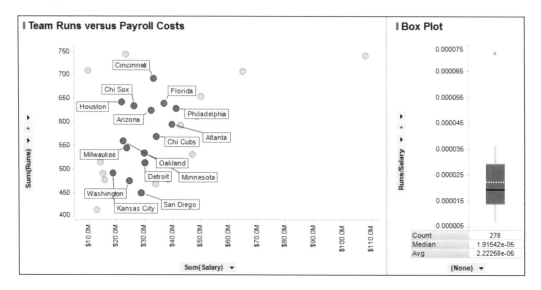

However, you can interact with the box plot in the opposite direction by selecting what we originally identified as outliers on the scatter plot and seeing where they appear on the box plot. It's interesting that these teams are all in the upper portion of the data distribution, so perhaps there is some justification for our visual bias. To explore this issue further, you would need to find some other variable or rationale to explain why this group of seven teams appears to outperform the other teams.

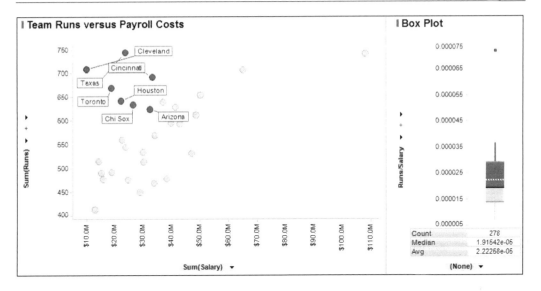

There is one final twist—now that our attention has been drawn to this upper portion of the data, we can confirm its full extent using the box plot. Box plots are marked in blocks, not individual items. If you select the upper portion (everything above the median), you'll find a few more teams marked on the scatter plot. I would put all those teams in group A for comparison with the remaining teams, group B, if I wanted to analyze this pattern further. It's important to stress that this is just data exploration and that the patterns, statistical or visual, that we perceive might have no explanation or rationale in the real world. You should hypothesize, gather more information, and test.

A hypothesis is a proposed explanation (or a theory in common language) for some phenomenon based on limited data or insight. To have any worth, a hypothesis must predict something that you can test against further observations or data. Your findings may lead to the rejection, confirmation, or refinement of the hypothesis.

Summarizing statistical measures using summary tables

Let's continue the statistical theme with something a little lighter: the **Summary Table** visualization, which is a simple tabular representation of statistical information. The configuration is straightforward. First, you need to select the columns in the data you want to report on; these will appear as rows in the table. Then you select from a comprehensive list of statistical measures you want to apply to those columns; these will appear as columns in the summary table. It's really a form of pivoting with a statistical focus.

We'll use the baseball data as a convenient example. Load up the baseball data and add a summary table using the **Insert** menu or by clicking on the summary table icon in the icon tray. Select some columns and statistical measures. I selected the ones you can see in the screenshot. That's pretty much it. There are no coloring or formatting options. You can sort it if it makes sense.

Column	Sum	Avg	Median	Min	Max	Q1	Q3
Games Played	36322.00	130.65	133.00	86	162	112.00	149.00
At Bats	124166.00	446.64	454.00	109	696	358.75	552.50
Runs	17401.00	62.59	61.00	12	129	45.00	78.00
Hits	34098.00	122.65	122.50	24	221	94.00	155.00
Doubles	6957.00	25.03	25.00	4	50	18.00	32.00
Triples	694.00	2.50	2.00	0	17	1.00	3.00
Home Runs	4033.00	14.51	12.00	0	51	7.00	20.00

The key thing to understand here is what the statistics mean, and that depends on the granularity of the data. Our data is at a player level, so **Sum(Runs)** is the total runs scored by all players; **Avg(Runs)** is the mean runs scored by players; and so on. You can add subsets if you want to break down the analysis, by league, for example, in the following manner:

1. Open the summary table's visualization properties, and select the **Subsets** property.

2. Add two separate custom expressions through the **Add | Custom Expression...** dialog, editing the expression and giving it a nice display name:

```
[League] = "AL"
[League] = "NL"
```

Subset custom expressions must evaluate as true or false.

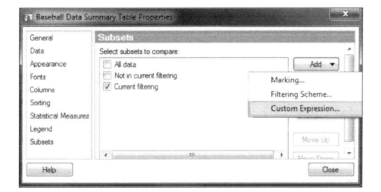

The result is a breakdown by league.

Column	(Subsets)	Sum	Avg	Median	Min	Max	Q1	Q3
Games Played	All Players	36322.00	130.65	133.00	86	162	112.00	149.00
	National League	19624.00	127.43	129.50	87	162	109.00	148.00
	American League	16698.00	134.66	139.00	86	162	122.00	150.00
At Bats	All Players	124166.00	446.64	454.00	109	696	358.75	552.50
	National League	64059.00	415.97	405.50	109	696	319.25	537.75
	American League	60107.00	484.73	483.00	218	679	406.00	575.75
Runs	All Players	17401.00	62.59	61.00	12	129	45.00	78.00
	National League	8835.00	57.37	52.00	12	129	38.00	76.00
	American League	8566.00	69.08	68.50	27	124	53.00	80.00
Hits	All Players	34098.00	122.65	122.50	24	221	94.00	155.00
	National League	17557.00	114.01	110.50	24	199	81.25	148.75
	American League	16541.00	133.40	126.50	44	221	109.00	163.00
Doubles	All Players	6957.00	25.03	25.00	4	50	18.00	32.00
	National League	3679.00	23.89	23.00	4	50	16.00	31.00
	American League	3278.00	26.44	26.00	5	50	20.75	33.00
Triples	All Players	694.00	2.50	2.00	0	17	1.00	3.00
	National League	367.00	2.38	2.00	0	17	1.00	3.00
	American League	327.00	2.64	2.00	0	15	1.00	4.00
Home Runs	All Players	4033.00	14.51	12.00	0	51	7.00	20.00
	National League	2028.00	13.17	10.00	0	51	5.00	19.00
	American League	2005.00	16.17	15.00	0	48	9.00	22.00

Visualizing complex multidimensional data using heat maps

The **Heat Map** visualization is actually two visualizations in one. At a basic level, it is a simple heat map, which we will get to shortly; at a more advanced level, it is also a dendrogram, or tree-structured graph.

Heat maps

A heat map is very similar in concept to a cross table, or even just a spreadsheet, except instead of numbers, each cell is configured to display a color that reflects an underlying number. It provides a very intuitive representation of the relative values of complex multidimensional data. Compare the following pictures of monthly temperatures for a selection of American states. They are identical, except that one shows the actual temperatures in °C and the other shows a heat map to represent the temperatures. Which visualization do you think conveys the temperature pattern better?

STATE	1	2	3	4	5	6	7	8	9	10	11	12
Arizona	5.99	8.08	11.47	15.63	20.88	25.26	26.93	25.72	23.15	16.92	10.36	5.70
Arkansas	4.43	6.97	11.75	16.59	21.25	25.49	27.63	27.22	23.05	16.79	10.97	5.55
California	9.40	11.11	13.02	15.14	18.19	21.08	23.33	23.03	21.14	17.43	12.64	9.27
Colorado	-2.50	-0.11	4.55	8.89	14.34	19.59	22.51	21.11	16.57	9.71	2.77	-2.33
Connecticut	-2.06	-0.48	3.71	10.04	15.48	20.62	23.54	22.55	18.50	12.23	6.65	0.91
Delaware	0.40	1.85	6.06	11.89	17.13	22.30	24.89	23.79	19.89	13.53	8.11	2.86
Florida	15.29	16.74	18.92	21.59	24.71	26.77	27.48	27.45	26.42	23.47	19.68	16.60

The second visualization is as follows:

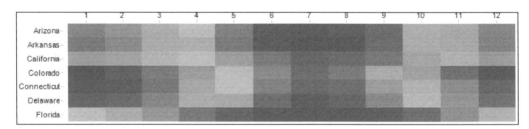

Let's look at how to configure a heat map in Spotfire. For this exercise, we're going to use hourly normal temperature data downloaded from the United States' National Climatic Data Center (http://www.ncdc.noaa.gov/cdo-web). This data, which was collected across almost 10,000 stations for the period 1981–2010, is not immediately usable. The temperatures (in Fahrenheit) have been entered as strings without decimal points and include flags, the station ID is given but not its location or name, and the data is in a wide format, with a column for each hour of the day, which makes it difficult to manipulate those temperature strings into numbers and convert to °C (which is how I like to look at temperature).

We need to download some additional information to cross-reference the station IDs to station names and states; we have to unpivot the data into a long skinny form, with a single temperature column and multiple rows for the hours of the day; and finally, we have to manipulate the temperature strings to get them into numbers we can use. All this is mentioned in passing to illustrate the importance of data manipulation and transformation in the task of creating visualizations. Fortunately, you won't need to do any of this, and the final dataset (`HourlyTemperatures.txt`), which has more than two million rows, is available for download from `http://www.insidespotfire.com`.

1. Load the temperature data into an analysis file and insert a new Heat Map visualization.

2. Open the heat map's visualization properties and configure the three axes: **Cell Values**, **X-axis**, and **Y-axis**. You configure these axes pretty much the same way as you would a cross table. The x- and y-axes are the variables that will frame the heat map, with the x-axis representing the horizontal axis (the columns) and the y-axis the vertical axis (the rows). The cell values are the numbers that will determine the colors in the map. We are going to use the hierarchy Month-Day-Hour as the x-axis and State as the y-axis. The cell values will be the average temperature.

3. Turn now to the **Colors** property. The default setting is to color by the cell values and apply a blue-gray-red gradient, but you can reconfigure this any way you like.

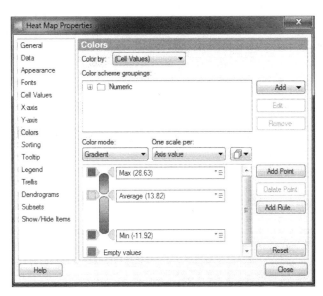

4. Set the Month-Day-Hour hierarchy slider to Month, and that's pretty much it.

The result is the representation of a lot of data in a pretty coherent pattern of color. You can clearly see seasonal patterns and differences between states. If you slide the hierarchy down to the hour level, filter to a particular day (21 June, for example), and zoom in on a few states, you can visualize different diurnal patterns too. Georgia gets as hot as Guam during the day but cools down more at night.

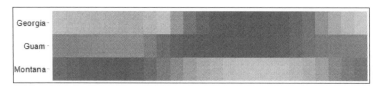

Dendrograms

A dendrogram is a tree-structured graph that can be added to a heat map to show hierarchical clustering. Spotfire offers a suite of clustering methods, distance measures, and other settings, including the option to import a dendrogram from a previous cluster calculation. It's beyond the scope of this book to explore these options, but the inline help in Spotfire is comprehensive.

We'll use the default settings to illustrate the power and analytical beauty of a good dendrogram:

1. Open the visualization properties of the heat map you've already created, and select the **Dendrograms** property.

2. We're going to do a row-based clustering analysis on the states, so select **Row dendrogram** in the **Settings for:** dropdown and check the **Show row dendrogram** Checkbox. If you want to verify or explore the settings for the **Calculated hierarchical clustering**, click on the **Settings...** button.

3. Click on the **Update** button next to the **Row Dendrogram** selection.

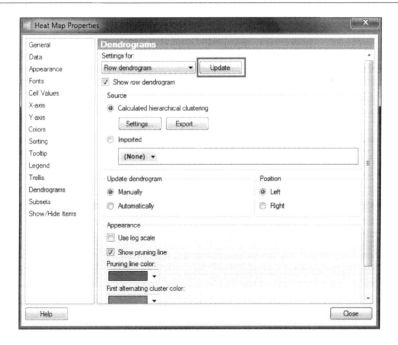

When you return to the heat map, you should see a very different picture, with the states organized into a hierarchical cluster. You can navigate this hierarchy by selecting individual nodes. You'll need a zoom slider to zoom in on areas of interest.

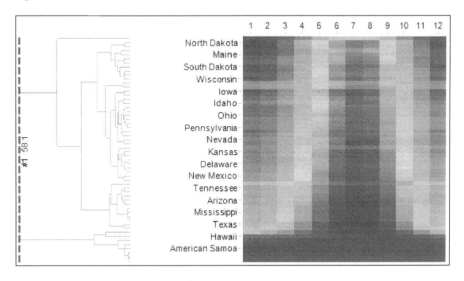

There is a major early fork in the hierarchy, and if we take a close look at this *hot* fork, we can see how easy it is to navigate the dendrogram. We can select the next bifurcation in the tree that separates Florida and Hawaii from hotter U.S. territories.

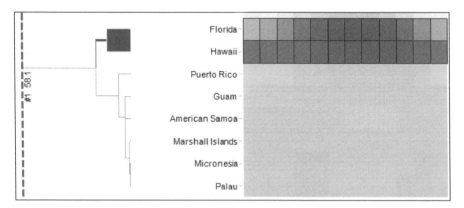

The dendrogram is a useful tool for data mining and the discovery of patterns in large datasets, and Spotfire provides a rich suite of options for doing this type of analysis.

Profiling your data using parallel coordinate plots

The **Parallel Coordinate Plot** visualization is used to compare a set of potentially diverse and unrelated properties that can nevertheless be attached to a themed series. A typical example would be comparing the specifications of a selection of desktop computers. The properties can be anything from keyboard color to processor speed, but they all apply to each PC in our selection.

The columns in a parallel coordinate plot are the properties we want to include, and their values, whether numbers or text, are normalized based on the value for numbers and an inferred value for strings based on natural string ordering. This normalization is the key to a parallel coordinate plot because it allows us to compare quantitative and qualitative information in the same plot. For example, if you include keyboard color and price in a comparison of 10 PCs, the color furthest down the sort order would be assigned the value of 100 percent, as would the highest price. The columns are plotted on the x-axis, and a line is created for each item in the series, showing how it compares with other items at each property point.

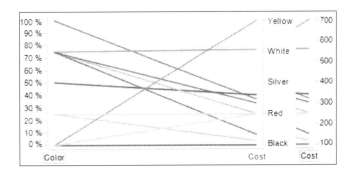

This type of plot is probably not appropriate for a high-level, executive presentation. It is fundamentally an interactive visualization for finding patterns in multivariate data. It might look like a line chart, but there is no sequence or independent variable, nor timeline. In the very simple PC example, you could choose a color and then see the prices available or choose a price and see the colors available. The line running from color 0% (Black) to cost 100% (700) is *not* a trend, it's just two unrelated comparison points.

Let's now work through a more substantial example to demonstrate the configuration and use of a parallel coordinate plot. Anyone can download consumer price index data (harmonized indices of consumer prices) from the European Commission's Eurostat website (`http://epp.eurostat.ec.europa.eu/portal/page/portal/eurostat/home/`). The data for mid-2014 shows price increases relative to prices in 2005 across 12 categories. You will need to model several downloaded datasets to create data columns for country, the 12 price index categories, and geographical and Eurozone classifications. Fortunately, the final datasets (`eurostatHICP.xlsx`) is available for download from `http://www.insidespotfire.com`.

1. Load the data into a new analysis file; create two pivots, one to provide a list by geographical classification and one for the Eurozone classification. Relate these pivots back to the main table.

2. Add a parallel coordinate plot using the **Insert** menu or icon tray, and open the plot's visualization properties.

3. Go to the **Columns** property, and select the 12 price categories as columns, leaving behind Country, Geographical Classification, and Eurozone Classification.

4. Go to the **Colors** property, and select **Country** as the column to color by. The **Line By** property should be left as **(Row Number)**.

5. Add three Table visualizations alongside the main plot: one for the main EurostatHICP table but showing only the country, one for the geographical pivot, and one for the Eurozone pivot. We will use these tables to interact with the parallel coordinate plot.

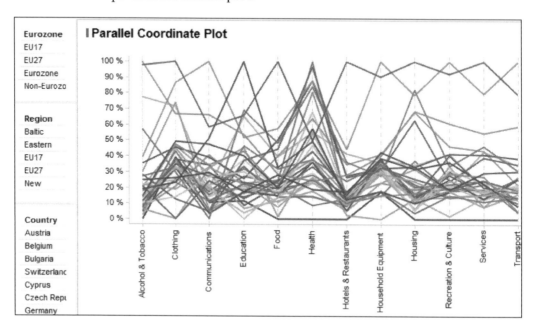

You can see why this plot is not really suitable as a general or intuitive visualization. We can see that a lot of countries have experienced an increase in health prices, and we can perhaps discern a reasonably coherent bunch of countries toward the bottom of the plot, but that's about as much as you can glean through simple inspection.

However, we can interact with the plot using the left-hand tables to select items of interest, either individual countries or one of the classifications we've created. Select **Eurozone** in the Eurozone list. You can see that the Eurozone countries show a fairly consistent pattern except for Latvia and Estonia (the two green lines), which have experienced relatively higher price increases in certain categories than the rest of the zone.

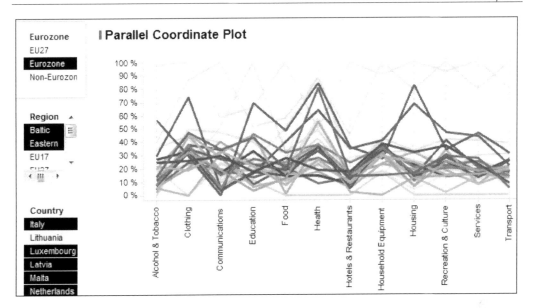

If you add in the other Baltic state, Lithuania, which is not in the Eurozone, you see a common Baltic pattern. Interestingly, it's also evident that the Baltic countries have experienced the lowest inflation in communication costs in the entire dataset, which includes some non-EU countries and the U.S.

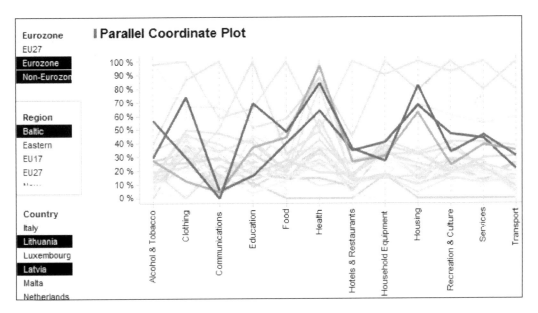

We could go on in this vein exploring patterns in the data. To communicate your findings to a general audience, you would probably create a guided, interactive dashboard and some companion visualizations to present your conclusions.

Exporting and publishing data and visualizations

There are many benefits in delivering Spotfire analyses to end users with direct access to the application, but this might not always be possible and you will need to export data or visualizations for consumption outside the tool. Users of the web player (Spotfire Consumer) might also want to export data for further analysis or copy visualizations into a report document.

Let's deal with that last requirement first. The **Export** dropdown in the web player menu provides a number of options:

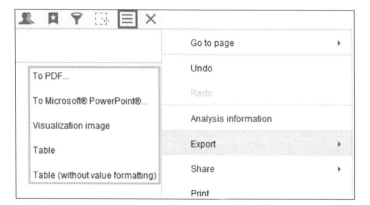

1. Export the active visualization as an image.

2. If the active visualization is a Table, Cross Table, or Summary Table, export the data as an ASP.NET Web Handler (ASHX) file, which can be opened with Microsoft Excel or a text editor. Only the data displayed in the Table, Cross Table, or Summary Table visualization will be exported, not the entire data table.

3. Select PDF or Microsoft PowerPoint for further options.

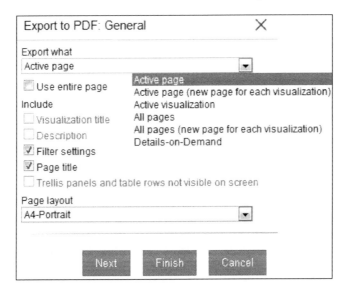

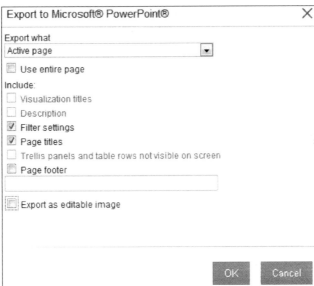

All of these options are available from the professional client via the **File | Export** options. In addition, you can export an entire data table from the client, independently of any visualization, and you can choose to export the data in one of four basic formats:

- Tab-separated text file
- TIBCO Spotfire Text Data Format (includes header information)
- TIBCO Spotfire Binary Data Format (faithful copy for export to another Spotfire file)
- Microsoft Excel

Summary

In this chapter, we have completed the tour of Spotfire visualizations that we began in *Chapter 2, Visualize This!*. You've covered quite a lot in this chapter, learning how to use the Cross Table to create dynamic pivots and cross tabulations; the Combination Chart to superimpose categorical information and trends; the Box Plot to create a statistically rigorous plot that retains full interactivity with other visualizations; the Summary Table for easy display of descriptive statistics; the Heat Map and its companion, dendrogram hierarchical clustering engine, as powerful tools for visualizing complex multidimensional data; and the Parallel Coordinate Plot as a good tool for exploring patterns in multidimensional data.

You've learned how to apply custom expressions directly to visualization properties and how to slice and dice visualizations using hierarchy nodes, understanding in the process the difference between calculated columns and custom expressions.

You've learned how to annotate visualizations with reference lines, fitted curves, and error bars; how to define color rules and organize document color schemes; and how to mash up data from different tables in a single visualization.

You've also learned how to export and publish data and visualizations for consumption outside Spotfire.

There are only two visualization types we haven't covered: the 3D scatter plot, which, apart from the z-axis, is exactly like a 2D scatter plot; and the map chart, which requires an entire chapter to itself, and is where we are headed in the next chapter.

7
What's Your Location?

The first six chapters of this book have shown you how powerful data visualization can be. You should understand by now the insight a bar chart or a scatter plot can add to a tabular representation of data.

Spatial analytics is a relatively new area of data visualization. We are all used to using **geographic information systems (GIS)** like Google Maps. It is much easier to give directions using an interactive map than using text instructions, and the language is universal. Moreover, this concept can be explored to create analytics contexts that are simply not possible with traditional tables and charts. If you stretch your imagination just a little, you will also quickly realize that you don't have to confine your analysis to geographic locations. Any spatial context — a silicon chip, an MRI scan, a baseball field — can be *mapped* and combined with other data to do spatial analytics.

The world of business intelligence lags behind popular culture, and spatial analytics is actually not mainstream yet. It is a technically challenging and complex form of analysis, but TIBCO has committed a lot of development time to making Spotfire a very accessible and state-of-the-art spatial analytics tool. The challenge has shifted to your imagination.

In this chapter, we will take a close look at the **Map Chart** visualization, which needs a chapter to itself. You will learn how to use Spotfire's spatial analytics capabilities to overlay data on images and multi-layered maps, putting spatial and geographic contexts on your analyses. Along the way, you will learn some important GIS concepts such as coordinate reference systems and geocoding. The map chart is a complex visualization to work with, but it is also probably the most intuitive because it connects directly with our inherent spatial awareness. This is as close as it gets to representing data in a native human form.

In this chapter, we will cover the following topics:

- Creating background map layers
- Key Spotfire concept—map chart layers
- Key mapping concept—coordinate reference systems
- Using automatic geocoding to accurately position locations from your data on a map
- Incorporating and using a feature layer
- Adding Web Map Service data to a map chart
- Using the map chart for nongeographic spatial analysis

Creating background map layers

As of Version 6.0, Spotfire comes with a tile-based web map supplied by TIBCO GeoAnalytics (http://geoanalytics.tibco.com/). This background map layer is created as a default base layer whenever you create a **Map Chart** visualization, but you must be connected to the Internet to access the full depth of the layer. Using a familiar zoom slider and hand tool, you can move quickly from a global view to a street map of a city, such as Mumbai, India, as shown in the following screenshot:

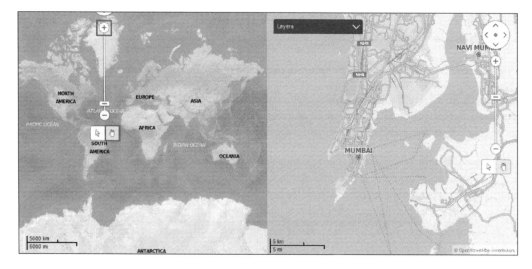

You can configure the level of cartographic detail in the map layer to include borders, labels, and roads, or you can build separate layers for each type of information and overlay them one on top of the other, allowing the user to choose which ones to show or hide.

Creating a map is very easy. First, load any small dataset containing some simple text values into a new analysis file. You need to have some nominal data in the analysis file before you can create any visualization. Next, create a map chart just like any other visualization, using the **Insert** menu or the map chart icon. Spotfire will create the map layer automatically, and you can begin zooming and exploring. There's not much you can do analytically, but for now take a look at the **Standard map Settings** tab to see how they change the presentation, as shown in the following screenshot:

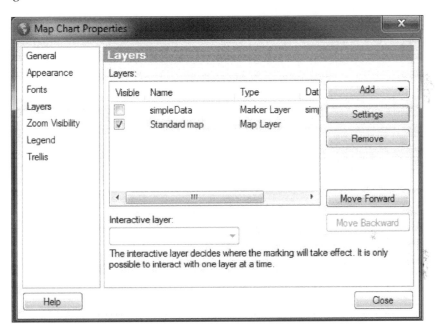

Change the map to a **Basic map**, and add three map layers using the **Add** dropdown, making one a **Labels** map, one a **Roads** map, and the third a **Borders** map.

You now have four map layers that you can show or hide to reveal increasing or decreasing levels of detail.

 Pay attention to the ordering of the layers. The order will determine which elements appear to the front or toward the back. You can move the layers forward or backward in the map chart **Layers** property page.

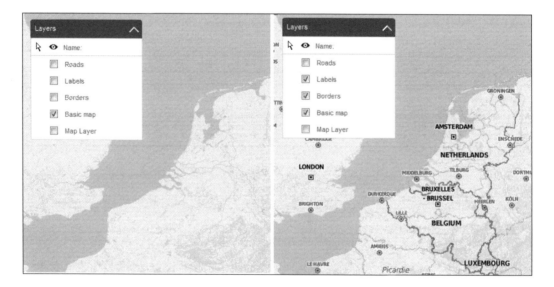

Key Spotfire concept: map chart layers

As you've just seen, Spotfire's standard map is always available as a background **Map Layer**, and you've seen how it can be divided into sub layers of detail. The map chart has four other types of layers to extend the range of spatial visualizations you can create.

The **Marker Layer** and **Feature Layer** are derived from datasets, and one marker or feature layer can be designated as the map chart's interactive layer. You can also change the interactive layer designation dynamically in the chart. Because they are linked to data, the markers on interactive marker layers and the features on interactive feature layers behave like other interactive elements in Spotfire and respond to marking and filtering.

The **Image Layer** and **Web Map Service (WMS)** Layer are linked to noninteractive content and their elements cannot be marked or filtered. WMS layers can be base maps or map composites that include geographically relevant information such as population density or forest cover. The Map Layer is also linked to noninteractive content and cannot be marked or filtered. The visibility of all layers can be changed at any time using the **Layers** control, provided it is enabled in the map chart's **Appearance** property **Show layers control in visualization**.

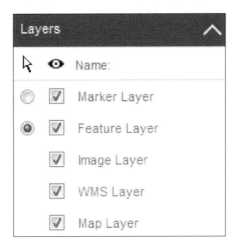

Key mapping concept – coordinate reference systems

Coordinate reference systems are used to project the three-dimensional Earth onto two-dimensional maps. There are many such models for expressing locations on Earth in a coordinate system. Spotfire supports more than 3,000 of them, but the geocoding data tables provided by Spotfire are expressed in the coordinate reference system EPSG:4326-WGS84, which we will use for all the geographic examples in this chapter. You don't need a coordinate reference system for plotting and layering data on two-dimensional images.

Using automatic geocoding to accurately position locations from your data on a map

So, we have a map, but we'd like to start superimposing our own data onto it. Let's plot the location of the weather stations we used in *Chapter 6, The World is Your Visualization*, for the heat map example, and let's plot them at different levels of detail, with and without geocoding:

1. Load the station inventory data (`stationInventory.xlsx`) into an analysis file, and create a map chart. You can download the data from `http://www.insidespotfire.com` as a Microsoft Excel or CSV file.

2. Spotfire will automatically create a Map Layer, as we have seen already, and it will add the station inventory data as a Marker Layer. To configure the marker layer, open the map chart's visualization properties, select the **Layers** property, select **stationInventory**, and click on **Settings**.

3. On the **Marker Layer Settings** page that opens, select **Positioning**. There are two ways to position your markers on the map: **Geocoding** and **Coordinate columns**.

4. If you want to check the coordinate reference system, go to **Layers | Settings | Data**. The default EPSG:4326-WGS84 suits our purposes well.

A set of default geocoding hierarchies is provided with TIBCO Spotfire Server as a ZIP file. A library administrator can import this file into the library and make the geocoding files available to users (instructions can be found in TIBCO's server installation documentation). You can also load these geocoding files manually into an analysis file, or you can provide a third-party file. To do any geocoding, you must have a geocoding file from some source.

Geocoding

Geocoding is in essence a way of matching a value, such as a city name or a country, to map coordinates. It can also extend to describing the geographic shape of the value as follows:

1. To apply geocoding to the station data, check the box next to **Geocoding** and use the **Geocode by** dropdown to select the **STATE** column in the stationInventory table as shown in the following screenshot:

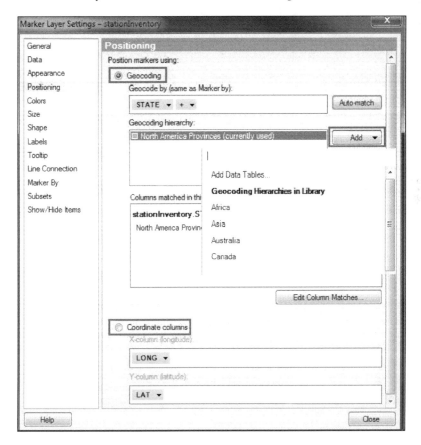

2. If you are logged into the Spotfire server and if you have access to the default geocoding hierarchies provided by Spotfire, all you have to do now is to click on **Auto-match**. Spotfire will find the most suitable hierarchy file for you, based on the values in the column you chose, import this file into your analysis, and match the column you've selected in the data with the column in the geocoding file. There is a Canadian province in the stationInventory data, so Spotfire should load a North American provinces geocoding table, even though the column is called STATE.

3. If you don't have access to the default geocoding hierarchies, you can download the file North American Provinces.sbdf from http://www.insidespotfire.com and load this into the analysis file.

4. You can click on **Edit Column Matches...** to match the columns yourself. You can also add any geocoding file you wish, either from the library or from an external source, such as a file or a database, using the **Add** dropdown.

 The marker layer behaves like a scatter plot; in this plot, you must decide which column in the data the markers are going to represent. In our example, this could be stations or states. The marker by level will be set automatically to the column you select for geocoding.

5. Apart from the position, you can also configure the color, size, and shape of the markers. Try coloring the markers by elevation, one of the station attributes in the data, using a traditional altitude scale. Because you aggregate the station data to the state level, you should select **Avg(ELEV)**. You could also choose to size the markers by **Count(ELEV)**, which is equivalent to a station count in each state, as shown in the following screenshot:

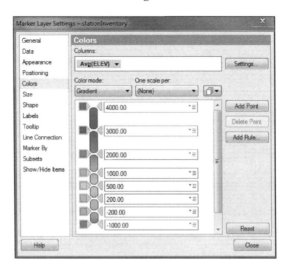

6. The result is not particularly exciting, giving you one marker for each state colored by the average station elevation in the state. However, it shows you how easy it is to geocode your data and superimpose it on a base map, as shown in the following screenshot:

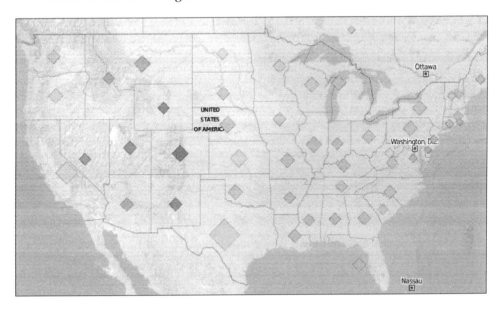

Coordinate columns

1. Now, let's do something a little more interesting. Because the station inventory data has latitude and longitude coordinates, Spotfire assigns these automatically as coordinate columns. If Spotfire doesn't automatically assign any latitude and longitude columns, you can easily select them yourself by checking the **Coordinate columns** option and using the **X-column (longitude)** and **Y-column (latitude)** dropdowns to select the columns.

2. Repeat the steps you followed to create the state-level map, except use the latitude and longitude coordinates and select **STATION_NAME** as the marker by column. There are so many stations in the dataset; the result is effectively a topographical map of the United States:

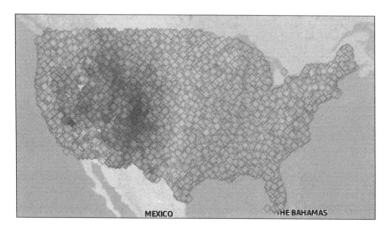

Incorporating and using a feature layer

Feature layers use "shapefiles" to represent features such as countries, rivers, and cities as vector-based polygons, lines, or points. Shapefiles are usually embedded as binary objects in a geocoding table, where they are linked to topological information such as map coordinates. The polygons, lines, and points can be filled with color and behave like markers in a map chart, allowing you to select a state outline, for example.

It is possible to manipulate and create shapefiles using a variety of free and paid software, but more often than not you will use a precompiled geocoded table with the shapes embedded. There are many free online sources for downloading shapefiles. The geocoding tables provided with Spotfire also include shapes in a column called Geometry.

Let's add a feature layer to our weather station map chart, and you'll quickly see how useful they can be. The datasets you need for this example are StationHourlyTemperature.sbdf, stationInventory.xlsx, and USA States.sbdf:

1. Import the datasets and the Spotfire geocoding table USA States into the analysis file.

2. Add a new map chart using the standard map, and, using the **Layers | Add** dropdown options, and add the USA States data table as a **Feature Layer**. The result should be a map of the United States with the shapes of individual states outlined. You should also be able to select individual states by clicking anywhere within the outline.

3. We'll color the states by the average temperature, as recorded in the hourly temperature data. Open the map chart's visualization properties, select **Layers**, then **USA States**, then **Settings**, and finally **Geocoding**. Set the **Geocode by** setting to **State**.

4. Now, select the **Colors** setting, and use the **Columns** dropdown to select **Temperature C** from StationHourlyTemperatures; set the aggregation to **Avg**.

5. Set the **Color mode** to **Gradient** and define a nice heat spectrum for the temperature range by adding some points to the gradient and choosing colors ranging from blue at the lowest temperatures to red at the highest. Save the color scheme as a **Document Color Scheme...** for future use.

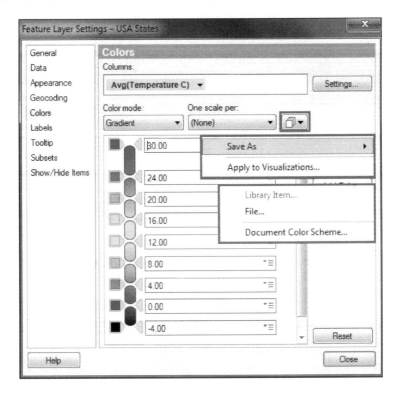

Always choose colors to suit the data, experimenting with the selections until you are happy with the result. Temperature gradients will differ from one dataset to another.

You should now have a map of the United States with each state outlined and selectable and colored by the average temperature for that state, which will look like the following image:

Geographic drill-down

Now, we're going to create a more detailed, state-level view of the individual stations on a second map chart based on marking (state selection) in the more global view as follows:

1. First, we need to create some table relationships. Open **Data Table Properties** from the **Edit** menu, select the **Relations** tab, and click on the **Manage Relations...** button. Create a new relation between **StationInventory** and **StationHourlyTemperature** based on **STNID = STNID**. Create a new relation between **StationInventory** and **USA States** based on **STATE = State**.

2. Duplicate the map chart you have just created by right-clicking on the chart and selecting **Duplicate Visualization**.

3. Open the **Layers** property of the second map chart and add **StationInventory** as a **Marker Layer**. Select **StationInventory** in the **Interactive layer:** dropdown.

4. In the layer's **Settings**, make the following entries:

Positioning	Coordinate columns using LONG and LAT
Marker by:	STNID
Colors	stationHourlyTemperatures.AVG(Temperature C), and reuse the temperature document color scheme you saved for the main map.
Size by:	None, and move the **Marker size:** slider until you have a size you like.
Label by:	STATION_NAME, with **Show labels for marked rows only**.

5. The StationHourlyTemperature data table is not complete, and most of the stations in StationInventory have no corresponding temperature data. For the purposes of our example, we should hide the stations that have no data. To do this, open the **Show/Hide Items** setting and add a rule to show stationHourlyTemperatures.AVG(Temperature C) with a value greater than -8. This setting will remove all the "empty" stations from the map and make it easier to read.

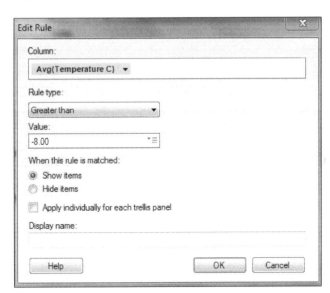

That's the basic setup complete, but there are a few more things we need to fine-tune to get the map working the way we want to use it as a drill-down as follows:

1. First, because the different layers cover each other and we would like to clearly see place names on the map layer alongside station markers on the StationInventory layer, we need to add a second map layer containing just labels and we need to move this layer right to the front. Add the layer from the **Layers** property, **Add** drop-down, and select **Labels** as the map type. Use the **Move Forward** button to move this new layer to the top of the layers list.

2. Second, we want this second map to respond to selections on the main map; so, open the layer settings for StationInventory, select the **Data** setting, and check **Marking** under **Data limiting | Limit data using markings:**. Remove any marking under **Marking:**. Do the same for the USA States layer.

3. Third, we want the map to zoom in automatically to the selected state. Select the **Appearance** property of the map chart and check the **Auto-zoom** option. Now, go into the StationInventory layer settings and ensure that **Include in auto-zoom** is checked in the **Appearance** setting. Open the USA States layer settings and ensure that **Include in auto-zoom** is not checked. If we didn't make this last setting, the larger states would zoom out too much and we would lose some map detail.

4. We want to make sure that we just see the state border, and not the solid polygon shape. To achieve this, go to **Layers | USA States | Settings | Appearance** and move the **Layer transparency** slider to the far right. While you are on this property page, make the polygon border color more pronounced (red, for example) and heavier (a thickness of 2 works well).

That's it! If you select a state on the main map, the second map should zoom in on this state, showing you the location of weather stations colored by the average temperature. Name this page `Temperature Profile`; we'll be developing it further in a later example.

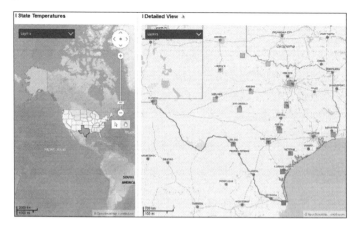

As an exercise, create a further drill-down based on station selection on the detailed view to get individual station details. It doesn't have to be a map; it could be a table or another visualization, such as a bar chart of average monthly temperatures for the selected station.

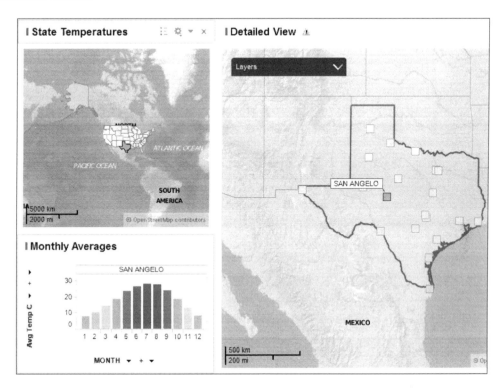

Adding Web Map Service data to a map chart

WMS is an Open Geospatial Consortium protocol for delivering geo-referenced map images over the Internet. There are many public WMS servers. The free ones are mostly provided by government agencies and research and educational organizations. Spatineo (http://www.spatineo.com/), a commercial spatial web services monitor, provides a free, searchable list of WMS resources, as does Skylab Mobilesystems (http://www.skylab-mobilesystems.com/en/wms_serverlist.html). The US government's open Data Catalog (http://geo.data.gov/) is a good resource for US-specific WMS links. However, there are lots of other lists; just search for WMS servers.

When you find a WMS server of interest, you want the WMS URL so you can paste it into a Spotfire map chart WMS layer setting. Not all the WMS links you find will work. Sometimes, the server will be down or no longer available.

Most WMS streams have multiple layers of information. Spotfire will show you the available layers, and you can choose which ones to include in your map. It's important to understand that you are streaming GIS data into your map chart from an external server, and you are dependent on the availability of this server and also on the form the WMS information takes. Also, just to reiterate, you cannot interact with WMS layers like you can with a feature layer.

Let's work through an example to see how WMS data works in a Spotfire map chart, as follows:

1. Open the visualization properties of the detailed map chart in the Temperature Profile page you created in the last example, select the **Layers** property, and add a WMS layer using the **Add** dropdown. Spotfire will require a URL for the map. Paste or type the URL `http://nowcoast.noaa.gov/wms/com.esri.wms.Esrimap/obs?service=wms&version=1.1.1&request=GetCapabilities`, and click on the **Update** button.

2. Assuming the link is valid and you are connected to the Internet, Spotfire will retrieve a collection of sublayers from the WMS server. Feel free to experiment with these sublayers, adding them across and removing them to see what appears on the map chart. Let's try **Weather Radar Mosaic** as an example.

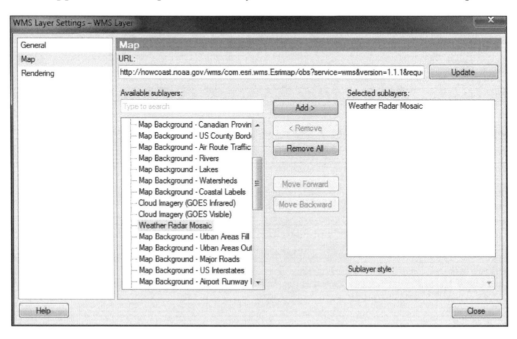

3. While still in the **WMS Layer Settings**, select **General**, and rename the layer appropriately: something like `Weather Radar WMS`.

The result is a WMS layer you can turn on and off with the layers control.

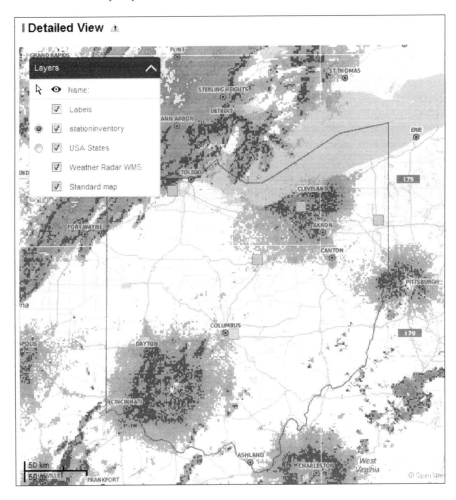

Add a second WMS layer, this time using the URL `http://webservices.nationalatlas.gov/wms/1million?SERVICE=WMS&REQUEST=GetCapabilities` and selecting the sublayer **1 Million Scale - Tree Canopy 100 Meter Resolution**. If you display the map chart legend with the **Tree Canopy** layer selected, you'll see a key for the underlying tree canopy. This key is provided by the WMS server.

You won't find any meaningful key for the weather radar feed. Different WMS streams have different degrees of presentation quality.

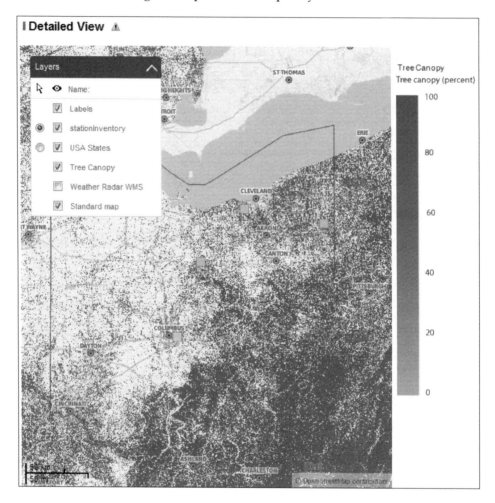

Using the map chart for nongeographic spatial analysis

The map chart can be used for any form of spatial analysis. For a simple application, all you need is a base image and some coordinate data. Think of the base image as the map layer and the coordinate data as a marker layer. With the right software, you could create relevant shapefiles and use them as a feature layer.

The base image could be a process diagram, a semiconductor wafer, an immunoassay plate, or a baseball field. It can be an image of anything of interest to you that is stable and fixed in time and upon which you can reliably plot data markers, which will be the variable part of your analysis. The markers could be process stage timings, semiconductor wafer failures, immunoassay well results, or stats for different baseball positions. The markers can be numbers, colors, or even mini pie charts.

There are a number of stages to creating a spatial visualization:

- Create or obtain a suitable image.
- Map out the image's coordinate space so you know where to place markers. This stage takes a little trial and error.
- Link the coordinates you define in stage 2 with some relevant data.

The default coordinate space for your image is its dimensions in pixels, so this gives you the maximum x- and y-coordinates. You can quickly build x- and y-reference axes using a spreadsheet and then load the coordinates with the image to help you map out the points of interest. We'll work through an example to illustrate the process from start to finish.

Consider a fictitious workflow for a website change process. The process map can be created using Microsoft Visio, or any suitable workflow software, and then saved as an image file. We can also create some fictitious process time data for this workflow, and we'll be using this data in the example.

The dataset (`WebPageProcess.xlsx`) and image (`ChangeProcess.png`) can be downloaded from `http://www.insidespotfire.com`.

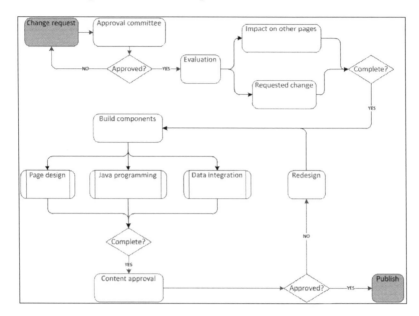

Let's get all this into Spotfire as follows:

1. Create a new map chart, select the **Layers** property, and remove any layers created by Spotfire, including the base map.

2. While still on the **Layers** property, use the **Add** dropdown to add a new **Image Layer**. When the **Image Layer Settings** window opens, simply browse to the image you want to import, which is `ChangeProcess.png` in our case. Once you've selected the image, close the dialog, select the map chart's **Appearance** property, and set the **Coordinate reference system** to None.

3. You should now see the process image but, to make it useful, we need to add a marker layer. The first step is to map out the coordinates and, to do this, we'll load up the reference axes I talked about and add the data as a marker layer. Add the dataset `coordinateMatrix.xlsx` to the analysis file, and then add this as a marker layer to the map chart. Make sure the coordinate reference system of the layer is set to None. Make the following settings:

Positioning	Coordinate columns set to x and y
Size by	None
Shape	A cross
Label by	Custom expression: `Concatenate([x] & "," & [y])` and **Show labels for: All**
Marker by	[Marker]

You can use this layer to assign coordinates to the elements in the process flow that we want to assign data to and interact with. Once this activity is complete, you can hide the matrix or just discard it.

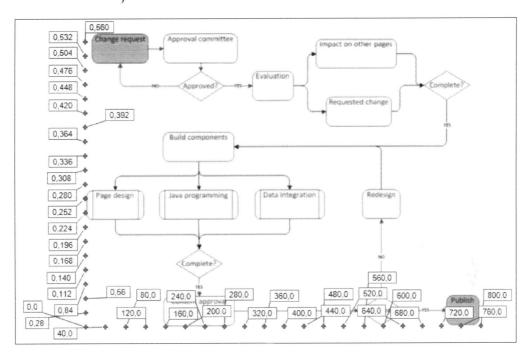

The final stage in creating an interactive spatial visualization is the plotting of the data. We're going to use the following dataset:

x	y	Average Elapsed Time	Target Elapsed Time	Average Process Time

The table includes the x- and y-coordinates that we worked out for the process elements plus some elapsed and process times. In the real world, you would collect this data and feed it to the visualization on a periodic basis. To complete the workflow analysis, execute the following steps:

1. Load the example data, `WebPageProcess.xls`, into the analysis file.

2. Now, add two calculated columns to the table:

   Total Elapsed Time: `Sum([Average Elapsed Time])`

   Percent Elapsed Time: `[Average Elapsed Time] / [Total Elapsed Time]`

   Format the [Percent Elapsed Time] column as Percentage (**Column Properties | Formatting**).

3. Open the map chart's visualization properties, select the **Layers** property, and add the data table as a new marker layer, remembering to set the coordinate reference system to none.

4. Make the following settings to the new layer:

Positioning	Coordinate columns set to x and y
Colors	[Percent Elapsed Time]; **Color mode: Segments**, with three segments (0–10, 10–20, and 20–33)
Size by	None, but use the **Marker size:** slider to fit the markers to the image
Shape	A square
Marker by	[Activity]

You have now superimposed a marker layer on the process flow image, and you can see which steps are taking the most time, and you can interact with these steps.

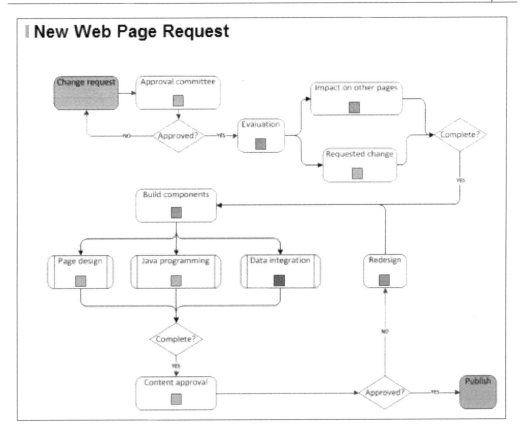

As an exercise, add to the visualization as follows:

- Use a calculated column to define a KPI (key performance indicator) for each activity (see *Chapter 5, Source Data is Never Enough*)
- Create a dropdown control to allow the user to choose whether to color by elapsed time, process time, or KPI (see *Chapter 3, Analyze That!*)

- Add two bar charts dependent on marking in the map chart to show the actual versus KPI target and elapsed versus process time (see *Chapter 2, Visualize This!*)

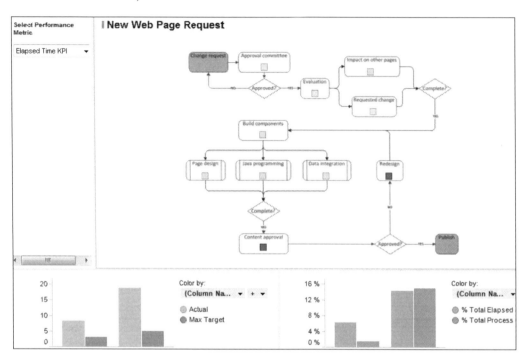

To maintain color scheme consistency across multiple user selections, save the color scheme as a `Document Color Scheme`, go to **Column Properties | Properties**, edit **DefaultContinuousColorScheme** or **DefaultCategoricalColorScheme**, and add the color scheme name (case sensitive) to the property. This will ensure that the color scheme is always applied to this column. If you don't set this property, Spotfire will not retain the scheme and apply a new, random, set of colors each time the user changes the selection.

This is the sort of analysis a Lean Six Sigma practitioner or anyone interested in the process improvement might perform. The beauty of the Spotfire map chart is that, as long as the process flow stays the same, it can be quickly analyzed against different data points and metrics.

Summary

In this chapter, we have taken a close look at the Spotfire map chart, which allows you to plot your data in a spatial context and to create interactive marker layers and feature layers, as well as reference maps, WMS, and image layers.

You have learned how to create a background map layer, how to use automatic geocoding to accurately position locations from your data on a map, how to incorporate and use a feature layer, how to add WMS data to a map chart, and how to use the map chart for nongeographic spatial analysis.

Geographically oriented location analytics is an obvious application of the map chart for most people. I hope the last section of the chapter on nongeographic spatial analysis made you think about the potential of plotting data against other spatial contexts and pictures that make immediate sense to you and to your analysis audience.

8

The Secret Life of Python

One of Spotfire's most powerful features is the access the platform gives frontend users to its **application programming interface** (**API**) through the programming language IronPython. API programming is typically the preserve of IT developers and usually occurs deep beneath the hood. Spotfire has made the API very accessible to all report developers and has integrated this into the everyday use of the platform. It's comparable to the use of VBA in Microsoft Excel.

To write API scripts, you need some programming experience and you also need to know how to use Spotfire's library of properties and methods, which is where this chapter will help you. Despite online reference documents and examples, it is a serious challenge to figure out how to do even quite simple tasks with the Spotfire API. This, unfortunately, is the downside of this otherwise wonderful facility. In this one chapter, you will learn things that might take you a year to figure out unaided, depending on your programming experience.

Even a basic use of API scripts will greatly enhance your ability to build professional analytics solutions. At the end of this chapter, you will see Spotfire in a whole new light, appreciating its potential to address the most complex informatics challenges and, in the hands of a skilled-up analyst, deliver intuitive self-service frameworks for others to use.

In this chapter, we will cover the following topics:

- Introduction to IronPython
- Overview of the Spotfire API
- Some useful .NET assemblies
- Creating scripts
- Referencing and manipulating the primary elements in an analysis file
- Manipulating visualization properties

- Manipulating color
- Manipulating filters
- Manipulating data already loaded into Spotfire
- Adding data to an analysis

Introduction to IronPython

Spotfire API scripts are written in IronPython. Python is a portable, object-oriented, interactive programming language that can interface with many system calls and libraries. IronPython is an implementation of Python that targets Microsoft's .NET Framework. It is beyond the scope of this book to provide a tutorial on Python. Please visit `https://www.python.org` and `http://ironpython.net` for comprehensive guides to the language. This section will give you a quick orientation, which should be enough to get you started with scripting, and you will get used to the syntax as we work through examples in this chapter. You will also need at least a rudimentary knowledge of programming concepts.

Control structures

All programming languages need to delineate the beginning and end of control structures such as conditional segments and iteration loops. Python does this using tabbed indents and colons. The opening statement of a control structure ends with a colon, and the next line of code is indented by a one-tab stop. If the structure deepens, the code indents by a further tab stop; if it comes back to a previous level, the code comes back to the corresponding indent:

```
if x == 1 then:
   if y == 1 then:
      # do action
   if y == 2 then:
      # do other action
if x == 2 then:
   # etc.
```

There are no end statements or punctuation marks, which does take a bit of getting used to.

The Python control structures are limited to the following:

- `if ... elif ... else`
- `for ... in`
- `for ... in range()`
- `try ... exception`

Comments are flagged using a hash symbol (#).

Libraries

To use a library, including a Spotfire library, you have to declare it at the beginning of the script: `from` *library namespace* `import` `class`.

Lists

You can build a list in Python by enclosing the elements in square brackets and separating them with commas. The system Array class includes an `Add` method for adding items to a list:

```
from System import Array
myList = ["element 1","element 2"]
myList.Add("element 3")
```

Lists can contain any variable type, but you cannot mix different variable types in the same list.

Functions

Functions are declared with the word `def`, followed by the function name and a list of parameters, followed by the function's statements. A return statement is optional. Functions can be used like subroutines to repeat a common piece of code:

```
def function name(parameter1, parameter2, …):
```

Object orientation

The depth and power of Python scripts are enabled by object-oriented programming, which is basically as simple as taking an object and either applying a method to it or getting or setting one of its properties. A *dot* notation is used to join the object to the property or method:

```
Result = Object.Property/Method
```

A list is an example of a simple object, and one of the methods available is `Add`, which adds an element to the list. An object can be as complex as an entire visualization, with all its associated properties and methods. Methods will often require you to provide additional parameters, usually enclosed by brackets.

Being aware of an object's existence, knowing how to reference this object, and knowing how to use its properties and methods are the keys to writing Spotfire IronPython scripts.

Overview of the Spotfire API

In essence, the Spotfire API is a collection of objects, methods, and properties that can be manipulated to do just about anything in a script that you would otherwise do through the graphical user interface. One notable exception is the creation and manipulation of text area property controls. You can create document properties and change their values through the API, but you cannot build or otherwise interact with the controls that are embedded in the text area.

It's also important to stress that the API contains a lot of material that even an advanced script writer will never need. This chapter will distill the API down to the essentials a typical script writer needs. The API is divided into primary namespaces, and the ones we will cover in this chapter are as follows:

- `Spotfire.Dxp.Application`
- `Spotfire.Dxp.Application.Filters`
- `Spotfire.Dxp.Application.Visuals`
- `Spotfire.Dxp.Application.Visuals.ConditionalColoring`
- `Spotfire.Dxp.Application.Visuals.FittingModels`
- `Spotfire.Dxp.Data`
- `Spotfire.Dxp.Data.Import`

Each of these namespaces contains a suite of classes, each with its own set of properties and methods. These classes are essentially the objects you need to manipulate to achieve something in a script. There is a lot of interdependency between the classes, including across namespaces, and often you need to reference one class through another.

For example, the `Spotfire.Dxp.Application` namespace has a class called `Visual`, one of the properties of which is `Title`. This property allows you to get or set the title of a visualization. However, to actually reference a particular visualization (to access this title property), you first need to reference the visualization's page, which is done through the `Spotfire.Dxp.Application` class `Page`, and to get the page, you have to use the `Spotfire.Dxp.Application` class `Document`.

Some properties, such as `Spotfire.Dxp.Application.Visual.Title`, are very easy to use: it's just a text value and you can get this by assigning it to a variable or set it by making it equal to a string variable or a value. Other properties expect a more complex type, often the property of some other class. Some properties are read-only (`get`), but there is sometimes a way to set these properties through alternative routes.

The API is a complex web of dependent classes, properties, and methods, but the succeeding sections will chart functional paths through this web for you and give you lots of practical working script examples. There is just one more item to get out of the way first, and that's the Microsoft .NET Framework.

Some useful external libraries

Sometimes, you need to import methods from IronPython or the Microsoft .NET Framework to help your script. The following table describes some libraries that you will find useful:

`import clr`	`clr` (common language runtime) is an IronPython module that provides some basic .NET functionalities, such as string methods
`import re`	Import this library if you want to use regular expressions
`from System.Collections.Generic import Dictionary`	Use this library to create dictionary objects, which are useful to store an indexed list
`from System.Drawing import Color`	Use this library to define your own custom colors
`from System.Drawing import Font`	Use this library to manipulate fonts
`from System import Guid`	Import this library if you want to reference system **global unique identifiers (GUID)**
`from System import Array,String,Object`	Use this library to get access to .NET array, string, and object methods

Microsoft provides a complete navigable guide to the .NET Framework class library at `http://msdn.microsoft.com/en-us/library/w0x726c2%28v=vs.110%29.aspx`.

Creating scripts

You use scripts by creating a button or an action link in a text area and typing the script code that you want to run whenever that button or link is clicked. As of Spotfire v6.5, you can also attach scripts to text area property controls and set them to execute whenever the underlying document property value changes. You must have a Script Author license to write scripts. Ask your Spotfire administrator to grant you the Script Author license if you don't have it.

1. Edit any text area, and click on the **Insert Action Control** icon:

2. Choose **Button** or **Link**, enter the text you want to display on the button or link under **Display text:**, select the **Script** icon, and click on **New...** to begin writing your script.

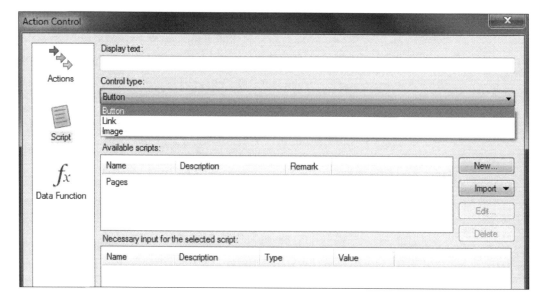

3. Give the script a name, and simply type (or paste) the script you want to run into the script area. You can run the script on the spot by clicking the **Run Script** button, or you can save the script by simply clicking **OK** until you are back at the text area. From there, clicking the button or link will run the script.

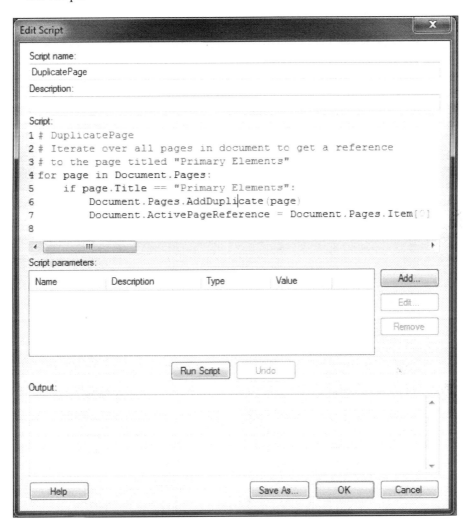

You can attach parameters (with associated values) to a script by clicking on the **Add** button next to the **Script parameters:** box on the **Edit Script** page.

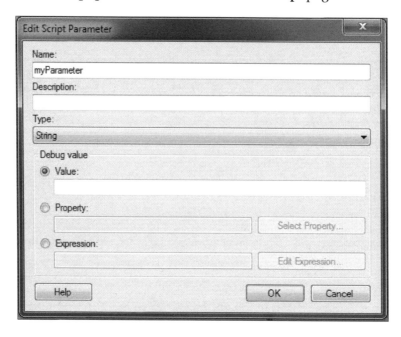

The parameter can be 1 of 14 types, but you will most often probably use String, Integer, and Real. The name you give the parameter, which must be a valid Python identifier (no spaces and a restriction on special characters), can be referenced directly in the script. Whatever value it is assigned will be available to the script. You can also link a parameter to a document, table, or column property or build a custom expression to calculate a value from a data table.

Referencing and manipulating the primary elements in an analysis file

No matter what you want to do with a Python script, you have to start with basic references. The analysis file is referred to as a **Document** in the API, and the Spotfire.Dxp.Application Document class and some classes in the Spotfire.Dxp.Data namespace provide the means for referencing what could be called the primary elements: pages, visualizations, properties, panels (such as filter schemes), markings, and data tables. Generally, you can directly reference an **active** element or iterate through the Document to find an element of interest, based on its name, for example. In some cases, you can reference an element directly based on some unique attribute, such as its name.

The important thing to understand is that you need to have a reference or a handle on an object such as a visualization before you can manipulate the more detailed properties of this object. For clarity, we will follow an important convention in the properties and methods tables presented in this chapter: objects and variables that you need to obtain or provide will be in italics, whereas literal property and method names from the Spotfire API will not. The example scripts should make the distinction very clear.

Please also understand the importance of indentation in Python if you are transcribing the scripts to try them out. You can download all the scripts from http://www.insidespotfire.com.

 General note: this chapter does not provide any instructions for setting up the analysis files in which to run the example scripts. You will need to set up your own files, with data and visualizations that mean something to you, to try the scripts for yourself. The examples are nevertheless designed to be straightforward and easy to apply.

Let's start with pages.

Pages

A single page is a page object; all the pages together is a page collection.

Action	Property or Method
Get or set the active (current) page	Document.ActivePageReference
Get all pages (page collection)	Document.Pages
Useful page properties	
Get or set the page title	*pageObject*.Title
	pageObject could be, for example, Document.ActivePageReference
Useful page methods	
Duplicate a page	AddDuplicate(*pageObject*)
Add a new page	AddNew(Page Name)
	Page Name is just the plain text name of the page.
Remove a page by reference	Remove(*pageObject*)
Reference a page based on position	Item[Position]
	Position is an integer index (0, 1, 2, … n). The first page in the analysis file is position 0.

Example script

Find the page "Primary Elements", duplicate it, and then put the focus back on Primary Elements by (re)making it the active page:

```
# DuplicatePage

# Iterate over all pages in document to get a reference
# to the page titled "Primary Elements"
for page in Document.Pages:
  if page.Title == "Primary Elements":
    Document.Pages.AddDuplicate(page)
    Document.ActivePageReference = Document.Pages.Item[0]
```

Here are three important principles that will recur in most scripts:

- Some methods and properties only work on collections (Document.Pages), whereas others refer directly to individual objects (page.Title).

- In condition statements, the equals symbol must be repeated (==, not =). It's like the difference between saying *is equal to* and *equals*, respectively, the latter being a variable value assignment, such as myVariable = "value".

- It's good practice to always include the script name at the beginning of the script and annotate the script with explanatory comments (# symbol).

Visualizations

Visualizations are referenced through their occurrence on a particular page:

```
for page in Document.Pages:
    for visualization in page.Visuals:
```

You identify the visualization of interest by iterating the loop; *visualization* can then be used as your visualization object reference.

Action	Property or Method
	Useful visualization properties
Get or set the visualization title	*visualizationObject*.Title
Show or hide the visualization title	*visualizationObject*.ShowTitle True or False

Action	Property or Method
Get or set the visualization type	*visualizationObject*.TypeId The visualization TypeId is a VisualTypeIdentifier, and you must use the VisualTypeIdentifiers **enumeration** when working with this property
	VisualTypeIdentifiers enumeration
	VisualTypeIdentifiers.BarChart
	VisualTypeIdentifiers.BoxPlot
	VisualTypeIdentifiers.BulletGraphMiniatureVisualization
	VisualTypeIdentifiers. CalculatedValueMiniatureVisualization
	VisualTypeIdentifiers.CombinationChart
	VisualTypeIdentifiers.CrossTable
	VisualTypeIdentifiers.GraphicalTable
	VisualTypeIdentifiers.HeatMap
	VisualTypeIdentifiers.HtmlTextArea
	VisualTypeIdentifiers.LineChart
	VisualTypeIdentifiers.MapChart
	VisualTypeIdentifiers.ParallelCoordinatePlot
	VisualTypeIdentifiers.PieChart
	VisualTypeIdentifiers.ScatterPlot
	VisualTypeIdentifiers.ScatterPlot3D
	VisualTypeIdentifiers.SparklineMiniatureVisualization
	VisualTypeIdentifiers.SummaryTable
	VisualTypeIdentifiers.Table
	VisualTypeIdentifiers.Treemap

Example script

Find "Visualization 1" on the active page, check if it's a scatter plot, and if it is, change it to a bar chart and change its name to "Visualization 2". Do the reverse if the visualization is a bar chart called Visualization 2:

```
# ChangeVisualizationType

# Import Visuals namespace to get access to
# VisualTypeIdentifiers enumeration
from Spotfire.Dxp.Application.Visuals import *

# Iterate over all visualizations on the active page to
# get a reference to the target visualization
for visualization in Document.ActivePageReference.Visuals:
```

```
# If the visualization is called "Visualization 1" and
# is a scatter plot, change it to a bar chart and change its name.
  if visualization.Title == "Visualization 1" and visualization.TypeId
== VisualTypeIdentifiers.ScatterPlot:
    visualization.TypeId = VisualTypeIdentifiers.BarChart
    visualization.Title = "Visualization 2"

# If the visualization is called "Visualization 2" and
# is a bar chart, change it to a scatter plot and change its name.
  elif visualization.Title == "Visualization 2" and visualization.
TypeId == VisualTypeIdentifiers.BarChart:
    visualization.TypeId = VisualTypeIdentifiers.ScatterPlot
    visualization.Title = "Visualization 1"
```

Properties

There are three types of properties in an analysis file:

- Document properties (Document)
- Column properties (Column)
- Data table properties (Table)

Properties are manipulated using the Spotfire.Dxp.Data DataProperty and DataPropertyRegistry classes, which are initially accessed through Document. Data.Properties. We're going to focus first on document properties because they are the easiest to manipulate and the property type you are most likely to want to manipulate. We'll look at column properties later on in this chapter. We're not going to look at table properties because they are rarely used.

To add a new property, you must first create a prototype using the DataProperty class and then add it as an instantiated property using the DataPropertyRegistry class.

Action	Property or Method
DataProperty class	
Create property prototype	CreateCustomPrototype(Property Name, DataType, DataPropertyAttributes)
	Property Name is a text value you supply for the property name. It must be unique and have no spaces or special characters.
	DataType is an enumeration, as is DataPropertyAttributes.

Action	Property or Method
DataType enumeration	
	`DataType.Binary`
	`DataType.Boolean`
	`DataType.Currency`
	`DataType.Date`
	`DataType.DateTime`
	`DataType.Integer`
	`DataType.LongInteger`
	`DataType.Real`
	`DataType.Single`
	`DataType.String`
	`DataType.Time`
	`DataType.TimeSpan`
DataPropertyAttributes enumeration **(There are other attributes, but these are the important ones.)**	
Make the property editable	`DataPropertyAttributes.IsEditable`
Make the property an array	`DataPropertyAttributes.IsListValued`
Include the property in the analysis file	`DataPropertyAttributes.IsPersistent`
Ensure the property can be copied to objects derived from the container	`DataPropertyAttributes.IsPropagated`
Make the property visible	`DataPropertyAttributes.IsVisible`
DataPropertyRegistry class	
Instantiate a prototype	`AddProperty(DataPropertyClass, `*prototypeReference*`)` `DataPropertyClass` is an enumeration with three possible values: `DataPropertyClass.Document`, `DataPropertyClass. Column`, or `DataPropertyClass. Table`.
Remove a property	`RemoveProperty(DataPropertyRegistry, DataPropertyClass, `Property Name`)` Spotfire expects a `DataPropertyRegistry` reference for the first parameter. This is simply `Document.Data. Properties`

Action	Property or Method
Get or set the value of a document property	Document.Properties [Property Name]

Example script

Create a new document property called NewProperty and give it the value 10:

```
# CreateDocumentProperty

# Import Data namespace to get access to the required classes
from Spotfire.Dxp.Data import *

# Remove any existing property called "NewProperty"
try:
  DataPropertyRegistry.RemoveProperty(Document.Data.Properties,
DataPropertyClass.Document, "NewProperty")
except:
  pass # i.e., do nothing if the property does not exist

# Create a property prototype
propertyPrototype = DataProperty.CreateCustomPrototype("NewPro
perty", 0, DataType.Integer, DataPropertyAttributes.IsVisible
| DataPropertyAttributes.IsEditable | DataPropertyAttributes.
IsPersistent | DataPropertyAttributes.IsPropagated)

# Instantiate the prototype
Document.Data.Properties.AddProperty(DataPropertyClass.Document,
propertyPrototype)
Document.Properties["NewProperty"] = 10

# Check the property's attributes
documentProperty = DataPropertyRegistry.GetProperty(Document.Data.
Properties, DataPropertyClass.Document, "NewProperty")
print documentProperty.Attributes
```

The Python `print` command is very useful for debugging scripts. If you run the script directly from the script window, any print statements you include will execute in the script's output window.

Data tables

We will be looking more closely at data tables later on in this chapter. For now, let's just look at how you reference a data table. It's very straightforward:

```
dataTable = Document.Data.Tables.TryGetValue(Name of the data table)
[1]
```

The `1` in square brackets at the end is important because the `Document.Data.Tables.TryGetValue` method returns a **tuple**, which is a type of list. The first item in the `TryGetValue` tuple is always a Boolean value indicating whether the table exists. The second item in the tuple is the actual data table reference (if the table exists). In Python, tuples are parsed using a number in a square bracket to indicate the item you want.

Marking

Markings are referenced through the `Spotfire.Dxp.Data DataManager` and `DataMarkingSelection` classes, through which you can reference markings for selection purposes and change marking names and colors.

Action	Property or Method
Reference a marking	`for marking in Document.Data.Markings:`
Get or set a marking name	`marking.Name`
Get or set a marking color	*marking*.`Color` You must use the `System.Drawing` library for color and use either `Color.FromArgb`(Integer) or `Color.FromName`(.NET color name)

Panels

The `Document.Pages` class has direct reference methods for filter and details-on-demand panels. All panels can be referenced by first getting the panel collection. We will look at filters in more detail later on in this chapter. We won't be looking at other panel types.

Action	Property or Method
Reference the filter panel on a page	`filterPanel = ` *page*`.FilterPanel` As already explained, `page` must be the `Document.ActivePageReference` or found through iteration over the `Document.Pages` collection.
Reference the details-on-demand panel on a page	`dodPanel = ` *page*`.DetailsOnDemandPanel`

Get a panel through the page's panel collection	`for panel in ` *page*`.Panels:`
	  `panelObject = panel`
	
	The `panel` here is the `PanelCollection` class, and it can be manipulated through this class's methods. We will cover this further when we look at filters in detail.

How to manipulate visualization properties

There are many reasons why you might want to manipulate visualization properties, not least to provide a more dynamic experience for the user. Visualization properties are manipulated using the `Spotfire.Dxp.Application.Visuals` namespace. This namespace is very large and includes some generic classes for manipulating items such as axes and then specific classes for each visualization type. Regardless of which class you wish to use, you must first find a visualization's object reference, as described in the previous main section. To recap:

```
for page in Document.Pages:
    for visualization in page.Visuals:
```

Only when you have identified the visualization you are interested in (by name or type usually) are you ready to use the methods and properties in Spotfire.Dxp. Application.Visuals.

The next step is to "convert" the visualization object identified using the `Spotfire.Dxp.Application Documents` class into a visual content object. This is achieved as follows:

```
visualContentObject = visualization.As[VisualContent]()
```

It is this `visualContentObject` you use for all visualization manipulations, and not the visualization object we used to set the visualization's title or type.

Casting the visualization object as a generic visual content works for most operations. You can also cast to a specific visual content type; an example would be `visualContentObject = visualization.As[ScatterPlot]()`. However, specific casting is usually unnecessary, even for operations that are restricted to a single visualization type.

Generic visualization properties

Some properties are common to all visualizations. The object in every case is the `visualContentObject` reference described in the previous section.

Action	Property or Method
Get or set the visualization's data table	*visualContentObject*`.Data.DataTableReference` Will return or must be set to a data table object. If you change a visualization's data table, you need to pay attention to all the table-dependent properties individually. We will cover this in a later section.
Get or set the visualization's description	*visualContentObject*`.Description`
Get or set the legend's font properties	*visualContentObject*`.Legend.Font` To set the font, you need to import the `Font` class from `System.Drawing` (see the example described later on).
Show or hide individual legend items	*visualContentObject*`.Legend.Items` You need to iterate through the legend items collection to access each item individually. You can use the item `Title` property to identify individual items.
Show or hide a visualization's legend	*visualContentObject*`.Legend.Visible`

Example script

Change the underlying data table for a visualization, change the legend font, and hide some legend items.

Please note: where the script refers to:

```
# ChangeDataAndLegend

# Import Visuals namespace
from Spotfire.Dxp.Application.Visuals import *
# Import Font from System.Drawing to manipulate fonts
from System.Drawing import Font

# Change the data table to stationInventory2
for visualization in Document.ActivePageReference.Visuals:
  if visualization.TypeId == VisualTypeIdentifiers.ScatterPlot:
    visualContentObject = visualization.As[VisualContent]()
    newDataTable = Document.Data.Tables.
TryGetValue("stationInventory2")[1]
    visualContentObject.Data.DataTableReference = newDataTable

# Show the legend item Data table and hide the rest
for legendItem in visualContentObject.Legend.Items:
  if legendItem.Title == "Data table":
    legendItem.Visible = True
  else:
    legendItem.Visible = False

# Change the legend font size
newFont = Font("Arial", 10)
visualContentObject.Legend.Font = newFont
```

To explore collections, use a loop and the Python command print. For example:
```
for legendItem in visualContentObject.Legend.Items:
  print legendItem.Title
```

Axes properties

All visualizations have axes except for the Table and Summary Table visualizations, and there are some general axes properties that can be manipulated through the `Spotfire.Dxp.Application.Visuals Axis` class and related classes. The main reference point is still `visualContentObject`, and although the class is referred to generically as Axis, it is always more specific when actually used (XAxis, for example). Other axis classes are indicated in the following table:

Action	Property or Method
Get or set the font of an axis label	*visualContentObject*.`Axis.Scale.Font` `Expects a System.Drawing Font.`
Get or set the label orientation of an axis	*visualContentObject*.`Axis.Scale.LabelOrientation` Expects the `LabelOrientation` enumeration, which has two values: `LabelOrientation.Horizontal` and `LabelOrientation.Vertical`.
Show or hide axis labels	*visualContentObject*.`Axis.ShowLabels`
Show or hide a scale	*visualContentObject*.`Axis.Scale.Visible`
Show or hide a manual zoom slider	*visualContentObject*.`Axis.ManualZoom` Doesn't apply to the cross table.
Show or hide an axis selector	*visualContentObject*.`Axis.ShowAxisSelector`
Get or set an axis expression	*visualContentObject*.`Axis.Expression` Axis here is one of the following related classes: • `XAxis` • `YAxis` • `ZAxis (3D scatter plot)` • `ColorAxis` • `HierarchyAxis` • `MarkerByAxis` • `SizeAxis` • `ShapeAxis` Doesn't apply to the cross table.

Example script

Change the y-axis and marker by expressions on a scatter plot, hide the x-axis scale selector, and make the x-axis label orientation vertical:

```
# AxisProperties
from Spotfire.Dxp.Application.Visuals import *

# Get the visualization reference
for visualization in Document.ActivePageReference.Visuals:
    if visualization.Title == "ELEV vs. STATE":
        visualContentObject = visualization.As[VisualContent]()

# Change the y-axis and marker by expressions
visualContentObject.YAxis.Expression = "Avg([ELEV])"
visualContentObject.MarkerByAxis.Expression = "<[STATE]>"

# Hide the x-axis selector and make the labels vertical
visualContentObject.XAxis.ShowAxisSelector = False
visualContentObject.XAxis.Scale.LabelOrientation = LabelOrientation.
Vertical
```

Visualization-specific properties

Space does not permit the detailed coverage of every property for every visualization type, but the following table will give you a good head start and orientation. The reference point in each case is, as usual, `visualContentObject`:

 At this point, you might care to take a look at the online API reference: https://docs.tibco.com/pub/doc_remote/spotfire/6.5.0/api/Index.aspx.

Action	Property or Method
Scatter Plot	
Get or set the Label By expression	*visualContentObject*.LabelColumn
Get or set the font used for labels	*visualContentObject*.LabelFont Expects a System.Drawing Font.
Show or hide labels	*visualContentObject*.LabelVisibility Expects the LabelVisibility.enumeration, which can have one of three values: LabelVisibility.None, LabelVisibility.All, or LabelVisibility.Marked.

Action	Property or Method
Get or set the amount of X jitter	*visualContentObject*.XJitter Expects a number between 0 and 0.5.
Get or set the amount of Y jitter	*visualContentObject*.YJitter Expects a number between 0 and 0.5.
Bar Chart	
Set whether bars should be 100% or stacked	*visualContentObject*.HundredPercentBars True or False.
Determine whether complete bar should be labeled	*visualContentObject*.LabelCompleteBar True or False.
Get or set label font	*visualContentObject*.LabelFont Expects a System.Drawing Font.
Get or set label orientation	*visualContentObject*.LabelOrientation Expects the LabelOrientation enumeration, which has two values: LabelOrientation.Horizontal and LabelOrientation.Vertical.
Get or set percentage decimal digits	*visualContentObject*.LabelPercentageDecimalDigits
Determine whether bar segments are labeled	*visualContentObject*.LabelSegments True or False.
Determine how labels should be made visible	*visualContentObject*.LabelVisibility Expects the LabelVisibility.enumeration, which can have one of three values: LabelVisibility.None, LabelVisibility.All, or LabelVisibility.Marked.
Get or set the bar orientation	*visualContentObject*.Orientation Expects the BarChartOrientation enumeration, which has two values: BarChartOrientation.Horizontal and BarChartOrientation.Vertical.
Get or set label format	*visualContentObject*.SegmentLabelInformationType Expects the LabelInformationType enumeration, which has two values: LabelInformationType.Value and LabelInformationType.Percentage.
Determine whether bars are sorted by value	*visualContentObject*.SortedBars True or False.

Action	Property or Method
Get or set the stack mode: None, Stack or Stack100Percent	*visualContentObject*.`StackMode` Expects the `StackMode` enumeration, which has three values: `StackMode.None`, `StackMode.Stack` or `StackMode.Stack100Percent`.
Box Plot	
Get or set the box width	*visualContentObject*.`BoxWidth` Range 0–100.
Get or set the relative marker size	*visualContentObject*.`MarkerSize`
Determine whether to superimpose a distribution	*visualContentObject*.`ShowDistribution` True or False.
| Get or set the color of a reference point | *visualContentObject*.`ReferencePoints.Color`<br><br>Need to iterate through `ReferencePoints` to find a specific item, and need `System.Drawing` to assign a color:<br><br>```
from System.Drawing import Color
for item in visual.ReferencePoints:
    if item.MethodName == "Median":
        item.Color = Color.Black
``` |
Get or set the line style of a reference point	*visualContentObject*.`ReferencePoints.LineStyle` Need to iterate through `ReferencePoints` to find a specific item, and need the `LineStyle` enumeration to define the style: `LineStyle.Single`, `LineStyle.Dot`, `LineStyle.Dash`, and `LineStyle.Double`.
Determine whether an individual marker is shown	*visualContentObject*.`ReferencePoints.Visible` True or False. Need to iterate through `ReferencePoints` to find a specific item.
Determine whether a statistics table is shown	*visualContentObject*.`Table.Visible` True or False.
Get or set the table font	*visualContentObject*.`Table.Font` Expects a `System.Drawing` font.
Set the measures shown in the statistics table	*visualContentObject*.`Table.Measures.Add(Measure)` Expects a string description of measure, such as "Median".
```

Action	Property or Method
Line Chart	
Get or set the LineByAxis expression	*visualContentObject*.`LineByAxis.Expression`
Get or set the line width	*visualContentObject*.`LineWidth`
Get or set the marker size	*visualContentObject*.`MarkerSize`
Determine whether line labels are shown	*visualContentObject*.`ShowLineLabels` True or False.
Determine whether marker labels are shown	*visualContentObject*.`ShowMarkerLabels` True or False.
Determine whether markers are shown	*visualContentObject*.`ShowMarkers` True or False.

Cross table visualization

The cross table behaves a bit like an axis visualization, but it does have some table-specific properties.

Action	Property or Method
Get or set the width of the table cells	*visualContentObject*.`CellWidth`
Define the header of the cross table	*visualContentObject*.`ColumnAxis.Expression`
Define the cell values of the cross table	*visualContentObject*.`MeasureAxis.Expression`
Show or hide column grand totals	*visualContentObject*.`ShowColumnGrandTotal` True or False.
Show or hide column subtotals	*visualContentObject*.`ShowColumnSubtotals` True or False.
Show or hide row grand totals	*visualContentObject*.`ShowRowGrandTotal` True or False.
Define the rows of the cross table	*visualContentObject*.`RowAxis.Expression`

Action	Property or Method
Get or set the font used in the table (rows, headers, and cell values)	*visualContentObject*.TableFont Expects a System.Drawing font.

Table visualization

The table visualization is quite different to axes-based visualizations and has its own set of properties to exploit. The main reference point is still visualContentObject.

Action	Property or Method
Get or set the number of columns to freeze for scrolling (left or right)	*visualContentObject*.FrozenCount
Get or set the number of rows to include in the table header	*visualContentObject*.HeaderHeight Expects a number between 1 and 20.
Clear any sorted columns	*visualContentObject*.SortedColumns.Clear()
Get or set the table font	*visualContentObject*.TableFont Expects a System.Drawing font.
Get or set the table header font	*visualContentObject*.TableHeaderFont Expects a System.Drawing font.
Add a data column to the display	*visualContentObject*.TableColumns.Add(dataColumn) The data column must be referenced as Data.DataTableReference.Columns ["Column Name"]
Clear all columns from the table	*visualContentObject*.TableColumns.Clear()
Remove a named column from the display	*visualContentObject*.TableColumns.Remove(*dataColumn*) The data column must be referenced as Data.DataTableReference.Columns [Column Name]

Script example

Set up a table to show only certain columns:

```
# SetupTable

from Spotfire.Dxp.Application.Visuals import *

# Get the visualization reference
for visualization in Document.ActivePageReference.Visuals:
  if visualization.TypeId == VisualTypeIdentifiers.Table:
    visualContentObject = visualization.As[VisualContent]()

# Clear existing columns
visualContentObject.SortedColumns.Clear()
visualContentObject.TableColumns.Clear()

# Define columns to add
columnList = []
columnList.Add("STATE")
columnList.Add("STATION_NAME")
columnList.Add("ELEV")

# Add columns to table
for column in columnList:
  visualContentObject.TableColumns.Add(visualContentObject.Data.
DataTableReference.Columns[column])
```

Trellising

Trellising can be changed through the `Spotfire.Dxp.Application.Visuals` `Trellis` class, again referencing the `visualContentObject`.

Action	Property or Method
Get or set trellising in a column layout	*visualContentObject*.Trellis.ColumnAxis.Expression
Get or set the font of the trellis header	*visualContentObject*.Trellis.HeaderFont Expects a System.Drawing font.
Get or set the number of columns when in Panels mode	*visualContentObject*.Trellis.ManualColumnCount

Action	Property or Method
Determine whether the layout is manual or automatic	*visualContentObject*.Trellis.ManualLayout True or False.
Get or set the number of rows when in Panels mode	*visualContentObject*.Trellis.ManualRowCount
Get or set trellising in a page layout	*visualContentObject*.Trellis.PageAxis.Expression
Get or set trellising in a panel layout	*visualContentObject*.Trellis.PanelAxis.Expression
Get or set trellising in a row layout	*visualContentObject*.Trellis.RowAxis.Expression
Get or set the trellis mode	*visualContentObject*.Trellis.TrellisMode Expects the TrellisMode enumeration, which can have one of two values: TrellisMode.Panels or TrellisMode.RowsColumns.

Error bars

Error bars may be used on scatter plots, bar charts, and line charts. They can be manipulated using the Spotfire.Dxp.Application.Visuals ErrorBars class, referencing the axis and visualContentObject.

Action	Property or Method
Determine whether error bars are enabled	*visualContentObject*.Axis.ErrorBars.Enabled True or False.
Determine whether to color the error bars with the marker color	*visualContentObject*.Axis.ErrorBars.UseMarkerColor True or False.
Get or set the fixed color used for drawing error bars when UseMarkerColor is False	*visualContentObject*.Axis.ErrorBars.FixedColor Expects a System.Drawing color definition.
Determine whether the axis range is extended to cover all error bars	*visualContentObject*.Axis.ErrorBars.IncludeInAxisRange True or False.

Action	Property or Method
Get or set the lower expression	*visualContentObject*.Axis.ErrorBars.LowerExpression
Get or set the upper expression	*visualContentObject*.Axis.ErrorBars.UpperExpression

Reference lines and curves

Reference lines and curves may be used on scatter plots, bar charts, line charts, combination charts, and box plots. They can be set up and configured using the Spotfire.Dxp.Application.Visuals.FittingModels namespace classes FittingModelCollection, ReferenceLineFittingModel, and ReferenceCurveFittingModel. The main reference point is still visualContentObject.

Action	Property or Method
Creating new curves (FittingModelCollection)	
Add a new curve by providing an expression for f(x)	*visualContentObject*.FittingModels.AddCurve(Expression) Expression is a string.
Add a new curve by providing an expression for f(x) using columns in a data table	*visualContentObject*.FittingModels.AddCurve(DataTableObject, Expression) Expression is a string.
Add a new horizontal line	*visualContentObject*.FittingModels.AddHorizontalLine(Expression) Expression is a string.
Add a new horizontal line using columns in a data table	*visualContentObject*.AddHorizontalLine(DataTableObject, Expression) Expression is a string.
Add a new vertical line	*visualContentObject*.FittingModels.AddVerticalLine(Expression) Expression is a string.
Add a new vertical line using columns in a data table	*visualContentObject*.FittingModels.AddVerticalLine(DataTableObject, Expression) Expression is a string.
Clear all lines	*visualContentObject*.FittingModels.Clear()

Action	Property or Method
Manipulating existing curves (ReferenceLineFittingModel and ReferenceCurveFittingModel)	

Before manipulating the properties of a curve, you need to get the `ReferenceCurve` object, which is the reference point for the properties listed as follows:

```
for item in visualContentObject.FittingModels:
    referenceCurveObject = item.Line (or item.Curve)
```

Action	Property or Method
Get or set the color of the reference line/curve	*referenceCurveObject*.Color Expects a System.Drawing color definition.
Get or set the custom display name of the reference line/curve	referenceCurveObject.CustomDisplayName
Determine whether the reference line/curve name and expression should be displayed as a label or tooltip	*referenceCurveObject*.Details To get at individual properties, you have to iterate over the collection. For example, ```for item in referenceCurveObject.Details:\n if item.Name == "Value":\n item.ShowInLabel = False\n item.ShowInTooltip = True```
Get the display name of the reference line/curve	*referenceCurveObject*.DisplayName
Get the expression that defines the reference curve	*referenceCurveObject*.Expression
Determine whether the reference line/curve is rendered in the background	*referenceCurveObject*.IsBackground True or False.
Get or set the line style of the reference line/curve	*referenceCurveObject*.LineStyle Expects the LineStyle enumeration: LineStyle.Single, LineStyle.Dot, LineStyle.Dash, and LineStyle.Double.
Get or set the width of the reference line/curve	*referenceCurveObject*.Width
Determine whether the line/curve is visible	*referenceCurveObject*.Visible True or False.

Script example

Add a red, dashed horizontal reference line to a bar chart, give it a custom name, and display this name as a label:

```
# AddHorizontalLine

from Spotfire.Dxp.Application.Visuals import *
from Spotfire.Dxp.Application.Visuals.FittingModels import *
from System.Drawing import Color

# Get the visualization reference
for visualization in Document.ActivePageReference.Visuals:
  if visualization.Title == "Elevation by Latitude":
    visualContentObject = visualization.As[VisualContent]()

dataTable = Document.Data.Tables.TryGetValue("stationInventory1")[1]

# Clear any existing lines and then add new line
visualContentObject.FittingModels.Clear()
referenceLine = visualContentObject.FittingModels.
AddHorizontalLine(dataTable, "[Average Elevation]")

# Style the new line
referenceLine.Line.Color = Color.Red
referenceLine.Line.CustomDisplayName = "Average Elevation"
referenceLine.Line.LineStyle = LineStyle.Dash
referenceLine.Line.Width = 2
referenceLine.Line.Visible = True
```

 Notice how a reference to the new curve is obtained at the point of addition by setting the variable `referenceLine` equal to the method used to create the line.

How to manipulate color

Color can be applied to a visualization in one of three fundamentally different ways:

- Category
- Rule
- Gradient

The use of these different approaches is constrained by visualization type, data type, and whether the data is categorical or continuous in nature. At a scripting level, the color is also handled differently for tables and cross tables, but let's start with the other visualizations: those with axes.

Color by category

Color by category is simply handled using the `Spotfire.Dxp.Application.Visuals ColorAxis` class we've already encountered. This class has a property called `Coloring`, to which we can apply a categorical color rule. As usual, the main reference object is `visualContentObject`.

Action	Property or Method
Create a new categorical color rule	`colorRule = ` *visualContentObject* `.ColorAxis.Coloring.AddCategoricalColorRule()`
Add values to the color rule	*colorRule* `.Item[Value] = Color` Value can be whatever you want but should match the anticipated values in the data column to which the categorical coloring will be applied. Color can be `Color.FromArgb`(Integer) `Color.FromName`(.NET color name)

If the values you assign to the coloring match any values returned by the column assigned to the visualization's color axis, they will be colored as defined in your script. In this way, you can anticipate column values that will appear in the dataset and predefine the colors you want to assign to them. You cannot assign colors to future values any other way in Spotfire.

Example script

Define colors for the values in a region column used on a color axis:

```
# SetRegionColor

from Spotfire.Dxp.Application.Visuals import *
from System.Drawing import Color
```

```
# Get the visualization reference
for visualization in Document.ActivePageReference.Visuals:
   if visualization.Title == "GDP By Region":
     visualContentObject = visualization.As[VisualContent]()

# Set up the coloring
visualContentObject.ColorAxis.Coloring.Clear()
colorRule = visualContentObject.ColorAxis.Coloring.
AddCategoricalColorRule()

# Set the color values
colorRule.Item["Asia"] = Color.FromName("Blue")
colorRule.Item["Europe"] = Color.FromName("CadetBlue")
colorRule.Item["North America"] = Color.FromName("DarkOliveGreen")
colorRule.Item["South America"] = Color.FromName("Gold")
colorRule.Item["Africa"] = Color.FromName("IndianRed")
colorRule.Item["Oceania"] = Color.FromName("Violet")
```

Color by rule

Color rules can be applied to string and numerical values. There are 5 color rules (string rules) for string values and 10 color rules (threshold, range, and top/bottom rules) for numerical values. Boolean expressions can be used for either.

The `Spotfire.Dxp.Application.Visuals.ConditionalColoring` Coloring class provides methods to assign colors to values using these rules. If none of the rules match, then the `DefaultColor` or `EmptyColor` will be used. These colors can also be defined.

The main reference point is *visualContentObject*.ColorAxis.Coloring. You simply add each rule individually directly to the color axis coloring. In all cases, Color must be defined using System.Drawing as Color.FromArgb(Integer) or Color.FromName(.NET color name).

Action	Property or Method
String rules	
Add a string rule	*visualContentObject*.ColorAxis.Coloring.AddStringColorRule(StringComparisonOperator, ConditionValue, Color)
	StringComparisonOperator is an enumeration with the following values:
	StringComparisonOperator.Equal
	StringComparisonOperator.NotEqual
	StringComparisonOperator.StartsWith
	StringComparisonOperator.EndsWith
	StringComparisonOperator.Contains
	ConditionValue requires the method CreateLiteral
	ConditionValue.CreateLiteral(Value)
Threshold rules	
Add a threshold rule	*visualContentObject*.ColorAxis.Coloring.AddThresholdColorRule(StringComparisonOperator, ConditionValue, Color)
	StringComparisonOperator enumeration:
	StringComparisonOperator.Equal
	StringComparisonOperator.NotEqual
	StringComparisonOperator.Greater
	StringComparisonOperator.GreaterOrEqual
	StringComparisonOperator.Less
	StringComparisonOperator.LessOrEqual
Range Rules	
Add a range rule	*visualContentObject*.ColorAxis.Coloring.AddRangeRule(ConditionValue, ConditionValue, Color)
	ConditionValue requires the method CreateLiteral
	ConditionValue.CreateLiteral(Value)

Action	Property or Method
Top and bottom rules	
Add a bottom N rule	*visualContentObject*.ColorAxis.Coloring.AddBottomNRule(Integer, Color)
Add a top N rule	*visualContentObject*.ColorAxis.Coloring.AddTopNRule(Integer, Color)
Boolean expressions	
Add a Boolean expression rule	*visualContentObject*.ColorAxis.Coloring. AddExpressionRule(Boolean Expression, Color)
General properties and methods	
Clear all rules	*visualContentObject*.ColorAxis.Coloring.Clear()
Get or set the default color	*visualContentObject*.ColorAxis.Coloring.DefaultColor If setting the color, you need to use System.Drawing (just as for color rules)
Get or set the "empty" color	*visualContentObject*.ColorAxis.Coloring.EmptyColor If setting the color, you need to use System.Drawing (just as for color rules)
Determine whether a coloring should be evaluated per trellis panel	*visualContentObject*.ColorAxis.Coloring. EvaluatePerTrellis True or False

Example script

Set the color for the top 5 values in a color by column:

```
# ColorTop5

from Spotfire.Dxp.Application.Visuals import *
from Spotfire.Dxp.Application.Visuals.ConditionalColoring import *
from System.Drawing import Color

# Get the visualization reference
for visualization in Document.ActivePageReference.Visuals:
  if visualization.Title == "GDP By Country":
    visualContentObject = visualization.As[VisualContent]()

# Clear any existing coloring
visualContentObject.ColorAxis.Coloring.Clear()

# Add the color rule
visualContentObject.ColorAxis.Coloring.AddTopNRule(5, Color.
FromName("Red"))
```

Gradient coloring

Axes with continuous data (numbers that have not been categorized) can be colored using a gradient, usually with defined segments. Continuous coloring is handled very much like categorical coloring, except you start with a continuous color rule and then add the intervals you require using the `Spotfire.Dxp.Application.Visuals. ConditionalColoring ColorBreakpointCollection` class.

Action	Property or Method
Add a new continuous color rule	`colorRule` = *visualContentObject*`.ColorAxis.Coloring. AddContinuousColorRule()`
Get or set the interval mode	*colorRule*`.IntervalMode` `IntervalMode` is enumerated as `IntervalMode.Segments` or `IntervalMode.Gradient`

Add a breakpoint	*colorRule*`.Breakpoints.Add(ConditionValue, Color)`
	
	`ConditionValue` is an enumeration with the following values:
	
	`ConditionValue.MinValue`
	
	`ConditionValue.MaxValue`
	
	`ConditionValue.AverageValue`
	
	`ConditionValue.MedianValue`
	
	`ConditionValue.CreateLiteralValue`(Value)
	
	`ConditionValue.CreatePercentValue`(Value)
	
	`ConditionValue.CreateExpression`(Expression)

Clear all breakpoints	*colorRule*`.Breakpoints.Clear()`

Coloring tables and cross tables

Tables and cross tables are handled a little differently to other visualizations. You first create a coloring entity through the `Colorings` property of the visualization; then, you map the coloring to a column(s); and finally, you define the rules and colors according to your preferred color mode using the same methods used for other visualizations.

Action	Property or Method
Create a new coloring entity	`coloring` = *visualContentObject*`.Colorings.AddNew`(Rule Name)
Map a color rule to a column	*visualContentObject*`.Colorings. AddMapping(CategoryKey`(Column Name)`, coloring)`
Clear all coloring	*visualContentObject*`.Colorings.Clear()`

Example script

Apply a color gradient to a table:

```
# ColorTable

from Spotfire.Dxp.Application.Visuals import *
from Spotfire.Dxp.Application.Visuals.ConditionalColoring import *
from System.Drawing import Color

# Get the visualization reference
for visualization in Document.ActivePageReference.Visuals:
  if visualization.Title == "GDP_Data":
    visualContentObject = visualization.As[VisualContent]()

# Clear existing coloring
visualContentObject.Colorings.Clear()

# Add the coloring entity
coloring = visualContentObject.Colorings.AddNew("GDP Gradient")

# Map the column
visualContentObject.Colorings.AddMapping(CategoryKey("GDP (USD
million)"), coloring)

# Add the gradient and intervals
colorRule = coloring.AddContinuousColorRule()
colorRule.IntervalMode = IntervalMode.Gradient
colorRule.Breakpoints.Add(ConditionValue.MinValue, Color.
FromName("SlateBlue"))
colorRule.Breakpoints.Add(ConditionValue.MaxValue, Color.
FromName("Red"))
colorRule.Breakpoints.Add(ConditionValue.MedianValue, Color.
FromName("Silver"))
```

How to manipulate filters

There are many ways in which filters can be manipulated in scripts, from the display of the filter panel, through how a filtering collection is organized, to the settings for an individual filter. Space does not permit a complete coverage of all the possible properties and methods, but we will look closely at filter settings.

No matter how you want to manipulate filters, you must traverse the hierarchy of filter objects: **filter panel** | **filtering collection** (data table) | **filter setting** (column). In an earlier section, we covered the filter panel object, which is accessed via the `Spotfire.Dxp.Application PanelCollection` class. With this reference to hand, we can move into the `Spotfire.Dxp.Application.Filters` namespace.

Action	Property or Method
Get a filtering scheme reference	*filteringScheme* = *filterPanel*. `FilteringSchemeReference`
Get a filter collection	*filterCollection* = *filteringScheme* [`dataTable`] `dataTable` must be a data table object
Get an individual filter	*filter* = *filterCollection* [Column Name] Column Name is a string.

Change a filter

What can you do with these objects? You can use the filter object to change a filter setting, but you need to take account of the filter type, of which there are six: Range, Item, Check Box, Radio Button, Text, and List Box. There is also a Check Box Hierarchy type for hierarchy columns. Each filter type has its own class of properties and methods. Once you have the filter item, you must *cast* it as whatever filter type it is before you can manipulate it. You can also change the filter type first.

Action	Property or Method

Get or set the filter type	*filter*.`TypeId`
	
	`TypeId` is enumerated by `FilterTypeIdentifiers`, which can have the following values:
	
	`FilterTypeIdentifiers.RangeFilter,`
	`FilterTypeIdentifiers.Itemfilter,`
	`FilterTypeIdentifiers.CheckBoxFilter,`
	`FilterTypeIdentifiers.RadioButtonfilter,`
	`FilterTypeIdentifiers.TextFilter,`
	`FilterTypeIdentifiers.ListBoxFilter,`
	`FilterTypeIdentifiers.CheckBoxHierarchyFilter`

Cast a filter item.	*filterObject* = `filter.As` [Filter Type] `()`
	
	Filter Type is one of the following:
	
	`RangeFilter, Itemfilter, CheckBoxFilter,`
	`RadioButtonfilter, TextFilter, ListBoxFilter,`
	`CheckBoxHierarchyFilter`

Reset a filter	*filterObject*.`Reset()`

Action	Property or Method
Set a range filter	*filterObject*.`ValueRange` = `ValueRange`(Start Value, End Value)
Set an item filter	*filterObject.Value* = `Value`
Set a check box filter.	*filterObject*.`Check`(Value) `filterObject.Uncheck(Value)` Unfortunately, you can only check or uncheck one item at a time, and so you need to use a loop to check or uncheck multiple values.
Set a radio button filter	*filterObject*.`Value` = `Value`
Set a text filter	*filterObject*.`Value` = `Value`
Set a list filter	*filterObject*.`IncludeAllValues` = `False` `filterObject.SetSelection(`[Value 1, Value 2, ... Value *n*]`)` You need this statement to remove the "All values" selection before you make your desired selections.

Script example

Set a list box filter to two values:

```
# ChangeFilterSetting

from Spotfire.Dxp.Application.Filters import *

# Get filtering scheme reference
filterPanel = Document.ActivePageReference.FilterPanel
filteringScheme = filterPanel.FilteringSchemeReference

# Get filter collection
dataTable = Document.Data.Tables.TryGetValue("GDP_Data")[1]
filterCollection = filteringScheme[dataTable]

# Get filter and cast it
filter = filterCollection["Region"]
filterObject = filter.As[ListBoxFilter]()

# Reset the filter and change the setting
filterObject.Reset()
filterObject.IncludeAllValues = False
filterObject.SetSelection(["Oceania", "Africa"])
```

Hide a filter group

Before we leave filters, I just want to give you a useful snippet. You can hide or show, expand or collapse filter groups by manipulating the FilterPanel TableGroups property. The following script shows only the filters you want on a page:

```
# HideFilters

from Spotfire.Dxp.Application.Filters import *

filterPanel = Document.ActivePageReference.FilterPanel
for group in filterPanel.TableGroups:
  if group.Name == "GDP_Data":
   group.Visible = True
   if group.Expanded == True:
    group.Expanded = False
  else:
   group.Visible = False
```

Manipulating data already loaded into Spotfire

There are many ways to manipulate the data in an analysis file using the Spotfire. Dxp.Data namespace, but the three most common activities are navigating a table to look up values, marking/selecting data, and creating and changing calculated columns. These are the three areas we're going to cover in this section.

Reading a table

The ability to read a data table using a script is a very useful tool, allowing you, for example, to drive actions based on the values in a metadata table. It's also very easy to do. You just need to define **cursors** for the columns you want to read and then iterate through the table's rows, inspecting the values of these cursors as you go. The data table object is the key to this activity; so, just to recap, you get a data table object as follows:

```
dataTable = Document.Data.Tables.TryGetValue(Name of data table)[1]
```

Action	Property or Method
Define a string cursor	`DataValueCursor.CreateFormatted(`*dataTable.*`Columns[Column Name])`
Define a numeric cursor	`DataValueCursor.CreateNumeric(`*dataTable.*`Columns[Column Name])`
Get the rows in a table	*dataTable.*GetRows(Cursor1, Cursor2, … Cursor3) To make this method meaningful, you need to iterate: for row in dataTable.GetRows(Cursor1, Cursor2, … Cursor3):
Get the current value of a cursor	*cursor.*CurrentValue

Example script

Provide the user with a search box to look up values in a table. The search box is referenced in the script through a document property:

```
# ReadTable

from Spotfire.Dxp.Data import *

# Define data table and cursors
dataTable = Document.Data.Tables.TryGetValue("GDP_Data")[1]
countryCursor = DataValueCursor.CreateFormatted(dataTable.
Columns["Country Name"])
gdpCursor = DataValueCursor.CreateNumeric(dataTable.Columns["GDP (USD
million)"])

# Read the table
for row in dataTable.GetRows(countryCursor, gdpCursor):
  # Use Trim() method to remove any spaces
  if countryCursor.CurrentValue.Trim() == Document.
Properties["SearchTerm"].Trim():
    Document.Properties["Gdp"] = gdpCursor.CurrentValue
    Document.Properties["SearchResult"] = ""
    # Exit the loop if a match is found
    break
  else:
    Document.Properties["Gdp"] = 0.0
    Document.Properties["SearchResult"] = "Not Found"
```

Marking and selecting data

Marking appears to the user as a very visual activity and one that is closely associated with a visualization, but it is in fact always a data operation. When you mark something in a visualization, you are actually marking the rows in the underlying data table. Using a script, you can select specific rows in a table independent of marking, which is not something you can do using the graphical user interface. You can also choose whether you want to apply a selection to a marking.

The `Spotfire.Dxp.Data DataTable` class provides a method for selecting data, and the `RowSelection` class allows you to turn this selection into a transferable index set, which is essentially a series of zeros and ones for each row in the table, a *one* meaning selected. The `DataMarkingSelection` class provides methods to turn data selections into markings or vice versa.

Action	Property or Method
Select rows in a data table using a Boolean expression	`rowSelection` = *dataTable*.`Select`(Expression) `dataTable` is a data table object; the expression must be a Spotfire expression that yields a Boolean value
Get the index for a row	*row*.Index The row object is obtained by iterating through the rows of a table, as we saw in the previous section
Get the index set for a row selection	*selectedIndexSet* = `rowSelection`.`AsIndexSet`()
Get the index value in an index set	*selectedIndexSet*[n] . This is just a standard Python string parsing, where n could be `row`.`Index`
Mark selected rows	*marking*.`SetSelection`(*rowSelection*, *dataTable*) Recall that the `marking` is obtained through `Document`.`Data`.`Markings`.
Get marked rows as an index set	`selectedIndexSet` = *marking*.`GetSelection`(*dataTable*)

Example script 1

Find values in a data table and mark the corresponding row(s):

```
# SelectRows

from Spotfire.Dxp.Data import *

# Define data table
```

```
dataTable = Document.Data.Tables.TryGetValue("GDP_Data")[1]

# Make a selection by expression
rowSelection = dataTable.Select("[Country Name] = 'Ireland' or
[Country Name] = 'India'")

# Mark rows
for marking in Document.Data.Markings:
  if marking.Name == "Marking":
    marking.SetSelection(rowSelection, dataTable)
```

Example script 2

Get marked rows and the corresponding data values. Use a text area control and corresponding document property to display the results:

```
# GetMarkedRows

from Spotfire.Dxp.Data import *

dataTable = Document.Data.Tables.TryGetValue("GDP_Data")[1]

# Get marked rows as a row selection
for marking in Document.Data.Markings:
 if marking.Name == "Marking":
  rowSelection = marking.GetSelection(dataTable)

# Cast rowSelection as an index set
selectedIndexSet = rowSelection.AsIndexSet()

# Define a cursor
countryCursor = DataValueCursor.CreateFormatted(dataTable.
Columns["Country Name"])

# Read the table and map the selected index set
resultString = ""
for row in dataTable.GetRows(countryCursor):
  if selectedIndexSet[row.Index] == 1:
    if resultString == "":
      resultString = countryCursor.CurrentValue
    else:
      resultString = resultString + ", " + countryCursor.CurrentValue

Document.Properties["SelectedCountries"] = resultString
```

Calculated columns

It can be very useful to build or change a calculated column using a script. It gives you the option, for example, of creating metrics on the fly based on business rules provided through a metadata table. Calculated columns can be created from scratch using the `Spotfire.Dxp.Data DataColumnCollection` class, and the existing calculated columns can be changed using the `Spotfire.Dxp.Data CalculatedColumn` class.

Action	Property or Method
Add a calculated column.	*dataTable*`.Columns.AddCalculatedColumn`(Column Name, Expression)
Cast a column as a calculated column. This step is necessary to use the CalculatedColumn class.	*calculatedColumn* = `dataTable.Columns`[Column Name]`.As[CalculatedColumn]()`
Change the expression for an existing calculated column.	*calculatedColumn*`.Expression`

Example Script

Add a new calculated column, or if this already exists, change its expression:

```
# AddChangeCalculatedColumn

from Spotfire.Dxp.Data import *

dataTable = Document.Data.Tables.TryGetValue("GDP_Data")[1]

# Define expression for calculated column
calculatedColumnExpression = "If([GDP (USD million)]>= Avg([GDP (USD
million)]), 'Above average', 'Below Average')"

# Determine whether the column already exists
createColumn = True
for column in dataTable.Columns:
  if column.Name == "GDP Comparison":
    createColumn = False
    break
```

```
if createColumn == True:
   dataTable.Columns.AddCalculatedColumn("GDP Comparison",
calculatedColumnExpression)
else:
   calculatedColumn = dataTable.Columns["GDP Comparison"].
As[CalculatedColumn]()
   calculatedColumn.Expression = calculatedColumnExpression
```

How to add data to an analysis

In *Chapter 5, Source Data is Never Enough*, we explored the notion that the source data might not be sufficient or in quite the right form for the analysis we want to do. It's always best to do as much data modeling and manipulation as possible at source, but if you need to do some additional data manipulation, scripting allows you to automate and control this activity.

Data can be added as columns or as rows, and it can be added from a variety of sources, including tables already present in an analysis file. The first step is to define or reference the data source using the `Spotfire.Dxp.Data.Import` classes. We can then move back to the `Spotfire.Dxp.Data` namespace to make the additions.

Define a data source

Data can come from many sources, and there is a class for each type. In this section, we're going to look at database sources, delimited text file data sources, information links, and sources within the analysis file. Once you have defined a data source, you can simply add an entire table, or you can use the source definition to add specific rows and columns, and we will cover this aspect in the sections that follow.

Action	Property or Method
Add a table from a defined data source	`Document.Data.Tables.Add(Table Name, `*`dataSource`*`)`
Database source	
Initialize new instance of a database source	`dataSource = DatabaseDataSource()`

Get or set the settings for a database source	`dataSource.Settings.ConnectionString`
	`dataSource.Settings.User`
	`dataSource.Settings.Password`
	`dataSource.Settings.SqlStatement`
	`dataSource.Settings.Provider`

Action	Property or Method
Delimited Text File	
Initialize a new instance of text data reader settings	`readerSettings = TextDataReaderSettings()`
Define column names	*readerSettings*.`SetColumnName` (Index, Column Name) Index begins at 0.
Define column to ignore	*readerSettings*.`AddIgnoreColumn` (Index)
Define column data types	*readerSettings*.`SetDataType` (Index, `DataType`) `DataType` is specified by the standard Spotfire DataType enumeration.
Define the delimiter	*readerSettings*.`Separator` tab = "/t"
Skip rows	*readerSettings*.`StartReadingRow` Integer (row 1 = 1)
Initialize new instance of a text file source	`dataSource = TextFileDataSource` (File Path, *readerSettings*) When entering a file path as a literal string, you need to double all the backslashes: `C:\\myDataFolder\\myDataFile.txt`.
Information links	
Initialize new instance of an information link source	`dataSource = InformationLinkDataSource` (GUID)
Define any parameters to be set when executing an information link	`parameterValue = Array[object]` (Value) (Value could be a document property linked to an input control.)

Compile a list of all parameters	`ilParameters = [InformationLinkParameter.`
	`CreateNamedParameter` (Name1, *parameterValue1*),
	`InformationLinkParameter.CreateNamedParameter`
	(Name2, *parameterValue2*), ... etc]

Add parameter values to the information link definition	`dataSource.Parameters =` *ilParameters*
Internal data tables	
Initialize new instance of a data table link source	`dataSource = DataTableDataSource` (*dataTable*)

Action	Property or Method
Initialize new instance of a data table link source with data selection	`dataSource = DataTableDataSource (`*dataTable, rowSelection*`)`

Add a column to a table

The addition of columns to a table require a sequence of coordinated actions and a few specialized objects. The basic action is to add an "add columns setting" definition from a defined source to a defined target. However, the `AddColumnsSettings` constructor has two elements that themselves require definition: the table joins and the columns to ignore. I don't know why the API is written this way. Defining the columns to include would be more intuitive, but it is what is! All columns, whether for a join definition or columns to ignore list, must be expressed or cast as **column signatures**.

Action	Property or Method
Create a column signature	`columnSignature = DataColumnSignature (`Column Name, `DataType)` `DataType` is defined by the standard Spotfire DataType enumeration
Define a column map	`columnMap = {`*columnSignature:columnSignature, columnSignature:columnSignature, ...,* `}` The curly braces define a dictionary set, which is required for the column map definition. The column signatures in this case are for the left and right sides of a join.

Define the add columns settings	`columnSettings = AddColumnsSettings (`*columnMap*`,`
	`JoinType,` *IgnoredColumns*`)`
	
	`JoinType` is enumerated by the following values: `JoinType.InnerJoin, JoinType.LeftOuterJoin, JoinType.RightOuterJoin, JoinType.FullOuterJoin.`
	
	`IgnoredColumns` is a list of column signatures. Any column not included in the list will be added. However, you can leave it blank when adding columns from a text file source, which has its own method for designating columns to ignore.

Add the columns	*dataTable*`.AddColumns (`*SourceTable, columnSettings*`)`

Script example

Add a column from an external CSV file to a data table in an analysis file. A text area control and the associated document property are used to allow the user to enter the file path to the external file:

```
# AddColumn

from Spotfire.Dxp.Data import *
from Spotfire.Dxp.Data.Import import *

# Define source and target and generate ignored columns list
targetTable = Document.Data.Tables.TryGetValue("GDP_Data")[1]
ignoredColumns = []
readerSettings = TextDataReaderSettings()
readerSettings.AddIgnoreColumn(0)
readerSettings.SetColumnName(1, "Country Name")
readerSettings.SetDataType(1, DataType.String)
readerSettings.AddIgnoreColumn(2)
readerSettings.AddIgnoreColumn(3)
readerSettings.SetColumnName(4, "G20")
readerSettings.SetDataType(4, DataType.String)
readerSettings.Separator = ","
filePath = Document.Properties["FilePath"]
sourceTable = TextFileDataSource(filePath, readerSettings)

# Define the table relationship
leftColumnSignature = DataColumnSignature("Country Name", DataType.
String)
rightColumnSignature = DataColumnSignature("Country Name", DataType.
String)
columnMap = {leftColumnSignature:rightColumnSignature}

# Build the column settings and add the column to the target
ignoredColumns = []
columnSettings = AddColumnsSettings(columnMap, JoinType.LeftOuterJoin,
ignoredColumns)

targetTable.AddColumns(sourceTable, columnSettings)
```

Add rows to a table

The addition of rows to a table follows a similar process to the add columns process. Just like adding columns, you have to define column signatures and a column map. Think back to *Chapter 5, Source Data is Never Enough,* and how we added rows using the graphical user interface: we matched *all* relevant columns in the two tables. Therefore, the column map will include all matches. You also have to define ignored columns, just as you do when adding columns to a table.

Action	Property or Method
Define the add rows settings	columnsSettings = AddRowsSettings (*columnMap, ignoredColumns*)
Add the rows	*dataTable*.AddRows (*SourceTable, columnSettings*)

Script example

Add rows from one table in an analysis file to another:

```
# AddRows

from Spotfire.Dxp.Data import *
from Spotfire.Dxp.Data.Import import *

# Define source and target
targetTable = Document.Data.Tables.TryGetValue("GDP_Data_first_half")
[1]
sourceTable = DataTableDataSource(Document.Data.Tables.
TryGetValue("GDP_Data_second_half")[1])
dataTable2 = Document.Data.Tables.TryGetValue("GDP_Data_second_half")
[1]

# Generate ignored columns list to disregard any nonshared columns
ignoredColumns = []
targetList = []
for column in targetTable.Columns:
  targetList.Add(column.Name)
for column in dataTable2.Columns:
  if column.Name not in targetList:
    ignoredColumns.Add(DataColumnSignature(column.Name, DataType.
Undefined))

# Define the table relationships
leftColumnSignature1 = DataColumnSignature("Country Abbreviation",
DataType.String)
```

```
rightColumnSignature1 = DataColumnSignature("Country Abbreviation",
DataType.String)
leftColumnSignature2 = DataColumnSignature("Country Name", DataType.
String)
rightColumnSignature2 = DataColumnSignature("Country Name", DataType.
String)
leftColumnSignature3 = DataColumnSignature("Region", DataType.String)
rightColumnSignature3 = DataColumnSignature("Region", DataType.String)
leftColumnSignature4 = DataColumnSignature("GDP (USD million)",
DataType.Integer)
rightColumnSignature4 = DataColumnSignature("GDP (USD million)",
DataType.Integer)
columnMap = {leftColumnSignature1:rightColumnSignature1, leftColumnSig
nature2:rightColumnSignature2, leftColumnSignature3:rightColumnSignatu
re3, leftColumnSignature4:rightColumnSignature4}

# Build the row settings and add the rows to the target
rowSettings = AddRowsSettings(columnMap, ignoredColumns)

targetTable.AddRows(sourceTable, rowSettings)
```

Summary

This chapter has introduced you to Python scripting and the Spotfire API. You have learned how to write basic IronPython scripts and how to use Spotfire and .NET classes. We have toured the Spotfire API, referencing and manipulating the primary elements in an analysis file, manipulating visualization properties, manipulating color, manipulating filters, manipulating data already loaded into Spotfire, and adding data to an analysis.

The Spotfire API can be difficult to figure out. The class descriptions and script examples in this chapter should demystify the API for you and provide you with practical script recipes that inspire you to begin creating your own applications. Working through the examples and writing your own scripts will help you to explore the online API resource to find new properties and methods to solve your analysis problems. The TIBCO website provides a complete guide to every class: https://docs.tibco.com/pub/doc_remote/spotfire/6.5.0/api/Index.aspx.

In the next chapter, we will develop a case study in self-service business intelligence that uses scripts as an integral component of the solution.

9

It's All About Self-service These Days

Traditional **business intelligence** (**BI**) places a strong emphasis on data control and the delivery of static dashboards and reports. The underlying data may be refreshed, maybe even in real time, but the metrics, KPIs, and configuration of the visualizations and reports remain the same unless someone, most probably an IT developer, updates or changes them.

The process for working with the customers of BI to build new reports or find new analytic insights is usually too slow. The customers tend to make ill-formed and indiscriminate requests because they are not quite sure what they want, are often precluded from truly agile development in which they can quickly change or drop things that have been built, and insure themselves in a way by keeping a long list of all possible requirements in the queue. Meanwhile, the IT professionals, perhaps overwhelmed with requirements, perhaps coping with limited resources, take too long to analyze the requirements and build the solutions. To compound matters, when the customers finally see the solution, they complain that it is not quite what they want or announce that the requirements have changed.

BI platforms often allow users to run ad hoc reports and analyses. Some provide a semantic layer to abstract a physical data structure into a representation that is familiar to end users. These are tentative steps toward self-service BI, but they are only the beginning, not least because the power to define new metrics, KPIs, and data representations remains restricted and the system or process for publishing BI to the enterprise remains slow and under the control of IT.

The rapidly growing demand for informatics, frustration with traditional IT, and the evolution of BI thinking within IT are leading to a growing interest in and delivery of self-service analytics, which is all about empowering end users to design and deploy their own reports and analyses within an approved and supported architecture and tools portfolio. One of the biggest drivers and enablers of self-service BI is the often superior understanding of the data and its applications among the consumers of BI, especially in a data-driven organization, a reality that the IT department can sometimes be unwilling to acknowledge.

Spotfire is built with self-service analytics as a core value, and it is an exemplary data exploration tool. Some might think it is too free and too individualistic; however, with a little imagination and technical know-how, the freedom and openness of the Spotfire platform can be harnessed to build sustainable and stable enterprise-grade self-service BI solutions.

In this chapter, we will explore this theme, starting with a look at guided analysis and finishing with the construction of a more sophisticated self-service application. We will cover the following topics:

- Building a guided analysis
- Key data concept—metadata
- Incorporating configurable business rules into your analysis
- A metadata-driven self-service analytics case study

Building a guided analysis

Spotfire can be used as a completely free-form data discovery tool; it can also be used to create static reports and dashboards. As a BI author, you will often want to build something in between: an analysis framework that allows the user to explore the data but within certain parameters and under the constraints imposed by the web player. A guided analysis can also simply give direction, helping users to navigate the data and gain insights quickly.

Some of the examples we've already worked through in this book have included guided analysis elements, such as drop-down options in text areas. The inline help in Spotfire highlights the following techniques:

- Create a cover page
- Write instructions in text areas
- Place links or buttons in text areas leading to relevant tools, pages, or views

- Use the **Step-by-Step** navigation mode or define page navigation using the **History Arrows** navigation mode
- Use customized filtering schemes

In the next example, we're going to reuse concepts already covered, include some of the techniques mentioned in the Spotfire user guide, and use some more advanced techniques to help guide an analysis. By now, you should be comfortable enough with Spotfire and a detailed set of instructions should not be required: so, the creation of the analysis will be outlined rather than stepped through in detail. We're going to create three pages, and we're going to use some fabricated retail data: StoreSales.csv, which can be downloaded from http://www.insidespotfire.com.

Before we create any pages, load the data file into a new analysis file.

Index page

The first page is an index that introduces the analysis options and provides links to the other pages. It consists of a text area with a layout defined by HTML and CSS (cascading style sheets) tags. You can download the HTML/CSS used to generate the following page from http://www.insidespotfire.com:

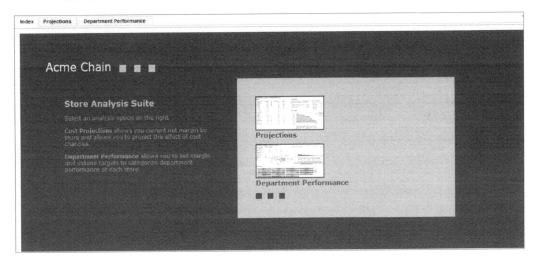

To insert the images and link them to pages in the analysis file, edit the text area, select the **Insert Action Control** icon, select **Actions**, select **Image** as the **Control type**, and add the page you want the action to navigate to from the available selections.

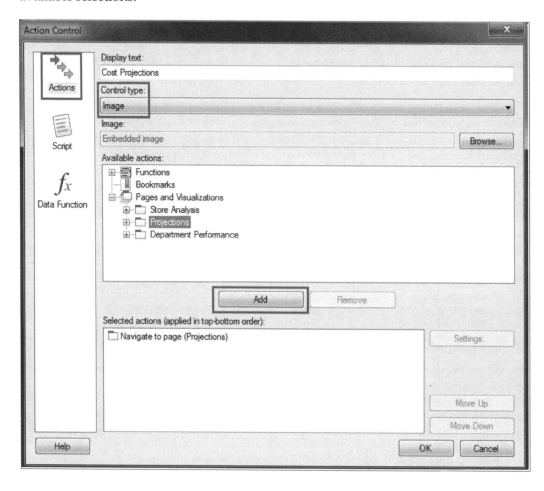

Once you've added the links, right-click on the text area and select **Edit HTML** to open the HTML editor. You will see the links embedded in the HTML as Spotfire controls; for example, `<SpotfireControl id="97df4e28318c43e78c8cf605363b4 e3e" />`. You can change the surrounding text and HTML tags and introduce your own custom inline CSS code to style the page. Just make sure you leave the Spotfire controls intact.

Projections page

The next page, Projections, shows the current net margin by store and gives the user sliders to project the effect of percentage decreases in costs or increases in sales. For example, a 2 percent drop in operational costs is projected to take two stores out of the red zone. The user can filter by department to see how individual departments affect the bottom line.

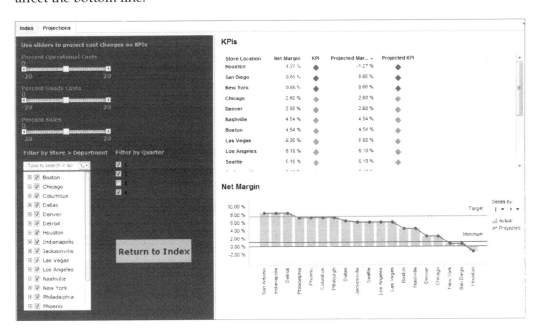

If you change the operational costs slider to **-2**, the San Diego and New York stores shift to an amber status.

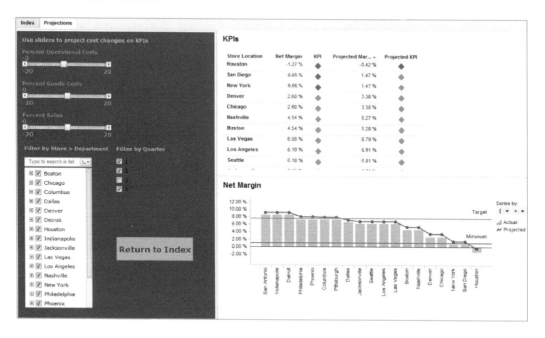

To build this page, you need to create the following components:

- **Sliders**: Create three sliders in a text area and associate them with new document properties called OpScaler, GoodsScaler, and SalesScaler. In each case, select **Numerical range** for **Set property value through:**. Assign a **Value interval:** of **1** in each case, and also **Min:** and **Max:** values of **-20** and **20**, respectively. Provide supporting text, such as `Percent Operational Costs`, `Percent Goods Costs`, and `Percent Sales`.

- **Hierarchy column**: Create the hierarchy column `DepartmentHierarchy`, which includes `[Store Location], [Department]`.

- **Custom filters**: Hide the main filter panel and add custom filters for **[DepartmentHierarchy]** and **[Quarter]** to the text area containing the sliders by right-clicking on the text area, selecting **Edit Text Area**, clicking on the custom filter icon, and selecting **[DepartmentHierarchy]** and **[Quarter]** from the filtering scheme list.

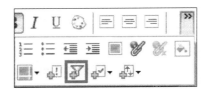

The layout and appearance of the text area can be improved using HTML.

- **Link to Index page**: Insert a navigation link to the Index page in the text area.

- **Calculated columns**: Create the following calculated columns:

Projected Operational Cost: `[Operational Cost]+[Operational Cost]*(${OpScaler}/100)`

Projected Goods Cost: `[Goods Cost] + [Goods Cost]*(${GoodsScaler}/100)`

Projected Sales: `[Sales] + [Sales]*(${SalesScaler}/100)`

Net Margin Store: `Avg((([Sales] - [Goods Cost] - [Operational Cost]) / [Sales]) OVER ([Quarter],[Store Location],[Department])`

Projected Net Margin Store: `Avg((([Projected Sales] - [Projected Goods Cost] - [Projected Operational Cost]) / [Projected Sales]) OVER ([Quarter],[Store Location],[Department])`

 Averaging over Quarter, Store Location, and Department allows the user to analyze the effect of filtering by quarter, store location, and department.

- **Graphical Table**: Create a graphical table with the following properties:

  Rows: [Store Location]

  Axes - Calculated value: Avg([Net Margin Store]); color bottom three red.

  Axes - Icon: Avg([Net Margin Store]); color rules: Green = Greater than value 0.075; Amber = Boolean expression [Axis.Icon]>0.01 and [Axis.Icon]<=0.075; Red = Less than or equal to 0.01.

  Axes - Calculated value: Avg([Projected Net Margin Store])

  Axes - Icon: Avg([Projected Net Margin Store]); color rules: Green = Greater than value 0.075; Amber = Boolean expression [Axis. Icon]>0.01 and [Axis.Icon]<=0.075; Red = Less than or equal to 0.01.

- **Combination Chart**: Create a combination chart with the following properties:

  Appearance: Sort x-axis by [Actual].

  X-axis: [Store Location]

  Y-axis: Avg([Net Margin Store]) as [Actual], Avg([Projected Net Margin Store]) as [Projected]

  Series: (Column Names) ([Axis.Default.Names]); Actual as bar, Projected as line.

  Lines and Curves: Horizontal Line 1: Fixed value: 0.01; Custom name: Minimum. Horizontal Line 2: Fixed value: 0.075; Custom name: Target.

Department Performance page

The final page for this example, the Department Performance page, allows the user to set margin and volume targets to categorize department performance at each store. The user can also filter to see how the performance changes through each quarter.

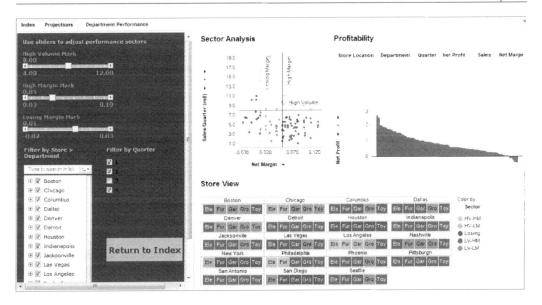

To build this page, you need to create the following components:

- **Sliders**: Embed sliders called High Volume, High Margin, and Losing Margin in a text area, and add supporting text. The **High Volume Mark** slider should range from 4 to 12 in increments of 8; the **High Margin Mark** slider should range from 0.03 to 0.10 in increments of 0.05; and the **Losing Margin Mark** slider should range from -0.02 to 0.03 in increments of 0.01.

- **Custom filters and navigation link**: Hide the main filter panel and add custom filters for [DepartmentHierarchy] and [Quarter] in the same way as for the Projections page. Add a navigation link back to the Index page.

- **Calculated columns**: Net Margin: `Avg(([Sales] - [Goods Cost] - [Operational Cost]) / [Sales]) OVER ([Quarter],[Store Location],[Department])`

  Net Profit: `[Sales] * [Net Margin]`

- **Hierarchies**: DepartmentHierarchy: **[Store Location] | [Department]**
- **Scatter Plot**: X-axis: `Avg([Net Margin]) as [Net Margin]`

  Y-axis: `Sum([Sales]) / UniqueCount([Quarter]) as [Sales/Quarter]`

 We need to average over a quarter to enable filtering by quarter. Doing this directly on the axis means the plot will dynamically recalculate as quarters are filtered in and out by the user.

Colors:

```
case
when Sum([Sales])/UniqueCount([Quarter])>=${Volume} and
Avg([Net Margin]) >=${HighMargin} then "HV-HM"
when Sum([Sales])/UniqueCount([Quarter])>=${Volume} and
Avg([Net Margin]) <${HighMargin} and Avg([Net Margin])
>${LosingMargin} then "HV-LM"
when Sum([Sales])/UniqueCount([Quarter])<${Volume} and Avg([Net
Margin]) >=${HighMargin} then "LV-HM"
when Sum([Sales])/UniqueCount([Quarter])<${Volume} and Avg([Net
Margin]) <${HighMargin} and Avg([Net Margin]) >${LosingMargin}
then "LV-LM"
when Avg([Net Margin]) <=${LosingMargin} then "Losing"
end as [Sector]
```

Labels: `UniqueConcatenate([Department])`

Marker by: `[Store Location] NEST [Department]`

Lines and Curves: Horizontal Line: Custom expression: `${Volume}`. Vertical Line 1: Custom expression: `${HighMargin}`. Vertical Line 2: Custom expression: `${LosingMargin}`.

- **Table**: Columns: `[Store Location], [Department], [Quarter], [Net Profit], [Sales], [Net Margin].`

  Limit data using markings: `Marking`

- **Bar Chart (for net profit)**: Appearance: Sort bars by value.

  Category axis: **DepartmentHierarchy**.

  Value Axis: `Sum([Sales]) * Avg([Net Margin]) as [Net Profit]`

  Colors: None.

- **Treemap**: Colors: Same as scatter plot.

Size: None

Hierarchy: DepartmentHierarchy set to Department.
(`PruneHierarchy([StoreSales].[Hierarchy.DepartmentHierarchy],1)`)

Trellis: `[Store Location]`

History Arrows

The final step is to remove the page tabs and switch to History Arrows mode to provide a more guided analysis. Right-click on any page tab, select **Page Navigation**, and select **History Arrows**.

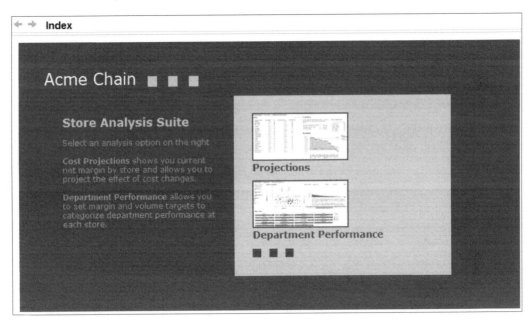

Now, the user is guided through the analysis through the navigation links you provide, combined with browser-style back and forward arrows. This type of guided analysis could be developed further to provide an analytic workflow, with the workflow laid out on the index page. You could also provide a button that uses a simple script to switch the page navigation mode from history arrows to tiled tabs, allowing users to deviate from the standard workflow to conduct more advanced or custom analysis.

Key data concept – metadata

Putting the prefix meta in front of a word means essentially that you are abstracting information in some way. A meta-analysis is an analysis of a set of analyses. Metadata is a term used to denote the description of data—*data about data*. This often means the data's structure, its column names essentially, but it can mean any abstraction of the data, such as purpose, date of collection, source, or standard.

Metadata is the key to bridging the gulf between the *raw* data sitting in databases and data warehouses in what are necessarily complex data structures optimized for performance and the everyday user of this data, irrespective of how familiar the user is with the data content. Metadata should be seen as an essential communication protocol for data analysis, particularly where a self-service approach is sought. It can be a common language through which user requirements can be expressed and understood by BI consumers, developers, and applications.

Incorporating configurable business rules into your analysis

Business rules are a form of metadata and usually play a central part in the creation of an analysis file. They govern the definition of metrics, KPIs, parameters, and even the application or customization of filters. They can be and often are hardcoded. They can be facilitated through the provision of user inputs, such as the input boxes we added to the pages in the guided analysis example. BI dashboards and analysis pages often include this type of flexibility, allowing users to essentially alter the business rules governing the analysis.

However, the level of configurability can be progressed to a deeper level, and this is where we begin to move from a world in which IT delivers informatics solutions directly to consumers via BI provisioners in the business who have the subject matter expertise and data skills to extend the informatics platform provided by IT. The challenge for IT is to make the platform extendable while retaining governance over the data and potentially other core aspects of the delivery.

A simple way to achieve this in Spotfire is to include a metadata table or tables in the analysis file that can describe pretty much any piece of metadata you wish to expose to configuration. It could be table column labels, a KPI, a list of options for a drop-down selection, or a color scheme. You will need to do the following:

- Write some IronPython scripts to read the metadata tables and apply the settings
- Ensure the settings relate correctly to the data structure and its expected values

- Ensure the settings conform to the visualization properties they affect
- Train the business provisioners on how to use the metadata tables correctly

In the simplest model, you do all of the preceding and allow the business provisioners to alter and use the metadata tables directly as part of a deployment process. The tables should be simple enough to export from a database to a spreadsheet, where they can be modified before being reimported back to a database location. The metadata configuration tables could be maintained under version control as spreadsheet files by the relevant business unit and imported directly into Spotfire as and when the business provisioner needs to change the report configuration.

In a more mature model, you would build a configuration interface in the Spotfire analysis file to guide the business provisioner's editing of the underlying metadata tables, ensuring that all settings are compatible with the analysis file and its data.

Only when there is a need to change the scope of the metadata or configuration options is there a need to engage IT to make those changes and any necessary alterations to the underlying visualizations and data model. The scope of metadata control is very wide, however, and metadata tables can be used to define and accommodate data structure changes and even define new data views, to completely alter visualization configurations, and to automate testing, eliminating the need for further IT involvement in every case.

Let's take a very simple example: say you want to allow a business provisioner to create new KPIs and add them as a color-by option to a particular visualization without any need to contact IT. Some constraints would apply:

- The KPI expression must obviously reference valid column names
- The **RAG** value must be "Red," "Amber," or "Green"
- The KPI must be applied to a specific visualization with a fixed data source

These constraints could be removed through the use of additional metadata properties, and you could break out the KPI definition into more user-friendly clauses, but let's keep the example simple to illustrate the principle.

The metadata table would have just two columns as follows:

KPI Name	KPI Expression
Any description	Valid Spotfire case expression with values conforming to the RAG constraint described in the preceding text

Example metadata table/spreadsheet

KPI Name	KPI Expression
Profitability	`case when [Sales]-[Costs]/[Sales] > 0.07 then "Green" when [Sales]-[Costs]/[Sales] <= 0.07 and [Sales]-[Costs]/[Sales] > 0.03 then "Amber" when [Sales]-[Costs]/[Sales] <= 0.03 then "Red" end`
Volume	`case when [Sales] > 5000000 then "Green" when [Sales] <= 5000000 and [Sales] > 1500000 then "Amber" when [Sales] <= 1500000 then "Red" end`

The analysis file would have a **Deployment page** for the business provisioner, and on this page, you would include a **Deploy Metadata** button with an associated script that does the following:

- Reads the metadata table row by row and gets the KPI Name
- Looks for the KPI Name as a calculated column in the target visualization data table and updates the expression with the KPI Expression from the metadata table
- If the calculated column is not found, creates a new one and adds the KPI Expression

The provisioner would load the updated metadata table and run the script, deleting the deployment page before publishing the analysis to consumers in the Spotfire library. The relevant page in the analysis file would have a drop-down list preconfigured to look for unique values in the metadata table's [KPI Name] column. The visualization would have a color-by property bound to the drop-down list property control.

Everyone works within an agreed analytic framework created by IT; yet, users can suggest and quickly get access to new KPIs. As long as the scope of the metadata-driven application is agreed by all stakeholders and conforms to relevant governance procedures, and as long as the development of the framework follows good software development practices, the possibilities are extensive and far reaching. Let's finish this chapter by exploring a more complex example.

A metadata-driven self-service analytics case study

Consider the following scenario for the fictional chain store we used for the guided analysis example:

A business unit has requested a KPI dashboard, but it's not sure exactly what data or KPIs it will need on an ongoing basis and wants to develop and control the dashboard, once it is built, with as little involvement from IT as possible.

We start with the following basic wireframe:

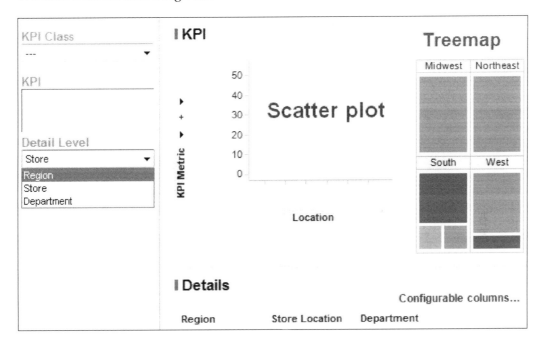

It's a good idea to set out your analysis design using **wireframes**, which are simply graphical outlines of the high-level content of your analysis: pages, visualizations, user inputs, and so on. Wireframes help you conceptualize the design and share it with other stakeholders, without any need for actual data or working visualizations.

We need IT to create this wireframe on top of a metadata definition that allows the business unit to define the KPI classes, source tables, and KPIs as required. The detail levels will always be Region, Store, and Department. What will the base template look like, what will the metadata look like, and what scripts will be needed to enable the template? Let's take a closer look.

Metadata

Let's start with the metadata. We will need three tables (all available as CSV files from `http://www.insidespotfire.com`):

Table	Description	Columns
BaseTable	List of stores. This table will be used to join any other tables added to the analysis so that marking and filtering will work across all loaded data tables.	`[Region]`, `[Store Location]`, `[Department]`
MetadataKpis	KPI names and expressions. This table will be used to populate KPI dropdowns, reference source data, and build the KPI base metric expressions.	`[KPI Class]`, `[KPI Name]`, `[KPI Metric Expression]`, `[Table Name]`, `[Data Source]`, `[Column List]`
MetadataBusinessRules	Business rules for KPI metrics. This table will be used to build the RAG clauses for the KPI metric expressions defined in MetadataKPIs.	`[Business Rule Name]`, `[Condition1]`, `[Condition 2]`, `[Description]`, `[RAG]`

The metadata design anticipates that there might be a need for more than one source table (`[Data Source]`) and that the KPIs might need to be classified into groups (`[KPI Class]`). The KPI class can be used as a convenient label for different data sources, as shown in the following example, but it is also flexible and can be used for a single data source:

Representative metadata content

BaseTable

Region	Store Location	Department
Midwest	Chicago	Electronics
Midwest	Chicago	Furniture
Midwest	Chicago	Garden
Midwest	Chicago	Groceries
Midwest	Chicago	Toys
Midwest	Columbus	Electronics
And so on for all the stores		

MetadataKpis

KPI Class	KPI Name	KPI Expression	Table Name	Data Source	Column List
Profitability	Margin	`((([Sales]-[Goods Cost]-[Operational Cost])/[Sales])*100`	StoreSales	`C:\Source Data\StoreSales.csv`	`[Region{String}],[Store Location{String}],[Department{String}],[Quarter{Integer}],[Sales{Real}],[Goods Cost{Real}],[Operational Cost{Real}],[Discount{Real}]`
Customers	Gender	`([Male Sales]/[Female Sales])*100`	StoreCustomers	`C:\Source Data\StoreCustomers.csv`	`[Region{String}],[Store Location{String}],[Department{String}],[Quarter{Integer}],[Sales{Real}],[Male Sales{Real}],[Female Sales{Real}],[Sales 20{Real}],[Sales 30{Real}],[Sales 40{Real}],[Sales 50{Real}],[Sales 60{Real}],[Sales 70{Real}]`

MetadataBusinessRules

Business Rule Name	Condition1	Condition2	Description	RAG
Margin	<3		<3%	Red
Margin	>=3	<=7	3-7%	Amber
Margin	>7		>7%	Green
Gender	>62		>62%	Red
Gender	<=62	>=56	56-62%	Amber
Gender	<56	>=48	48-55%	Green
Gender	<48		<48	Amber

Source data

The source data tables, which could be views created by IT in the data warehouse or views created by a business information designer in Spotfire, have only one constraint: they must contain the columns [Region], [Store Location], and [Department]. All other columns are flexible. Any business user(s) adding new KPI metrics just needs to know the column names.

We can use the following datasets to build the example: `StoreSales.csv`, `StoreCustomers.csv`, and `StoreStaff.csv` (all available from `http://www.insidespotfire.com`).

Base template

The base template needs to have the components outlined in the following text. To build the template, you will need to load some source data, even just a single row. Once the visualizations are configured, the source table is removed from the analysis file. The configurations will no longer be valid, but this is taken care of by the deployment scripts. The idea is to create a generic, blank template that is deployed using metadata tables, source tables, and scripts.

KPI Page

- **Source data**:

   Start the analysis file build by loading the base table, empty KPI and business rules metadata tables, and one of the source tables.

- **User inputs**:

   KpiClass: drop-down list with values set through unique values in [MetadataKpis].[KPI Class].

   SelectedKpi: List box with values set through unique values in [MetadataKpis].[AvailableKpis]. Please note that you will need to create the calculated column [AvailableKpis] first (see the following text).

   DetailLevel: drop-down list with fixed values "Region," "Store Location," and "Department."

- **Calculated columns**:

   MetadataKpis

   AvailableKpis: if([KPI Class]="${KpiClass}",[KPI Name])

   Source data table

   KPI Metric: The integer value 1 (the correct expression will be set at deployment by metadata and scripts).

   KPI RAG: The string value "1" (the correct expression will be set at deployment by metadata and scripts).

- **Hierarchies**:

   BaseTable

   StoreHierarchy: **[Region]** | **[Store Location]** | **[Department]**

- **Document properties:**

  HierarchyLevel: integer value (set to 1).

  TreemapTrellisLevel: string value.

  TreemapHierarchyLevel: integer value (set to 1).

- Scatter plot

  Data table: source data (StoreSales, for example).

  X-axis: `<PruneHierarchy([BaseTable].[Hierarchy.StoreHierarchy],${HierarchyLevel})>`

  Y-axis: `Avg([KPI Metric])`

  Colors: `<[KPI RAG]>`

  Marker by: `<$esc(${DetailLevel})>`

- Treemap

  Data table: source data.

  Colors: UniqueConcatenate([KPI RAG])

  Size: `UniqueCount($esc(${DetailLevel})) as [${DetailLevel}s]`

  Hierarchy: `<PruneHierarchy([BaseTable].[Hierarchy.StoreHierarchy],${TreemapHierarchyLevel})>`

  Trellis: Panels split by <${TreemapTrellisLevel}>

- Table

  Data table: source data.

Once the template is built, remove the source data table (**Edit | Data Table Properties**, select table, and click on **Delete**). Save the analysis file as `KpiTemplate_Blank.dxp`.

IronPython scripts

As you can see, the metadata and base template are actually quite simple. The complexity in this design is all in the scripts, and this is where IT involvement is probably, though not necessarily required. Once the scripts are written, however, the template will be flexible enough to support new KPI classes/source tables and new KPI metrics.

Three scripts are required:

- **RefreshMetadata**: Implemented as a button on a dedicated deployment page, this script deploys new metadata and source tables
- **ChangeDataTable**: Implemented to run each time the property `KpiClass` changes, this script switches the data table on all visualizations accordingly and assigns a default KPI metric
- **ChangeMetric**: Implemented to run the properties `SelectedKpi` and `DetailLevel` changed each time, this script alters the visualization configuration to reflect the selected metric or detail level

The scripts can be downloaded from the publisher's website or from `http://www.insidespotfire.com`. The scripts are outlined in the following text using pseudocode.

Deployment page

Create a deployment page with a single button called Refresh Metadata and associate the `RefreshMetadata` script with this button. You would remove this page when publishing the template to the user community. Whenever the metadata files are modified at source, this script is run to rebuild and update the template, whether it is blank or already populated with data.

The `RefreshMetadata` script reads the MetadataKpis table to determine what needs to be added to the template and what configuration changes need to be made (refer to the representative metadata content shown earlier in this chapter).

For convenience, we are using CSV files as data sources, but the source entry in the metadata table could be a database connection and table reference or even a piece of SQL. You would just have to incorporate the necessary code into the script to process the information. The key point is that the script can be as complex as it needs to be to ensure that the metadata tables are simple and business friendly.

If the business provisioner wants to add a new KPI, they just need to add a new entry to MetadataKpi. If a new table is required, a data requirement might have to be submitted to IT to create the necessary view, but if the business provisioner has direct access to the data, even this contact with IT is not necessary, just an update to MetadataKpis.

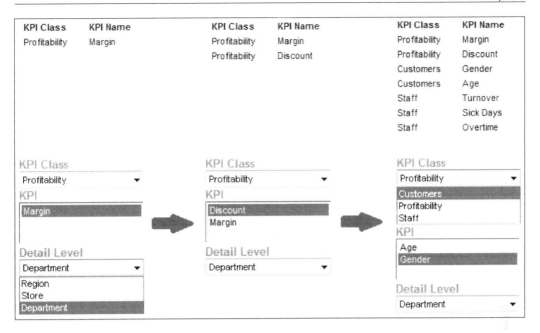

The KPI name is used to look up the `MetadataBusinessRules`. The business provisioner can maintain these business rules and change them as required, simply redeploying the template to publish the change to the consumers of the analysis (refer to the representative metadata content shown earlier in this chapter).

The deployment script that makes all of this possible is outlined as follows:

```
# RefreshMetadata
# Declare libraries
# Define the metadata table objects
# Refresh their content
# Get a list of tables already loaded
# Set up cursors for columns in MetadataKpis and MetadataBusinessRules
# Initialize dictionaries for holding key:value pairs
# Read MetadataKpis to get a list of required source tables
   # Use the dictionaries to store key:value pairs for
TableName:DataSource, TableName:ColumnList, TableName:KpiName,
TableName:KpiExpression, and TableName:KpiClass
# Load the source tables
   # Use TableName:ColumnList to define the columns in each case
   # Use the TextDataReaderSettings() method with TableName:DataSource
to import the table
# Relate all imported tables to the base table
# Set filter propagation to mutually exclude filtered out rows
```

```
# Add a calculated column [KPI Metric] using TableName:KpiName and
TableName:KpiExpression. This script sets up a nominal KPI expression,
which is changed/updated dynamically at runtime by the script
ChangeMetric (described later in the chapter)
# Read MetadataBusinessRules to create nominal [KPI RAG] and [KPI
Description] case statements and add them as calculated columns. These
expressions will be updated dynamically at runtime by the script
ChangeMetric
# Add a Region>Store>Department hierarchy column
# Assign document properties for drop-down controls
# Ensure visualizations are pointed at a data table
# Set the columns to display in the table plot
```

Runtime scripts

The ChangeDataTable and ChangeMetric scripts perform similar lookups in the metadata tables as users make selections at runtime. You need to associate the ChangeDataTable script with the KPI Class dropdown control (right-click on the control and select **Edit control...** and then **Script**. Select the script and select the option **Execute the script selected below:**). Associate the ChangeMetric script with the Selected KPI and Detail Level controls.

The ChangeDataTable script makes some default assumptions about the KPI and the level of detail to use, but as soon as the user selects a KPI or detail level, the ChangeMetric script changes the configuration to reflect this change:

```
# ChangeDataTable
# Declare libraries
# Define the metadata table objects
# Set up cursors for columns in MetadataKpis and MetadataBusinessRules
# Get a nominal metric expression from MetadataKpis for the KPI Class
selected by the user (document property KpiClass) and update the
calculated column [KPI Metric]
# Set the document property SelectedKpi to correspond to the nominated
KPI
# Get the corresponding KPI RAG and KPI descriptions from
MetadataBusinessRules, create the case statements, and update the
calculated columns [KPI RAG] and [KPI Description]
# Point visualizations at the correct data table
# Set the columns to display in the table plot
# ChangeMetric
# Declare libraries
```

```
# Define the metadata table objects
# Set up cursors for columns in MetadataKpis and MetadataBusinessRules
# Get the metric expression from MetadataKpis for the KPI selected
(document property SelectedKpi) and update the calculated column [KPI
Metric]
# Get the corresponding KPI RAG and KPI descriptions from
MetadataBusinessRules, create the case statements, and update the
calculated columns [KPI RAG] and [KPI Description]
# Set the hierarchy levels to match the selection made in the document
property DetailLevel
# Point visualizations at the correct data table
# Set the columns to display in the table plot
```

The complete self-service solution can be summarized as follows:

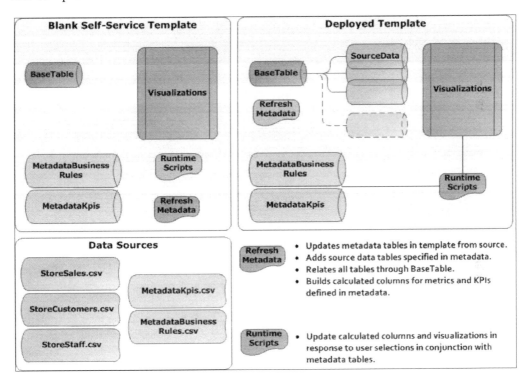

We'll finish with a screenshot of one selection showing a margin KPI by department on the scatter plot, automatically rolled up to show a department summary by store in a treemap. The take-home message here, however, is the empowerment of the owners of this data and analysis to modify parameters and add new domains and metrics over time without any further IT development.

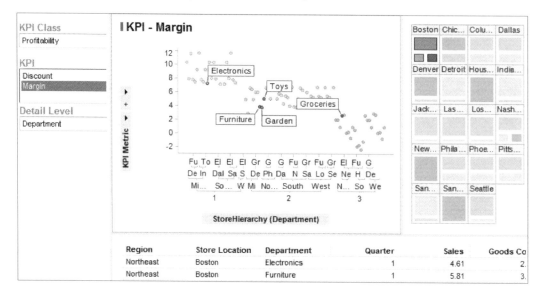

Summary

In this chapter, we started by looking at the concept of guided analysis and we worked through a relatively sophisticated example of how a guided analysis can be constructed. We moved on to consider the importance of metadata as an essential communication protocol for data analysis, particularly where a self-service approach is sought. If you talk to BI professionals or read about the subject, you will find strong recognition for the importance of metadata dictionaries and semantic layers, but you will also find an acknowledgment that we are poor at implementing business-targeted metadata.

This chapter should give you a sense of how metadata can be a common language through which user requirements can be expressed and understood by BI consumers, developers, and applications. You should now see how easy it can be to incorporate configurable business rules into an analysis using metadata tables.

This chapter finished with a metadata-driven self-service analytics case study. This example is a significant advance from our opening foray into Spotfire as described in *Chapter 1, Show Me the Data*, and it relies on some fairly advanced programming skills. You might not wish to develop your Spotfire programming skills to this degree, but perhaps the case study gives you some food for thought and a practical basis to discuss self-service BI options with those who have these skills.

We are almost at the end of the book now, and all that remains is to take a peek over the horizon at some of the other components that Spotfire offers. Up to now, we have focused on the core components of server, web player, and client, but believe it or not, there is a lot more to the Spotfire platform than this *core* functionality. The final chapter will take a cursory look at these additional components.

10
Beyond the Horizon

This book has focused on what most people would understand as the core implementation of TIBCO Spotfire: analysts working in a professional client (Spotfire Analyst) to build analysis files and then publishing those files to a wider audience through the web player (Spotfire Consumer) and the Spotfire library. The Spotfire server manages authentication, functional licensing, and access to the library content.

We delved quite deeply into what the Spotfire client can do, including the advanced functionality of IronPython scripting. In this chapter, we'll take a short tour of some additional components that add even further power to the platform. We'll start with **TIBCO Enterprise Runtime for R (TERR)**, which is an essential tool for advanced and predictive analytics, and progress to consider some of the advanced data handling capabilities of Spotfire. Along the way, we'll look at some new mobility options.

In this chapter, we will cover the following topics:

- TIBCO Enterprise Runtime for R (TERR)
- JavaScript
- TIBCO Spotfire Mobile Metrics
- Event analytics
- Spotfire data connectors
- TIBCO Spotfire Advanced Data Services

TIBCO Enterprise Runtime for R (TERR)

R is a language for data manipulation and statistical computing available as free software under the terms of the Free Software Foundation's GNU general public license. It has a wide range of statistical modeling and graphical techniques, but it is also highly extensible through the use of thousands of community-developed packages published through **Comprehensive R Archive Network (CRAN)**. It is one of the most popular tools for statistical modeling and analysis and is used, for example, in data cleaning, data exploration and visualization, statistical analysis, and the predictive modeling of complex systems. Go to `http://www.r-project.org` for more information.

R has always been a supported feature of Spotfire, but up to the release of Version 5.0 of the platform, you had to install a TIBCO Spotfire Statistics Services server, configure it with an R engine, write your R programs in that environment, and create and register data functions to provide input to the R program and use its output in a Spotfire analysis file. Furthermore, the R installation was not part of TIBCO Spotfire and had to be obtained under separate open source software license terms.

Version 5.0 of Spotfire launched TERR as a compatible R installation and embedded it in the Spotfire professional client, giving you the option to deploy R code directly in Spotfire analysis files. Furthermore, Spotfire now leverages TERR to provide a host of built-in modeling functions and tools that you can incorporate into your analysis. For further reading on TERR, visit `https://docs.tibco.com/products/tibco-enterprise-runtime-for-r-3-0-0`, which includes documentation on the compatibility of R packages with TERR.

Data functions

To use TERR with a dataset, you first define a data function using **Register Data Functions...** in the **Tools** menu. Data functions have three principal components:

- The R program script to be run—you can type the code from scratch, paste it from the clipboard, or import it as a script function definition

- Input parameters—you specify the input type (value, column, or table) and allowed data types

- Output parameters—you specify the output type (value, column, or table) and allowed data types

You can run a data function immediately, or you can save it to the Spotfire library, after which you can select **Data Function...** in the **Insert** menu to associate it with a table and explicitly define the input(s) and output(s), which can be new columns or document properties. You can also edit the data function at any time by selecting **Data Function Properties** in the **Edit** menu.

Expression functions

You can use TERR to write custom functions and then use those functions directly in calculated columns and custom expressions. You simply open the **Data Function Properties** dialog from the main **Edit** menu, select the **Expression Functions** tab, and type or paste your R code. You give the function a name, specify its return data type, and categorize the function's type (binning, conversion, date and time, and so on). Now, whenever you use the **Calculated Column...** or **Custom Expression...** builder, your custom function will be listed among the built-in functions, categorized as you specified in its definition.

Predictive modeling

TERR provides a lot more than access to data functions; it also supports a suite of built-in predictive modeling tools. These tools are powered by TERR but you don't need any knowledge of R code to use them.

TERR can be used to fit a model using either regression analysis (numerical) or classification analysis (categorical). Both are accessible from the **Tools** menu.

After you run a model over some data, Spotfire automatically generates a **Model Page**, giving you a comprehensive set of outputs:

- **Model Summary**
- **Table of Coefficients**
- **Residuals vs. Fitted**

- **Variable Importance**
- Choice of additional diagnostic visualizations

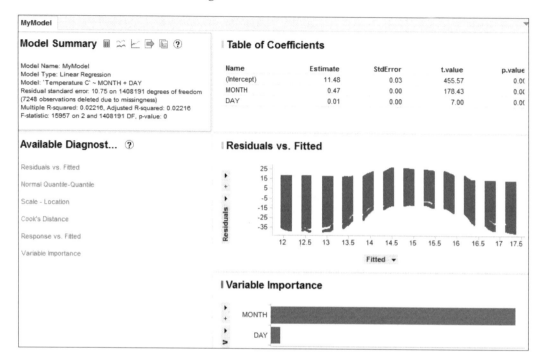

The **Model Summary** panel provides five tools to help you refine and evaluate the model and predict from it. From left to right, they are **Edit model**, **Evaluate model**, **Predict from model**, **Export from model**, and **Duplicate model**.

The Evaluate Model tool allows you to compare the model with another data table that includes the values you are trying to predict using the model. When you run the Predict from model tool, Spotfire inserts prediction columns into the source data table, from where you can easily work up your own visualizations and analysis to present the findings as you wish.

Apart from the model page, TERR also generates a set of supporting tables:

- `MyModel_fitSummaryTable`
- `MyModel_fitPlotData`
- `MyModel_coefTable`
- `MyModel_varImpTable`

Holt–Winters forecast

You can use TERR to do a Holt–Winters forecast for any data that can be mapped to a time series. The Holt–Winters algorithm, named after Charles C. Holt and his student Peter Winters, is a **triple exponential smoothing** technique that models the level, trend, and seasonal components of a time series. The smoothing parameters are selected, either automatically or by the user, to minimize the sum of the squared one-step-ahead prediction errors. You can also select how far out in time you wish to project the forecast.

The great thing is that all of this is handled by TERR and integrated as a **Lines & Curves** option for any time series plot, as shown in the following screenshot:

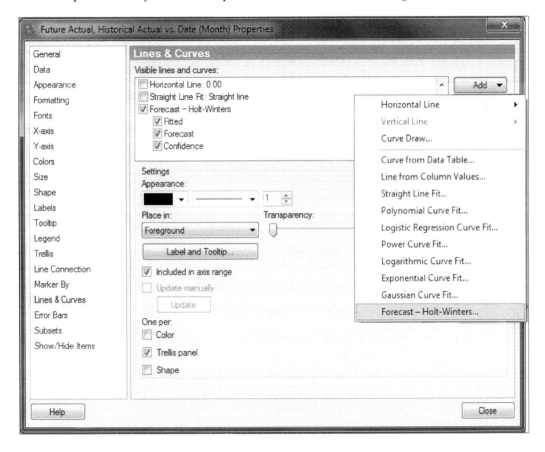

The Holt–Winters forecast creates three curves: a fitted curve showing the general variation of the measure of interest, a forecast curve predicting the future trend, and a confidence interval, or funnel, for the future trend. For example, if you apply a Holt–Winters forecast to the market interest rate data we used in the earlier chapters, you can see how a forecast based on data for January 1987 to February 1989 compares with the actual values (provided in a separate table) for subsequent months up to December 1992.

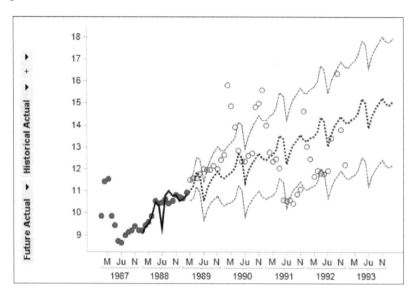

JavaScript

Since Spotfire v6.0, it is possible to add JavaScript to text areas using the HTML editor. It is beyond the scope of this book to review all the things you can do with JavaScript, but a common use is to improve the appearance and usability of websites by creating interactive elements such as menus and calendar pickers for date inputs. Treat the Spotfire text area as a website. You can also use JavaScript to change the content of property controls and even run IronPython scripts.

If you right-click on a text area, select **Edit HTML**, and click on the **Insert JavaScript** icon, a window will open in which you can type or paste the required JavaScript code and save it for deployment in other text areas. You can also assign parameters to the JavaScript in similar fashion to IronPython scripts.

To apply JavaScript code to text area content, including Spotfire controls such as buttons, you tag the target element with an identifier and then reference that identifier in the script. For example, if you want to run an IronPython script every time the mouse cursor rolls over some text or image, format the text area with the following HTML tags:

```
<div id="mouseover">Some text or an image</div>
<div style="DISPLAY: none" id="autoExec"><SpotfireControl id="f7dd0eef
477b4897b7b42052430b112b" /></div>
```

The style display attribute for the Spotfire control hides the button containing the script you want to run. The JavaScript, which could include two script parameters, one for the text and one for the button, would be as follows:

Mobile Metrics

TIBCO Spotfire Mobile Metrics was released with Spotfire v6.0 as a new, standalone tool to deliver key performance indicators (KPIs) to mobile devices (iOS, Android, and Windows) and Windows 8 PCs. It is implemented through Microsoft **Internet Information Services (IIS)** and requires a dedicated Microsoft SQL Server database.

You can group sets of KPIs into different feeds, allowing you to target specific audiences with the mobile KPI dashboard(s) most appropriate for them. The information latency can be as real time as you wish to give your mobile clients an up-to-date picture of performance. The tool also has a comment functionality, allowing users to socialize their response to the information and their insights with colleagues directly from their mobile device.

The consumer app is available to everyone as a free download from the relevant app stores. You, as a KPI provider, supply a URL and login credentials to give access to your mobile metrics website. The display is slightly different with each app/operating system, but all show an intuitive set of Traffic Light tiles and allow drilling down into deeper levels of detail and trend analysis. You can also link each KPI directly to another analytics solution, such as a Spotfire analysis file, for deeper analysis.

The next screenshot shows the iPhone app with demo data provided by TIBCO. The left-hand picture is the starting position; the center picture is a Drill Down on **South - Sales**; the right-hand picture is a Drill Down on **Florida - South - Sales**.

Setting up KPI sets

You set up KPIs using TIBCO Spotfire Metrics Modeler, a web-based metrics application service that allows you to do the following:

- Connect to and query different data sources
- Define KPIs for the data returned by database queries
- Deliver those KPIs to users via the Metrics Viewer Service
- Build different feeds to group and categorize KPI sets for context or security reasons
- Schedule data refresh and set caching parameters to store refreshed content in memory between refreshes

The metrics modeler can connect to the following data sources: Microsoft SQL Server, Oracle, Teradata, Microsoft Excel, Google Spreadsheet, and **Microsoft Online Analytical Processor (MSOLAP)**.

To build a KPI set, create a database connection, write a query to obtain the information and metrics you need, and add that query to a KPI set. Then, configure the set with additional metadata to map the query dataset to KPI set definitions (dimensions and measures), threshold settings for a visual indication of performance (traffic lights), and other formatting and presentation settings. KPI sets are maintained in a KPI library.

You need to be familiar with dimensional modeling to create a KPI set and to understand the *cardinality* of the relationships between dimensions, that is, whether the relationship is one-to-one, one-to-many, or many-to-many.

The metrics modeler allows you to create feeds, which not only allow you to group KPI sets for publishing but also allow you to preview your KPIs as end users see them.

Event analytics

TIBCO's event analytics bundle combines multiple components to build, in TIBCO's words, an "Understand–Anticipate–Act" analytic cycle. This system allows you to stream data in real time through a predefined workflow, apply business rules, generate forecasts based on current and historical values, apply statistical models, and present the findings to decision makers and analysts, allowing them to take preemptive action.

It has many business applications across multiple industries:

- **Financial Services** — FX trading systems, pricing, smart order routing, real-time profit and loss, auto-hedging, transaction cost analysis, compliance, algorithmic trading, and market data processing

- **Intelligence** — Signals processing

- **Manufacturing** — Supply chain monitoring

- **Retail and e-commerce** — Real-time inventory and offers, dynamic pricing, and customer engagement

- **Telco** — Network monitoring

- **Online Gaming and Social Media** — Fraud detection, cyber security, and user behavior analytics

So how does it work?

TIBCO StreamBase

The first component of the event analytics bundle is TIBCO StreamBase, an event processing platform that joined the TIBCO suite of products when the company acquired StreamBase Systems in June 2013. StreamBase has over 150 pre-built connectivity and visualization options that integrate with a variety of real-time data feeds, messaging systems, high-capacity data stores, alternative programming languages, and real-time interactive dashboards. It has over 40 market data/venue adapters, over 50 general adapters, connectivity to general purpose and analytic databases, multiple visualization options, and APIs for C++, C#, Java, .NET, and Python.

The StreamBase engine differs from traditional database models by processing the inbound data while it is in flight, streaming through the server, rather than storing, indexing, and processing the data through queries. It can perform a multitude of actions on the streaming data, applying aggregating functions, computing new values, applying filters, performing buffered sorts, joining split streams of data, and populating shared data tables to facilitate lookups.

To help you work with this complex data application, TIBCO provides a graphical development environment called **StreamBase Studio**, which allows you to design, test, and deploy streaming applications. You build the workflow using a palette of operators, each of which has a set of properties that you can configure to manipulate and redirect data streams and static data sources.

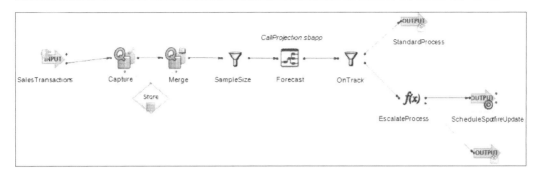

For example, you could set up a workflow that captures key sales metrics for the members of a sales team directly from a transactional system, merge those metrics with historical data from a data warehouse to analyze the trend, and run the numbers through a predictive algorithm to forecast whether individual sales personnel are on track to meet their targets. The workflow can also be used to initiate additional actions based on the results of the forecast.

StreamBase and TERR

The next component in the event analytics bundle is TERR, which we covered at the beginning of the chapter. The idea here is to pass the data captured by StreamBase to a predictive algorithm, which could be a built-in forecast or a custom algorithm developed by a data scientist and implemented in TERR.

In our relatively simple example of projecting sales targets, we could project an individual's sales against a predefined target for the year. The StreamBase workflow can include actions based on the output of the predictive analytics, updating other analysis and even e-mailing alerts.

In a more complex example, an event analytics workflow could be used to track a manufacturing process in real time, streaming data from instruments through predictive models and outputting the results to KPI and other types of analytics dashboards.

Contextual analysis and mobile metrics

The final components in the event analytics bundle are contextual analysis and mobile metrics. The predictive output from TERR gives you the basic alert, but you will probably also want to dig deeper into the causes and context of the alert. The StreamBase workflow can trigger a Spotfire Automation Services job to update a prebuilt analysis file containing supporting visualizations with the projected data, placing the sales trend in context and allowing an analyst or manager to reach more informed conclusions and decisions.

The relevant KPIs and predictions can also be updated in a Spotfire Mobile Metrics implementation, giving the relevant audience a real-time Traffic Light overview of the sales team's performance, alerting relevant managers whenever an individual is trending below or above target, providing some detail on those trends, and even providing a link to a more detailed, contextual analysis. All of this can be delivered in a personalized way to any mobile device.

Spotfire data connectors

Way back in *Chapter 1*, *Show Me the Data*, we covered some standard ways in which Spotfire can access data: delimited text files and Excel spreadsheets, SAS datasets, and basic database connections to mainstream databases such as Oracle and Microsoft SQL Server. In *Chapter 5*, *Source Data is Never Enough*, we looked at information links and in-database analytics, but we still confined the discussion to those mainstream data sources.

In the world of **Big Data**, there are many data sources that don't fit any of the preceding categories and that require specific connectors. Since Spotfire v4.5, TIBCO has been expanding the number of data connectors available. Spotfire now has almost 20 native connectors, including Apache Hadoop/Hive, Cloudera Hive and Impala, HP Vertica, Oracle Essbase, SAP HANA and NetWeaver Business Warehouse, Teradata, IBM DB2 and Netezza, and Cisco ("Composite") Information Server.

To install these connectors, a Spotfire administrator must first deploy the relevant connector package on the Spotfire server. The connector is then automatically rolled out to clients that log in to the server. In most cases, a driver must also be installed on the machine running the data connector.

Once the connector is installed and configured, you treat it like you would any data link, saving a shared data connection to the library or adding a local data connection to an analysis. Some connectors support a basic, username–only authentication protocol; others have more complete authentication models.

TIBCO provides further information on its website: `http://support.spotfire.com/sr_spotfire_dataconnectors.asp`.

Hadoop

Apache Hadoop is a key enabling technology for Big Data analytics and is widely used to manage large amounts of data, particularly unstructured or semi-structured data. Hadoop is not so much a database as a combined data processing framework and distributed file system for data storage.

You need to use a programming platform such as MapReduce to process data in Hadoop. Using this Java-based platform instead of a more traditional query language gives you a lot of power and flexibility but also adds a lot of complexity and requires specialist programming skills. Apache Hive provides the SQL-like language HiveQL to translate SQL-type queries into MapReduce operations.

Cloudera is a provider of Apache Hadoop–based software, support, and services. Another supported Hadoop provider is Hortonworks. Spotfire has connectors for both providers.

It's important to stress that Hive is batch-oriented and not well suited to interactive data analytics. It's best used to extract information from large quantities of unstructured data, put some structure on it, and then feed it to an agile analytic tool such as Spotfire.

Columnar databases

HP Vertica is a distributed, columnar database designed to handle large, fast-growing volumes of data and provide very fast query performance across parallel nodes. A columnar database organizes data in a columnar fashion, meaning that you can extract designated columns over billions of rows in conventional database terms in a matter of seconds. The database indexes each column to allow it to respond to queries and return just the required columns, skipping the other columns and therefore saving time scanning them. The time-saving becomes considerable when you reach large data volumes.

SAP also offers a high-performance analytic appliance called HANA, which is an in-memory, column-oriented, relational database management system designed to handle both high transaction rates and complex query processing on the same platform.

Online analytical processing

Oracle Essbase and Microsoft SQL Server Microsoft Analysis Services are multidimensional database management systems optimized for **online analytical processing (OLAP)**, rather than online transaction processing. These products are probably best known for their facility to *slice and dice* OLAP cubes.

Teradata

Teradata is a *massively parallel processing* system running a *shared-nothing architecture*, which means that each node in the distribution is independent and self-sufficient and there is no single point of contention across the system. It is a powerful data warehouse solution that offers scale and speed. It is used across a wide range of industries.

IBM offers competing products (DB2 and Netezza), as does Pivotal Greenplum, and Spotfire has native connectors for these systems too.

Cisco information server

Cisco's composite data integration platform collects data from multiple sources across the enterprise into a unified, logical virtualized data layer for consumption by frontend business and analytics tools such as Spotfire. Cisco information server has its own connectors for many of the data management systems mentioned previously.

The main take-home message of this section is that Spotfire can hook into most of the data management systems on the market, whether they are designed to process unstructured data, provide quick parallel processing of human queries, or build multidimensional "cubes." Many of these systems offer their own multitiered business intelligence and analytics solutions. Spotfire, though by no means unique in this regard, provides a central analytics integration point to explore and analyze data from disparate sources. When you add TERR and Mobile Metrics to the mix, you have a lot of options in your toolkit.

TIBCO Spotfire Advanced Data Services

We're going to finish this chapter with a look at TIBCO Spotfire Advanced Data Services, which is an on-demand data integration service that allows you to create aggregated and mashed-up views of business objects from multiple source applications and deliver those views directly to Spotfire users or via the information and library services on the Spotfire server. The resulting data views are well suited for self-service visual data discovery.

In addition to all the standard database connections and specialized data connectors supported by Spotfire, Advanced Data Services can also connect to database applications such as Oracle E-Business Suite, Salesforce.com, SAP BW, SAP ERP, and Siebel CRM, as well as other applications through web services APIs.

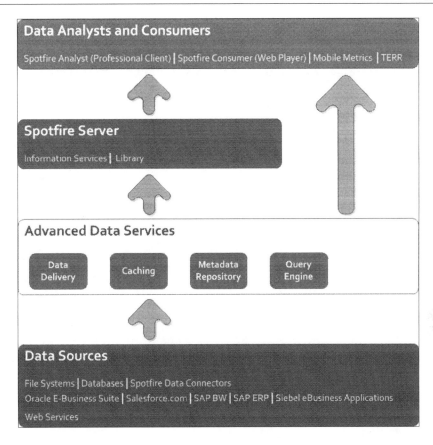

Data delivery

The Advanced Data Services platform supports multiple data delivery mechanisms: SQL (ODBC and JDBC), web services (HTTP, SOAP, and JSON), messaging (JMS), URIs, Java, and application APIs.

Caching

The diversity of data sources and data usage types that converge on the Advanced Data Services platform via multiple connectors and network connections requires load management. The platform provides a set of connectivity tuning tools to help ensure that the right balance is achieved and that the system is not, for example, wasting resources trying to refresh large volumes of archived data in real time and compromising the refreshing of data from a time-critical transactional database.

The system can offload queries to a caching layer to uphold time-critical transactions, it can speed data access to slow sources using an optional caching layer, and it allows users to schedule data updates at specified frequencies so that data is available for analysis when they need it.

Metadata modeling

The metadata modeling engine is the brain of the system. A graphical interface studio allows developers to create metadata transforms for source API-based applications to create a common **logical layer** in Spotfire. The goal is to create reusable views that hide the physical data integration complexity from end users, providing them with a more logical presentation that makes sense to their business context.

For example, an end user might wish to view or analyze all available information on a business object such as a customer, but they might not want, or might not have, the required skills to negotiate multiple sources of information and figure out how those sources are related in a data sense or how a metadata label in one source is equivalent to the label in another. For example, is "ZMKT_CUST_NM" in SAP BW the same thing as "ACC_NAME" in Oracle E-Business Suite?

Therefore, the IT department does all that work up front, creating a single logical view of customer information and freeing the end users to apply their business analysis and data visualization skills at the Spotfire frontend. The logical layer can be updated by IT when necessary, but day-to-day dependency on IT development is essentially eliminated.

There are benefits for IT as well because this logical layer can eliminate the need to build and maintain additional data warehouses or data marts, thereby reducing infrastructural capital and resource costs.

Query engine

At the heart of Advanced Data Services is a query processing engine that securely queries, accesses, federates, abstracts, and delivers data to consume business solutions on demand. The engine uses distributed query-plan optimization and data-streaming technologies to create a query plan that optimizes processing and performance.

As you might imagine, processing such diverse data streams, queries, and mashups requires careful monitoring, and this is achieved using a feature-rich graphical user interface console to monitor queries through the system.

Summary

In this chapter, we have looked at some optional Spotfire components. Most are unlikely to be universally deployed, although we've seen that one of them, TERR, assuming you have Spotfire v5.0 or later, is actually available to all users of the professional client. TERR is definitely worth a look, if only to use the built-in advanced analytics tools, and if you have any interest in predictive analytics then TERR is a must.

We saw how JavaScript can extend the functionality of text areas. If you want to deliver clear and personalized KPIs to your mobile user community, then we've seen how easy it can be to get up and running with TIBCO Spotfire Mobile Metrics.

For those interested in the analysis and monitoring of complex data streams in real time, the event analytics bundle, incorporating StreamBase, offers a powerful and sophisticated solution. This chapter should also have given you a good appreciation for the breadth of Spotfire's data modeling and connectivity capability. With just an overview of the range of data connectors supported by Spotfire and the capabilities of TIBCO Spotfire Advanced Data Services, you should now have a greater sense of the extent of Spotfire's potential as a hub for data integration, modeling, exploration, and visualization.

We've been to the horizon and looked beyond it and have come to the end of this book. The main purpose of this relatively short primer was to launch you into the rich analytics landscape of the Spotfire platform. If it has also stretched you a little and stimulated you to develop your analytics skills further, all the better.

Index

used, for slicing data 133, 134
used, for slicing visualizations 169-174
histogram 38
History Arrows, guided analysis 283
History Arrows navigation mode 275
Holt-Winters forecast, TIBCO Enterprise
       Runtime for R (TERR) 303, 304
HP Vertica 311
hypothesis 185

I

Image Layer 203
Import button, Library Administration
       interface 108
inbuilt filters
  using, in Spotfire 16-18
in-database analytics
  used, for optimizing complex data
       manipulations 153, 154
in-database views
  creating 155-157
Index page, guided analysis 275-277
Information Designer
  about 109
  Columns 110
  Data Source 110
  Filter 110
  Information Links 111
  Join 110
  Procedure 111
  using 147
information link
  building, to multiple source
       data tables 147-151
  building, which writes data back to
       database 151-153
Information Links, Information Designer
  about 111
  Caching section 112
  Conditioning section 112
  Description section 112
  Elements section 112
  Filters section 112
  Join path section 112
  Parameters section 112

Prompts section 112
Properties section 112
inner join 149
interactivity
  increasing, property controls used 81-85
Internet Information Services (IIS) 100, 306
IronPython
  about 225
  URL 226
IronPython scripts, metadata-driven
       self-service analytics case study
  ChangeDataTable 292
  ChangeMetric 292
  deployment page, creating 292, 293
  RefreshMetadata 292
  runtime scripts 294-296
item filter 65

J

JavaScript 304, 305
jobs, Automation Services
  running 118
Join, Information Designer 110

K

KPI Page, metadata-driven self-service
       analytics case study
  calculated columns 290
  document properties 291
  hierarchies 291
  scatter plot 291
  source data 290
  table 291
  treemap 291
  user inputs 290
KPI sets, Mobile Metrics
  setting up 307

L

libraries 227
Library Administration interface
  Export button 108
  folder permissions 106-108

Import button 108
using 106
Library Administrator 106
Line Chart visualization 49-51
list box filter 65
lists
about 227
used, for annotating data 90-92
logical layer 314

M

map chart
using, for nongeographical spatial
analysis 217-222
Web Map Service data, adding to 213-215
map chart layers 203
Map Chart visualization 199, 200
Map Layer 203
marked items
details, obtaining of 90
Marker Layer 203
marking
about 43, 239
behaviors, setting 45-49
color, changing 44
metadata 284
metadata-driven self-service analytics
case study
about 286, 287
base template 290
IronPython scripts 291
metadata 288
source data 289
metadata modeling, TIBCO Spotfire
Advanced Data Services 314
metadata table/spreadsheet
example 286
metrics
creating, calculated columns used 124
Microsoft Active Directory 102
Microsoft Excel spreadsheet
importing, into Spotfire 9-11
Microsoft Online Analytical Processor
(MSOLAP) 307
Mobile Metrics
about 306

KPI sets, setting up 307
Model Page 301
multiple source data tables
information link, building to 147-151
multiple sources
data, merging from 138

N

narrow tables
versus wide tables 142
nongeographic spatial analysis
map chart, using for 217-222
nonparametric statistics 182
normal data distributions
reference link 182

O

object orientation 227
ODBC
about 24
connection, setting up in Microsoft
Windows 7 25, 26
connection, using in Spotfire 27-29
on base percentage (OBP) 124
online analytical processing (OLAP) 311
Open Database Connectivity. *See* **ODBC**
optional components, Spotfire
Spotfire Advanced Data Services 101
Spotfire Desktop 101
Spotfire Statistics Services 101
OVER functions 133

P

pages
about 233
example script 234
panels 240
parallel coordinate plots
used, for profiling data 192-196
Parallel Coordinate Plot visualization 192
parametric statistics 182
Pareto chart 179
Pie Chart visualization 51, 52

Thank you for buying
TIBCO Spotfire – A Comprehensive Primer

About Packt Publishing

Packt, pronounced 'packed', published its first book, *Mastering phpMyAdmin for Effective MySQL Management*, in April 2004, and subsequently continued to specialize in publishing highly focused books on specific technologies and solutions.

Our books and publications share the experiences of your fellow IT professionals in adapting and customizing today's systems, applications, and frameworks. Our solution-based books give you the knowledge and power to customize the software and technologies you're using to get the job done. Packt books are more specific and less general than the IT books you have seen in the past. Our unique business model allows us to bring you more focused information, giving you more of what you need to know, and less of what you don't.

Packt is a modern yet unique publishing company that focuses on producing quality, cutting-edge books for communities of developers, administrators, and newbies alike. For more information, please visit our website at www.packtpub.com.

About Packt Enterprise

In 2010, Packt launched two new brands, Packt Enterprise and Packt Open Source, in order to continue its focus on specialization. This book is part of the Packt Enterprise brand, home to books published on enterprise software – software created by major vendors, including (but not limited to) IBM, Microsoft, and Oracle, often for use in other corporations. Its titles will offer information relevant to a range of users of this software, including administrators, developers, architects, and end users.

Writing for Packt

We welcome all inquiries from people who are interested in authoring. Book proposals should be sent to author@packtpub.com. If your book idea is still at an early stage and you would like to discuss it first before writing a formal book proposal, then please contact us; one of our commissioning editors will get in touch with you.

We're not just looking for published authors; if you have strong technical skills but no writing experience, our experienced editors can help you develop a writing career, or simply get some additional reward for your expertise.

Building Dashboards with Microsoft Dynamics GP 2013 and Excel 2013

ISBN: 978-1-84968-906-9   Paperback: 268 pages

Easily build powerful dashboards with Microsoft Dynamics GP 2013 and Excel 2013

1. Build a dashboard using Excel 2013 with information from Microsoft Dynamics GP 2013.

2. Make Excel a true business intelligence tool with charts, sparklines, slicers, and more.

3. Utilize PowerPivot's full potential to create even more complex dashboards.

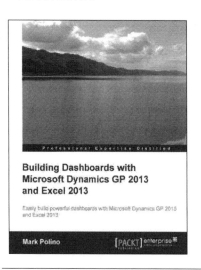

Building Dashboards with Microsoft Dynamics GP 2013 and Excel 2013

Easily build powerful dashboards with Microsoft Dynamics GP 2013 and Excel 2013

Mark Polino

IBM Cognos Business Intelligence

ISBN: 978-1-84968-356-2   Paperback: 318 pages

Discover the practical approach to BI with IBM Cognos Business Intelligence

1. Learn how to better administer your IBM Cognos 10 environment in order to improve productivity and efficiency.

2. Empower your business with the latest Business Intelligence (BI) tools.

3. Discover advanced tools and knowledge that can greatly improve daily tasks and analysis.

4. Explore the new interfaces of IBM Cognos 10.

IBM Cognos Business Intelligence

Discover the practical approach to BI with IBM Cognos Business Intelligence

Foreword by Steve Villeneuve, Director, Product Management, Interactive Analytics & BI, Business Analytics, IBM

Dustin Adkison

Please check **www.PacktPub.com** for information on our titles

Instant Creating Data Models with PowerPivot How-to

ISBN: 978-1-84968-956-4   Paperback: 58 pages

Build better business intelligence with this practical guide to creating Excel data models with PowerPivot

1. Learn something new in an Instant!
   A short, fast, focused guide delivering immediate results.

2. Detailed, step-by-step interactive tutorial guide to learning PowerPivot.

3. Carefully organized topics for users of all levels.

4. Learn how to make your data accessible and attractive

Clojure Data Analysis Cookbook

ISBN: 978-1-78216-264-3   Paperback: 342 pages

Over 110 recipes to help you dive into the world of practical data analysis using Clojure

1. Get a handle on the torrent of data the modern Internet has created.

2. Recipes for every stage from collection to analysis.

3. A practical approach to analyzing data to help you make informed decisions.

Please check **www.PacktPub.com** for information on our titles

65002713R10194

Made in the USA
Middletown, DE
21 February 2018